A Mythical Image

A Mythical Image: The ideal of India in German Romanticism

by A. Leslie Willson

*Nichts ist dem Geist erreichbarer
als das Unendliche.* —NOVALIS

Duke University Press   Durham, N. C.   1964

Library of Congress Catalogue Card number 64-14083

Printed in the United States of America by
Heritage Printers, Inc., Charlotte, N. C.

For
Hermann J. Weigand
genial scholar,
good friend

Acknowledgments

The author acknowledges his gratitude to the Research Council at the University of Texas for a grant which gave him the freedom of a leave of absence to re-examine the early form of this study, a dissertation at Yale University; to the Council on Research at Duke University for publication support; and to the editors of the following journals for permission to incorporate the articles listed into the body of this work.

"Herder and India: The Genesis of a Mythical Image," *PMLA*, LXX (1955), 1049-1058.

"Rogerius' 'Open-Deure': A Herder Source," *Monatshefte*, XLVIII (1956), 17-24.

"The *blaue Blume*: A New Dimension," *The Germanic Review*, XXXIV (1959), 50-58.

"Friedrich Majer: Romantic Indologist," *Texas Studies in Literature and Language*, III (1961), 40-49.

Foreword

German Romanticism engaged in burning metaphysical and aesthetic quests and in a revival of the unity perceived between the arts and the religion of the Middle Ages. It experimented imaginatively with the untested, unprobed fantasy of the subconscious mind, with studied, ingenuous style, and with conscious, skilful irony. It strived for the reunion of man and nature and was enthralled with the allurement of an infinitely perfect but unattainable goal. One magically precipitated image of that goal and a summary of Romantic aspirations was the Indic ideal.

The influence of India on German literature has been a generally neglected field of investigation. Evidence of such an influence is strikingly apparent, but until 1901 bare mention at the most was made of it in literary histories. Arthur F. J. Remy's dissertation, "The Influence of India and Persia on the Poetry of Germany"

(Columbia, 1901), amounted to little more than an outline because of the confining boundaries he set for himself. A much more valuable work, the dissertation by Paul T. Hoffmann, "Der indische und der deutsche Geist von Herder bis zur Romantik" (Tübingen, 1915), is restricted to an investigation of India and gives a rather complete account of the sources from which Herder developed an attitude toward Indic culture that was transplanted into fertile Romantic minds. A most important contribution is Hoffmann's recognition of Friedrich Majer, the Romantic Indologist and mythographer, as a chief agent in the sowing of seeds of fascination for India.

It was the expansive Romantic spirit which first felt the bond linking fundamental human activities such as religion, language, and art, and it was this questing spirit which felt compelled to search for a common origin for these universal human disciplines. The Romanticist was uniquely equipped for such a quest because he was historically oriented and because he was philosophically moved to elaborate grand human themes. To interpret human experience, the Romanticist availed himself of every variety of myth, the "unconscious fiction," in the words of Ernst Cassirer. The theoretical element and the element of artistic creation perceived by Cassirer in myth appealed to the artistic and theoretical qualities innate in the Romantic author.

Modern poetry has truly evolved from ancient myth, says F. C. Prescott, who maintains that the mind of the poet is mythopoeic. The most mythopoeic of poetic minds was that of the Romanticist, who was capable of the act of belief which Cassirer finds paradoxically basic to myth-making. The Romantic poet imbued the world of nature with emotion, a testimony to his belief in the reality of conflict among the powers of nature. The substratum of feeling which Cassirer finds in myth was supplemented by the Romanticist with a substratum of thought which manifested itself in deliberate but still intuitive theoretical probings, essays toward unknown but suspected affinities. The boldness of the Romantic imagination would seem to indicate that the Romantic authors subscribed to Aristotle's thesis that a convincing impossibility is preferable to an unconvincing possibility for the purposes of the poetic arts.

Myth "is at once an external reality and the resonance of the in-

ternal vicissitudes of man," according to Jerome S. Bruner, and it is
in this seeming contradictory sense that the term *mythical image* is
used here. The phrase does not mean the image of myth but the
image of India as a source of inspiration to the poetic imagination
of the German Romanticist and, in that role, as a basis for ideal
reality. Thomas Mann wrote that mythical knowledge resides in the
gazer and not in that at which he gazes. The mythical image formed
by the Romanticist in his view of India and its culture is unreal, but
it is true in his ideal world and in his imaginative projection of that
world through his art. It is a dynamic picture which the Romanticist
sought to transform into reality through a unification of the wisdoms and a reconciliation of the cultures of the Orient and the
West. A restatement of Western values embossed with the stamp
of the mythical image, in the symbolism of a new mythology, meant
a deeper understanding of man's place in the cosmos. Friedrich
Schlegel's definition of a historian as a retrospective prophet, a con-
jurer of the past, found an extension in the Romantic author, whose
ideal assimilation of mythic reality vivified an immediate poetic
present.

In order to strive for a clear depiction of German Romantic involvement with the mythical image of India, it is necessary to follow
the entangled path Indic culture took to the West, particularly to
Germany, in some detail. Therefore in Part I of this book, "The
Sources of the Image," a survey begins with the travel literature
which furnished the West with Indic lore from before the time of
Alexander the Great and culminates in the first Sanskrit translations in the last quarter of the eighteenth century.

Part II, "The Delineation of the Image," is concerned with the
unwitting contribution of Johann Gottfried Herder to the config-
uration of the image of India which was drawn basically from a
variety of travel books and was focused finally in a form perceptive
to the Romantic mind through the discovery of the Sanskrit play,
Sakuntala.

"The Scrutiny of the Image," Part III, considers the elaboration
of the ideal impression of India on the part of Romantic translators
(working from English sources), mythologists, and philosophers. If
the section on the Romantic philosophers seems to be tenuous, it is
because the ideal image had necessarily a very flimsy philosophical

base. So little was known about Indic philosophy at the time that the philosophers had only dessicated crumbs to work with. That, even so, the ideal image of India manages to come to the surface is testimony to its penetration and permeation through the intellectual strata of the age. The inclusion of Hegel and Schopenhauer among the Romantic philosophers is not meant as a re-classification, but simply is a convenience for the inspection of the Indic ideal as it was perceived by them: hesitantly and warily, even reluctantly, by Hegel, and ambivalently by Schopenhauer, whose introduction to the mythical image resulted in his large indebtedness to the philosophy of India.

Not all the German Romantic poets are considered in Part IV, "The Projection of the Image," and more detailed consideration is given the members of the so-called Early Romantic group. The zenith of the acceptance and poetic transformation of the image occurred in the works of the earlier generation of Romanticists. Ideal Indic or Orient-colored symbols and metaphors among the later Romantic poets are either superficial or have the character of a diluted epigonistic enterprise. In this part, two authors resist designation as Romantic: Jean Paul and Friedrich Hölderlin. How far either may be endowed with certain aspects of the characteristics of Romantic authors is not germane here. They are included because they share with their Romantic fellow poets in the appropriation and transmutation of the mythical image of India.

The ideal image of India was not a tenacious manifestation and consequently faded rapidly. The concluding part of the study, "The Reflection of the Image," is an examination of the brief revival of the Indic ideal in E. T. A. Hoffmann's *Der goldene Topf*, though not of its reflections in other Hoffmann works, such as *Meister Floh*. Its glints and sometimes inescapable ironic guise in works by Heinrich Heine are illustrated. Its weak and diffused glow is finally traced in Adalbert Stifter's mournfully nostalgic tale of *Die Narrenburg*.

Goethe's engagement with India, although not properly pertinent to the study of the mythical image because of his modification of the ideal image to conform to Goethean artistry and ethics, is nevertheless discussed briefly in footnotes. Just as Goethe's immense intellect hovered ever near the German Romantic authors, now enticed and now repelled by them, the poet also took the measure of the Indic ideal, accepting or rejecting it in accordance with his emphasis on formal beauty and man's ethical purpose.

The term *romanticism*, which is both useful and vexatious, defies exact definition. It must particularly be kept in mind that neither French nor English Romanticism is the equivalent of the German movement. The Romantics of English literature have more in common with the genius, unbridled emotion, and self-dedication to feeling and freedom of German literature's pre-Romantic *Sturm-und-Drang*. The preferred German Romantic literary vehicle—though not the most perfect—was the novel, a form ignored by the representative English Romantics: Byron, Shelley, Keats, Blake, and Coleridge. The aesthetic leaning of the German Romanticists, to whom the artist and the poet were the most glorious, though harried and imperfect, of men, led to a decadent aesthetic trend of Romanticism in France and to the development of the rich beauty and fatal enchantment of symbolist poetry.

German Romanticism began as a programmatic poetic enterprise, initially almost exclusively the work of two men, Friedrich Schlegel and Novalis. Schlegel succeeded in promulgating the theory, but failed at its poetic realization, while Novalis contributed admirably to both. They and the other German Romanticists who gathered in Jena were short-lived as an aggregation of dedicated theorists and practitioners of Romanticism, but their influence was expansive. The mythical image of India, as a phenomenon of German Romanticism, found its greatest expression, its apotheosis, in its creative transfiguration by these poets. The turn of the century, around 1800, was the moment of its greatest triumph. Through the study of the image as it is projected by Romantic authors, a new dimension is revealed in the literature of Romanticism and a brilliant new stratum is uncovered in the intellectual landscape of the time.

Contents

A Mythical Image

I. The Sources of the Image

1. So heeft doch Godt de saken sulcks beschickt, dat den Bramine
Padmanaba *alle het volgende aen Dom. Rogerius ontdeckt.*
— JACOBUS SCEPERUS

Even in ancient times the fame of the wonder and wisdom of India
spread westward in a tangled array of hearsay and falsehood, en-
meshed in which the truth still defies the unraveling fingers of
scholars. It was principally through the Greeks that tales of India
first came to the West, and it was they who first began to shape the
mythical image.

A pre-Alexandrian interpenetration of religious and philosophic
thought between Greece and India is suggested by the legends surrounding the coming of the immigrant god Dionysus to Greece and
his peripatetic procession to or from India. Megasthenes, who held
an ambassadorial post at Patna at intervals between 302 and 288

B.C., and whose work on India survives only in fragments quoted by succeeding historians, wrote of the conquest of India by Dionysus. He mentions cities named after Dionysus and affirms that important evidences exist attesting to Dionysus' Indic birth, but unable to justify or reconcile conflicting legends Megasthenes drops the subject as being too tedious to write about.[1] Euripides in his *Bacchae*, although firmly holding to the Theban birth of Dionysus, nevertheless heralds the triumphant homecoming of the god from Asia.[2] Pliny has him entering Thebes in a chariot drawn by elephants.

Orphism, the secret religious rites growing out of the Dionysian mysteries in the sixth century B.C., had in common with contemporary Indic thought the belief in the transmigration of souls, the reincarnation of human beings in animal or plant form, the "wheel of birth" from which the adherent of Brahma as well as of Dionysus had to free himself to become once more divine.[3] Pythagoras (*ca.* 582—*ca.* 507 B.C.), about whom there persisted a tradition of a journey to India,[4] taught the doctrine of palingenesis and as a corollary emphasized the kinship of all living creatures.[5] Empedocles (*ca.* 495—*ca.* 435 B.C.) also was a believer in the transmigration of souls and a universal kinship of all living things,[6] persuasions which have an Indic counterpart.

1. J. W. McCrindle, tran. and ed., *Ancient India as Described by Megasthenês and Arrian* (London, 1877), pp. 36-37.

2. Robert Graves, in *The Greek Myths* (2 vols.; New York, 1959), suggests that "the main clue to Dionysus' mystic history is the spread of the vine cult over Europe, Asia, and North Africa" (I, 107). Jane Harrison, in *Prolegomena to the Study of Greek Religion* (New York, 1955), notes the barbaric Asiatic women with whom Euripides invests Dionysus as companions on his return to Greece (p. 372).

3. John Burnet, in *Early Greek Philosophy* (New York, 1957), denies that any Indic influence was possible in Greece during the sixth century B.C. He mentions Pyrrho of Ellis (*ca.* 360-270 B.C.) as the first Greek philosopher in whom Indic influence can be proven. Burnet suggests, too, that common tenets of Orphic and Indic thought might have a mutual generic source in a northern area vaguely called "Scythia" (p. 82 and n. 2).

4. McCrindle, p. 121; see also [William Macintosh], *Travels in Europe, Asia and Africa* (2 vols.; London, 1782), I, 311. The German translation of Macintosh was published in two volumes in Leipzig in 1785.

5. Burnet, pp. 92-93. Burnet mentions that Herodotus' report of Pythagoras' having imported the doctrine of the transmigration of souls from Egypt is of no consequence since the Egyptians did not believe in the doctrine at all (pp. 88-89).

6. Burnet quotes two Empedoclean fragments which verify these tenets: "For I have been ere now a boy and a girl, a bush and a bird and a dumb fish in the sea" (No. 117, p. 223), and "For all things were tame and gentle to man, both beasts and birds, and friendly feelings were kindled everywhere" (No. 130, p. 225).

The first historian who made clear references to India was Hecateus of Miletus (549-486 B.C.), but among all the early authors who transmitted fantastic tales of the East to the Greeks it was Ctesias of Cnidus (*fl.* 400 B.C.) who identified the abundant astonishing wonders of nature to be found in India. Ctesias resided a number of years in Persia as the private physician to Artaxerxes Mnemon, and during his sojourn collected materials for his treatise on India, the first such work written in Greek. It was this work, unreliable in fact but enthralling in fable, which made India the goal of adventurous longing among the Greeks and perhaps contributed an impulse to Alexander's expedition into India.[7] Alexander's conquering penetration into the Indic heartland (about 326 B.C.) spurred a spate of narratives and memoirs written by members of his retinue, and for a time India was open to the West.[8] Seekers of knowledge wandered among the Hindus, according to tradition, and brought back greater and more enduring treasures than the con-

7. O. Doberentz, "Die erd- und völkerkunde in der weltchronik des Rudolf von Ems," *Zeitschrift für deutsche Philologie*, XIII (1882), 46-47. See also McCrindle, p. 6.

8. McCrindle, p. 7, lists the following scientific and military men who, among others, preserved a record of their Indic service with Alexander: Aristobolus, Baeto, Diognetus, Kallisthenes, Nearchus, and Onesikritus. Their works are all lost, but the substance is found in Arrian, Pliny, and Strabo.

Alexander was the best-known figure of antiquity in the Middle Ages. An epic of late antiquity, falsely attributed to Kallisthenes, related his life and conquests and determined the Alexander image for more than a thousand years. It was translated into Latin soon after its appearance about A.D. 300 by Julius Valerius, and again in the tenth century by Archbishop Leo. By the time of the Middle Ages the work existed in thirty languages. A translation of letters purported to be by Alexander to his teacher Aristotle is preserved from eleventh-century England, one of many heroides associated with the Alexander figure. Valerius' work was translated into French by Alberich von Besançon in the early twelfth century, a version used by Pfaffe Lamprecht between 1140 and 1150 for his Alexander epic, which was the first German epic on a secular subject taken from a foreign source. In Lamprecht's version the powerful Alexander is taught the medieval virtue of moderation by an Indic ascetic. In this epic also occur the fantastic maidens who blossom forth from flowers and perish with the flowers' withering, an imaginative conception used by Wagner in *Parsifal*. Treatments of Alexander and the fabulous campaign in India were made in epic form by Rudolf von Ems about 1250 and by Ulrich von Eschenbach about 1270, later by Seitfrit in the middle of the fourteenth century. The first prose treatment of the theme was done by Johannes Hartlieb in 1444 (published 1472); see reprint in *Deutsche Literatur*, Reihe Volks- und Schwankbücher, Vol. II: *Volksbücher von Weltweite und Abenteuerlust*, ed. Franz Podleiszek (Leipzig, 1936). Hans Sachs (1494-1576), who adapted an astonishing number of mythological and ancient historical themes, used Alexander material in several works between 1557 and 1563. The inexhaustible sources inspired some fifty plays and novels in Germany between 1775 and 1935. See also Elisabeth Frenzel, *Stoffe der Weltliteratur* (Stuttgart, 1962), pp. 26-29.

queror dreamed of: "Pythagoras, Democritus, Anaxarchus, Pyrrho, Appollonius [*sic*], and others, went to India in order to converse with the Brahmins of that country."[9] Works on India were produced by Deimachus, like Megasthenes an ambassador of Seleucus Nicator to Patna, by Patrokles, the admiral of Seleucus, by Timosthenes, the commander of the fleet of Ptolemeus Philadelphus, and by Megasthenes.

The *Indica* of Megasthenes provided the principal source from which succeeding writers for centuries drew their commentaries on India. It can be surmised that, for his era, Megasthenes was encyclopedic in his description of India, its soil and rivers, its climate, the flora and fauna, the government, the customs of various ethnic groups, and, to a lesser extent, the art and religion. He relates the conquest of India in ancient times by Dionysus and again by Heracles. With admiration he notes that the people of India were free men, no person being allowed to be held as a slave. He lists (erroneously) seven castes and remarks that the "philosophers," though the smallest in number, are pre-eminent in dignity. Here he alludes to the Brahmans, about whom he comments further that

on many points their opinions coincide with those of the Greeks, for like them they say that the world had a beginning, and is liable to destruction, and is in shape spherical, and that the Deity who made it, and who governs it, is diffused through all its parts. They hold that various first principles operate in the universe, and that water was the principle employed in the making of the world. In addition to the four elements there is a fifth agency, from which the heaven and the stars were produced [*akaśa*, the ether]. The earth is placed in the centre of the universe. Concerning generation, and the nature of the soul, and many other subjects, they express views like those maintained by the Greeks.[10]

Megasthenes lauds the people of India for their frugality, honesty, truthfulness, virtue, and appreciation of beauty. Although much of what he writes about Indic wonders is farfetched, most is credible, though at times exaggerated. Megasthenes summed up the knowledge the ancient Greeks had of India and became the authority for writers on India after him.[11]

9. Macintosh, I, 311.

10. McCrindle, p. 101, quoting Strabo's citation of Megasthenes on the philosophers of India. For further statements of Megasthenes on India in the present discussion, see McCrindle, pp. 27, 36-41, 69-70, and 97-101.

11. McCrindle, quoting Schwanbeck (*Megasthenes Indica* [Bonn, 1846]), lists the

Almost half a millenium after Megasthenes, Arrian (*ca.* A.D. 96– *ca.* 180) was able to present an accurate description of the geography and the inhabitants of the subcontinent of India, drawing principally on Aristobulus, Eratosthenes, Megasthenes, and Nearchus. Concerning the Hindus he wrote of

their delicate and slender form, their dark complexion, their black, uncurled hair, their garments of cotton, their living entirely upon vegetable food, their division into separate tribes or casts [*sic*], the members of which never intermarry, the custom of wives burning themselves with their deceased husbands.[12]

Thus was the sometimes authentic and often fanciful image of India handed down through generations to Roman times.

Trade with India, over long and arduous land routes to the Mediterranean and then by water to the Italian boot, flourished in the Roman age. The consumption of spices and aromatics must have been very great, for such wares were used in religious ceremonies of every kind.

But the vanity of men occasioned a greater consumption of these fragrant substances than their piety. . . . We consume in heaps these precious substances with the carcases of the dead (says Pliny): We offer them to the Gods only in grains.[13]

Although the products of India and other Eastern nations found their way westward through the centuries, the tedious and dangerous routes made direct intellectual commerce impossible. The Western world was long waiting to learn more about India than was provided in scanty outline by the Greek historians and in the hearsay offered by merchants.

The first report, meager though it was, given to the West about India by an educated traveler was that of Marco Polo (1254?-1323?) in 1298. He relates very little about the customs of the Hindus and seems most taken with the marvelous tales of large rubies on Cey-

---

following imposing list of writers in Greek and Roman times after Megasthenes who treated India: Agatharchides, Alexander Polyhistor, Apollodorus, Eratosthenes, Hipparchus, Marinus of Tyre, Mnaseus, Polemo, Ptolemy, and Strabo among the Greeks, and Pliny, Pomponius Mela, Seneca, Solinus, Terentius Varro of Atax, and Vipsanius Agrippa among the Romans (p. 8 n.).

12. William Robertson, *An Historical Disquisition concerning the Knowledge which the Ancients had of India* (London, 1791), p. 21.

13. *Ibid.*, pp. 54-56.

lon, diamonds in Northern India, and great bats on the coast of Coromandel. He does mention the burning of widows with their husbands and the refusal of the Hindus to kill beast or bird or anything that lives. He also calls attention to the abstinence from wine among the inhabitants and says that the Brahmans are the most truthful men in the world (a trait impressed also upon Arrian).[14]

The earliest report after that made by Marco Polo was furnished by the Venetian Nicolo Conti (*fl.* 1419-1444), who traveled in India during the first half of the fifteenth century (before 1439). In the second part of his narrative concerning India, entitled "de ritu moribusque Indorum," Conti gives a lengthy description of the burning of widows, general customs with regard to the dead, and some words about the Brahmans and various religious festivals. Only after 1510, when the Portuguese gained a stronghold in India, following the expedition of Vasco da Gama in 1497, did more and more information concerning India become available to the West. Most of these reports were in the form of travel literature or missionary narratives, among them being the "Livro de Duarte Barbosa," written before 1516, and those of de Barros, do Couto, and the cardinal J. P. Maffeus in his *Historiarium Indicarum*.[15]

Although according to Pietro della Valle (1586-1652), whose *Viaggi* appeared in Rome from 1650 to 1653, there must have been some recent work on the Hindus published before 1615, W. Caland (the editor of the most recent Dutch edition of Abraham Rogerius) was able to show that della Valle's Francesco Negrone was actually Francisco Negram, whose work never appeared in print but was preserved at the Monastery of St. Franciscus in Lisbon. In 1630 the first cohesive description of the religious rites of the Hindus appeared in Henry Lord's treatise on the sect of the Banians, a book "more curious than scientific."[16]

The most important early publication about India was doubtless *De Open-Deure tot het Verborgen Heydendom* by Abraham Roger-

14. Marco Polo, *The Book of Ser Marco Polo*, trans. and ed. Col. Sir Henry Yule, 3rd ed. rev. Henri Cordier (2 vols.; London, 1926), II, 341, 342, 363, and 367, n. 1.

15. W. Caland, ed., *De Open-Deure tot het Verborgen Heydendom*, by Abraham Rogerius, Linschoten-Vereeniging, X ('S-Gravenhage, 1915), xxii-xxiii. Volume III of *Allgemeine Historie der Reisen zu Wasser und zu Lande oder Sammlung aller Reisebeschreibungen* (21 vols.; Amsterdam, 1747-1777), ed. J. J. Schwabe, contains a relation of Dutch explorations in the area by C. Houtmann in *De erste Schep Vaert* (Amsterdam, 1595).

16. Caland, pp. xxiii-xxiv.

ius, published at Leyden in 1651 by his widow. Rogerius went as a Protestant missionary from Holland to Pulicat, the first Dutch settlement on the Indian mainland, in 1630. He spent ten years on the coast of Coromandel and five years more at Batavia (now Jakarta, capital of Indonesia), preaching in both Dutch and Portuguese. In 1647 he returned to Holland and settled in Gouda, where he died in 1649. A nineteenth-century scholar noted that this book "is still, perhaps, the most complete account of S. Indian Hinduism, though by far the earliest."[17] Certainly Rogerius' work was the most capacious source for information concerning Hindu customs and religious myths and rites until almost the end of the eighteenth century. William Robertson, the Scottish historian, says (in 1791) that by gaining the confidence of an intelligent Brahman, Rogerius acquired information concerning the manners and religion of the Hindus, more authentic and extensive than was known to Europeans prior to translations from Sanskrit (1785).[18] The *Open-Deure* was translated in a comparatively short time into German and French.[19] An estimable virtue of Rogerius' work is commented upon by Caland, who says that it contains an impressive and objective description of Hindu religious rites, in general free from the restrictive and zealous criticism which brands the works of many other missionaries.[20]

Although the Brahmans were forbidden to reveal the mysteries of their religion to foreigners, Rogerius was able to present his treatise on the Hindus because he persuaded a number of Brahmans to take him into their confidence. As he says, he acquainted himself

with a few Brahmans . . . who are people gifted generally with excellent understanding and aptitude, whose wisdom even Pythagoras and Plato were not ashamed to seek out, from whom both of the latter (it may be supposed) derived all their philosophy and transmitted it to the Greeks: for which reason those Brahmans are even today considered the most adroit, intelligent, and commodious among the heathen.[21]

17. A. C. Burnell, quoted by Caland, p. xxii.
18. Robertson, p. 338.
19. Abraham Rogers, *Offne Thür zu dem verborgenen Heydenthum*, trans. Christoph Arnold (Nürnberg, 1663); Abraham Roger, *Le Theatre de l'Idolatrie, ou la Porte Ouverte*, trans. Thomas la Grue (Amsterdam, 1670).
20. Caland, p. xxii.
21. My translation; Rogers, *Offne Thür*, Vorrede: "mit etzlichen Bramines . . . welches mit fürtrefflichem Verstand und Geschikklichkeit gemeiniglich begabte Leute sind; derer Weisheit auch Pythagoras und Plato sich nicht geschämt / zu besuchen;

Jacobus Sceperus, a minister in Gouda who wrote the dedicatory epistle to the original Dutch edition of the *Open-Deure*, speaks of Rogerius' success with the chief Brahman informant, Padmanâbha. This Brahman had shorn the head of one of his concubines, a woman of high caste, to whom such treatment was a great disgrace. Consequently he made enemies of her friends and relatives and drew upon himself the wrath of the foreign governor (presumably in a Portuguese settlement) and was forced to flee and seek asylum with the Dutch administrator at Pulicat. It was through the agency of the Dutch governor, with whom he was on excellent terms, that Rogerius became acquainted with the Brahman. Sceperus says that Padmanâbha, a man of great wisdom, was often at the home of Rogerius and that they spoke together about the Hindu religion, even though the Brahmans supposedly were not permitted to reveal their religion to the Christians nor to disclose the vedic laws or the mysteries of their worship to the Sudras, the common people in their own nation. Although Padmanâbha did not know Dutch, both he and Rogerius could converse in Portuguese. Many times the Brahman brought others of his rank to Rogerius' house, among them a Brahman named Dammersa, who was more fluent than Padmanâbha in Portuguese and thus more comfortably could express ideas about the religion.[22]

Aside from the value of Rogerius' book as an unbiased authoritative depository of Hindu religious and cultural lore, it contains as a supplement the first direct adaptation of a Sanskrit work into a Western tongue: two of the three hundred "centuries" (*śatakas*) of Bhartrihari, supposedly in literal translation but actually more in a paraphrase. Caland errs in his statement that this version of a fairly comprehensive Sanskrit work is the very first that came to the West.[23] Bhartrihari's lyric collection in the prose version by Rogerius was the first Sanskrit work to be adapted directly into a Euro-

---

von denen sie beede (wie vermutlich) fast all ihre Philosophiam entlehnt / und den Griechen überbracht haben: Dannenhero diejenigen Bramines noch heut zu Tag für die geschikktesten / verständigsten / und bequemsten unter den Heyden gehalten werden."

22. Caland, p. xxxvi.

23. *Ibid.*, p. xxv. Caland disputes the claim that Rogerius wrote the work in Latin originally; see pp. xxvii-xxviii.

pean language, but one other Sanskrit work, the fables of Bidpai (or Pidpai or Pilpai), had made its way West through an astonishingly devious route of successive translations.[24]

The majority of the lyric creations of the middle period of Indic letters (around the eighth century) present a very special and sharply defined genre. The small poems, concise and formed by a few strokes, offer a picture, a situation, or an emotion. The lyric, kin in many respects to the gnomic aphorism of prose, was developed to a great fulness by the Sanskrit poets. But the grace and fine observation of the genre, along with its terse form, make translation almost impossible. Sanskrit meter does not lend itself easily to reproduction, and one must depend upon prose paraphrases or inadequate versions in the form of the lyric current in the language into which the translation is made.[25] It is not surprising then, and certainly is no reflection upon Rogerius, who could not read the Sanskrit original (and was moreover no poet), that Bhartrihari's lyrics were paraphrased in prose.

An inclination for reflection and speculation is a trait firmly established as an essential part of the Hindu spirit. Aphorisms are found throughout the literature of India: in religious and scientific writings, in fables, dramas, epics, and also in the lyric. Such sayings of wisdom were given poetic expression in very original, striking thoughts and in forms sharp, clear, and often very artistic. These gnomic gems are found generally scattered throughout Sanskrit literature; very few are in works which are exclusively made up of aphorisms. Such a work, however, is the collection of *śatakas* by

24. The first Sanskrit work to make its way to the West, the *Panchatantra*, written in the fourth century A.D., was translated into Pahlavi (Middle Persian) and then in Arabic was carried across North Africa to Spain, where it was translated into Hebrew by Rabbi Joël early in the thirteenth century and then into Spanish in 1251. A Latin translation of the Hebrew version, *Directorium humanae vitae*, was made by Johannes von Capua between 1263 and 1278; the Latin edition, published in Germany in 1480, served then as a source for the German translation by Antonius von Pforr, *Das Buch der Beispiele*, first printed in Urach in 1480 or 1481, ostensibly the basis for *Das Buch der Weisheit*, published in 1483. See *Das Buch der Weisheit*, facsimile edition, ed. Rudolf Payer von Thurn (Vienna, 1925), pp. iii-iv. See also Johannes Hertel, *Das Pañcatantra, seine Geschichte und seine Verbreitung* (Leipzig, 1914). The work was translated into Italian (from the Latin version) by A. F. Doni, *La moral filosofia* in 1552, and from the Italian edition into English in 1570 by Sir Thomas North, *The Morall Philosophie of Doni*; see Heinrich Zimmer, *Philosophies of India* (New York, 1956), p. 92 n.

25. Leopold von Schroeder, *Indiens Literatur und Kultur* (Leipzig, 1887), p. 563.

Bhartrihari, especially the second and third parts (those found in Rogerius' volume).[26]

The Chinese writer and pilgrim, I Tsing, says that Bhartrihari, who lived around the middle of the seventh century, was a poet, grammarian, and philosopher. Tradition says that he was also a king. His wisdom is supposed to have come to him after bitter reflection over a wasted youth. It is said that he became a Buddhist monk, but after a time was so filled with longing for the world that he returned to a lay status (an act permissible in Buddhist canon law). During his lifetime he is supposed to have wavered, unsure of his vocation, seven times, on one occasion even having a chariot waiting at the monastery gate to take him back into the world.[27] L. D. Barnett, in The Heart of India, says: "Again and again, when he had drained the cup of passion to the dregs, he sought peace for his soul in religion; but his heart was still restless under the ragged gown of the monk, and time after time drove him back to the world that he had hoped to abandon."[28] According to Rogerius, when Bhartrihari turned out his three hundred wives upon the death of his father, they and their descendants became a numerous sub-caste of the poet's own caste.[29]

Bhartrihari wrote three śatakas, that is, three series of lyrics, each containing ten chapters, with each chapter made up of ten lyric epigrams, giving a total of one hundred for each series. The first, the "Century of Love," is a record of changeful passion, treated in gracious and thoughtful lyric form. The second śataka, the "Century of Polity," is concerned with his lightly ironic scorn for the statesmanship of princes; but he nevertheless bears witness to the ideal of moral and ethical behavior among men and stresses character as contrasted with expediency. The third group of lyrics is called the "Century of a Stilled Heart" and is dedicated to the renunciation of the world. It represents Bhartrihari's disillusionment with life, but emphasizes certain convictions which had become deeply rooted in his philosophy.[30]

26. Ibid., pp. 667-668.
27. Ibid., pp. 563-564; see also Herbert H. Gowen, A History of Indian Literature (New York, 1931), pp. 411-412.
28. L. D. Barnett, The Heart of India (London, 1908), pp. 115-122.
29. Rogers, Offne Thür, pp. 462-464.
30. Gowen, pp. 411-412; Von Schroeder, p. 564.

Only the latter two hundred of the three hundred lyrics were adapted by Rogerius. The Brahman Padmanâbha, who paraphrased the lyrics in Portuguese for the missionary (who then translated them into Dutch prose), did not, for some reason, want to transmit the "Century of Love."[31] In two chapters of the *śatakas* published, the tenth aphorism is missing, but Rogerius says he was told by Padmanâbha that the original also contained this omission.[32]

Even before Rogerius' book appeared, Adam Olearius (*ca.* 1603-1671), a member of the first German linguistic society, the "Fruchtbringende Gesellschaft," had published a communication on India sent him by Johann Albrecht von Mandelslo (1616-1644), a member of the ambassadorial party which made a journey to Persia by way of Moscow between 1633 and 1639 as the representatives of Duke Frederick of Holstein. The book, published in 1645 after the death of its youthful author, was in such demand that Olearius published a second edition in 1647 and yet another in 1658.[33] When public interest in such information spread abroad, an English translation of the voyages and travels of the ambassadors, with a more complete presentation of Mandelslo's narrative taken from a French edition, was published in 1662,[34] and a second English edition appeared in 1669. A much enlarged edition of books published by

31. Padmanâbha's refusal to translate the erotic *śatakas*, as reported by Rogerius, has given rise to a series of errors and mistranslations. Rogerius uses the word *verduytschen* in the sense of "to translate," since in the same paragraph only a few lines previously he had used *vertaelt* "translated." The German edition has *verdolmetschet* for *vertaelt* but then has *verteutschen* for *verduytschen* (p. 462). From *verteutschen* one could possibly construe that Padmanâbha spoke German. However, the French edition of Rogerius' work goes even farther: *traduit* for *vertaelt*, but *en Flamen* for *verduytschen* (p. 291). This confusion, for Rogerius made it quite clear that he communicated with Padmanâbha in Portuguese, has resulted in erroneous statements such as the following by Mrs. Dauer in her dissertation on the influence of Buddhism on German literature: "he . . . translated Bhartṛhari with the help of a Brahman, whom he calls Padmanabha, and who was well versed in the Dutch language." (See Dorothea W. Dauer, "Buddhistic Influence on German Literature and Thought to the End of the Nineteenth Century." Unpublished Ph.D. dissertation, University of Texas, 1953, p. 146.)

32. Caland, p. 169.

33. Adam Olearius, ed., *Mandelslos Schreiben von seiner ostindischen Reise an Ad. Olearius*, by J. A. von Mandelslo [Schleswig], 1645). Also Adam Olearius, ed., *Oft begehrte Beschreibung der newen orientalischen Reise* . . . , by J. A. von Mandelslo (Schleswig, 1647); and Adam Olearius, ed., *Des . . . Johann Albrecht von Mandelslo morgenländische Reisebeschreibung*, by J. A. von Mandelslo (Schleswig, 1658).

34. Adam Olearius, *The Voyages & Travels of the Ambassadors*, trans. John Davies (London, 1662); see Preface.

Olearius, collected in the Hamburg edition of 1696, contains the sayings of Bhartrihari as reproduced by Rogerius, but does not give credit to the Dutch missionary nor comment in any manner on the source of the aphorisms.[35]

Other, but less renowned and widely read, travel accounts which had currency before 1750 were by Saar, Hofmann, Von der Behr, Schweitzer, Fricken, Bernier, Dellon, de Bruyn, Schouten, Valentin, Hamilton, and Downing.[36] Several of these accounts appeared in translation soon after their original publication, testifying further to the interest in travel literature exhibited by readers of the period.

Philipp Baldeus (1632-1672), a Dutch missionary who spent ten years on the coasts of Malabar and Coromandel, but who relied principally on Rogerius for his knowledge of Hinduism, can hardly be considered an impartial and unprejudiced reporter upon the religion of India because he was a bigoted critic and saw in the customs of the Hindus only an insult to God and Christianity and an opportunity to offer a refutation through a display of his own erudition. Baldeus at times was able to comment positively on Hindu traits. He mentions that the natives of Malabar hold respect and honor very highly and are not the coarse barbarians which some eminent Europeans consider them to be, rather they shame the Europeans in regard to courtesy. He says, further, that the Brahmans are outwardly endowed with the greatest virtue one could ask for, and that they are sober, alert, clean, modest, congenial, and moderate in eating and drinking—but they are quite lascivious, as is the whole nation. He traces historically the belief in metempsychosis, citing Appian (*fl.* second century) for evidence of its being held even by Germanic tribes. The inhabitants of Ceylon, he says, are intelligent, have a good memory, and are sober, moderate, and clean and neat in their persons.[37] But such positive remarks are rare. One critic, in a study on the sources for Johann Gottfried Herder's *Ideen zur Philosophie der Geschichte der Menschheit*, says that Baldeus' criticism of Hindu religious beliefs is false because he extracts the

35. Adam Olearius, *Viel vermehrte Moscowitische und Persianische Reisebeschreibung* (Hamburg, 1696), following the appendix concerning the wars of the Tartars against the Chinese, pp. 95-112.

36. For the works of these travelers, see Bibliography.

37. Philipp Baldeus, *Beschreibung der ostindischen Kusten* [sic] *Malabar und Coromandel* . . . (Amsterdam, 1672), pp. 191, 404-408 (esp. p. 407 for Appian), and p. 411; translated from the Dutch edition.

ancient Indic customs and teachings from their frame of reference to place, time, and character of the people, and as a measure for judging them takes conditions far removed in time and place. He criticizes the Indic legends of the creation as nonsense and calls phallic worship a bestiality.[38]

That Rogerius is quite without prejudice in his account of the customs and religion of the Hindus has already been mentioned. Mandelslo remains comparatively disinterested, although at times he cannot suppress a shudder. Because both Rogerius and Mandelslo are relatively uncritical and inform truthfully and unemotionally, rather than criticize, their dispassionate narratives roused and sustained interest in India.

In the calm tone which pervades his work Mandelslo admires the Indian landscape, relating that at Surat there were "pleasant Country houses, which being all white, a colour it seems the *Indians* are much in love with, afford a noble prospect amidst the greenness whereby they are encompassed." He observes that the inhabitants of Bengal "bear religious worship to the River *Ganges*, and hold the water thereof to be so holy that, who wash themselves therein are cleansed from all their sins."[39] He is particularly fascinated by the array of sects which he encounters, and he enumerates the demeanor, the customs, and the dress (or undress) of each group.

Mandelslo was a very young and inexperienced man and no scholar, and it is Rogerius who mentions the holy scriptures of the Hindus and the language in which the holy books are composed. He calls attention to "Samscortamish," a language esteemed by the Brahmans as is Latin in Europe by the scholars, a language which contains all the secrets of the heathen.[40] He also gives a relatively thorough description of the Vedas, information which he must have gotten from Padmanâbha or the other Brahmans whom Padmanâbha persuaded to visit him. He says that the Veda is the law book of the heathens, containing all the beliefs they are to hold, along with ceremonies they must observe. He notes that the book is written in Sanskrit and emphasizes its poetic form. The first part treats

38. Johannes Grundmann, "Die geographischen und völkerkundlichen Quellen und Anschauungen in Herders 'Ideen zur Geschichte der Menschheit.' " Dissertation, Leipzig, 1900, p. 72. Grundmann says that Herder names Baldeus as a source probably only because of the missionary's (very slight) translation of Indic writings.

39. Olearius, *Travels*, pp. 16-17, 118.

40. Rogers, *Offne Thür*, p. 8.

primary causes, primeval matter, angels, souls, rewards to the pious, and the punishment of evildoers. It discusses the genesis of all creatures and their eventual destruction. It explains what sin is and how sins can be forgiven, as well as who those are who commit sins and why they do so. The second part expounds upon rulers, who are supreme and to whom all people are subject. The third part is given entirely to morals, admonishes men to be virtuous, and pledges the reader to hate all immorality. The fourth part contains prescriptions for temple ceremonies and the observation of sacrifices and feast days.[41] Any reader of Rogerius would recognize that the compilers of such lofty tenets in poetic garb were not an uncivilized people, not barbarians—heathen though they might be.

Rogerius is impressed with the high esteem which belongs to the Brahman caste by reason of the holy ordinances of the Vedas. According to the holy books, he says, no Brahman may be executed, no matter how atrocious his crime. He calls attention also to the privilege accorded the Brahmans, in that only they are allowed to read the Vedas. Another Brahmanical privilege (and, indeed, in some parts a duty) is their intimate participation in the marriage rite, the observation of the *lex primae noctis*, the deflowering of the bride on her wedding night.[42]

Concerning the origin of this highest Indian caste, Mandelslo writes: "These *Bramans* [*sic*] . . . make it their boast, that they came out of the head of their God *Brama*, of whom they say there were many other Productions, which came but out of his arms, thighs, feet, and other more ignoble parts of his body; but that they have this advantage, that they have their being from the brains of that great God." This later version of the Mandelslo narrative, emendated copiously by Olearius, calls upon the only European authority of the time, Abraham Rogerius, in telling of the Brahmanical history of the Creation:

Abraham Rogers . . . relates . . . that the *Bramans* affirm, that their great God, whom they somtimes [*sic*] call Wistul, somtimes Etwara, bethinking himself . . . to make a World, had assumed the Figure of a little Childe, and having cast himself upon a Leaf, which he had found swimming upon the Water, and playing Childishly with his great Toe in his

41. *Ibid.*, pp. 56-57.
42. *Ibid.*, pp. 5, 56, 854; also, for *lex primae noctis*, see Olearius, *Travels*, p. 58.

mouth, there came out of his Navell a Flower, which they call *Tamara*, of which Flower was produced the first of all men, whom they call *Brama*.[43]

In addition to this, Mandelslo presents several different versions of the Creation which he obtained from various Hindu sects encountered on his journey through India.[44]

Mandelslo also comments upon, and is especially horrified by, the Hindu custom of *suttee*, the burning of widows on the funeral pyres of their husbands. He was a witness, on one occasion, to such a ritual death and dwells upon the event in great detail.[45] Alexander Hamilton, a traveler to India in the first quarter of the eighteenth century, whose laudable objectivity approaches that of Rogerius, suggests that the introduction of the practice of *suttee* came about at a time when there was a proliferation of the poisoning of husbands by disgruntled wives.[46]

In his reasonable and matter-of-fact way Mendelslo describes the sect of *Goêghy*, the yogis, who in consonance with their beliefs are sworn to poverty and in mortification cover their bodies with ashes. He remarks upon their view that God is an invisible light with whom their souls are reunited at their death.[47] Hamilton's account of yogis lacks the metaphysical overtones of Mandelslo but illustrates his tolerant attitude and the droll sarcasm which his commentary at times adopts:

There is another sort called Jougies, who practice great austerities and mortifications. They contemn worldly riches, and go naked, except a bit of cloth about their loins, and some deny themselves even that, delighting in nastiness and an holy obscenity, with a great shew of sanctity. They never cut nor comb their hair, and besmear their bodies and faces with ashes, which makes them look more like devils than men. I have seen a sanctified rascal of seven feet high, and his limbs well proportioned, with a large turband of his own hair wreathed about his head, and his body bedaubed with ashes and water, sitting quite naked under the shade of a tree, with a pudenda like an ass, and an hole bored through his prepuce, with a large gold ring fixed in the hole. This fellow

43. Olearius, *Travels*, p. 66.
44. *Ibid.*, pp. 70, 71-72, 74-75, 77, 120.
45. *Ibid.*, p. 41.
46. Alexander Hamilton, *A New Account of the East Indies* (Edinburgh, 1727), in John Pinkerton's *Voyages and Travels* (17 vols.; London, 1808-1814), VIII, 363.
47. Olearius, *Travels*, pp. 71-72.

was much revered by numbers of young married women, who, prostrating themselves before the living Priapus, and taking him devoutly in their hands, kissed him, whilst his bawdy owner stroked their silly heads, muttering some filthy prayers for their prolification.[48]

Emphasizing the belief held by the Brahmans that fire is the great cleanser, Mandelslo describes a temple rite of purification: the approach of the priest to the sepulcher, his nearing the lamp, his muttering of "certain Prayers" (the German text has *viel Dinge*), and the priest's rubbing his hands over the fire and stroking his face in a gesture of laving. This kind of purification is observed, Mandelslo says, because the Brahmans believe that fire has a far greater power of purifying than water, and after this ceremony they may lift up clean and pure hands to God.[49] To Mandelslo, unversed in Sanskrit, the priests "muttered a lot of stuff," an observation made by other travelers as ignorant of the language and details of Hindu temple rites as he.

Rogerius also describes a Brahmanical rite, a morning purification, where water, subservient to fire, is offered to the new sun: when the sun rises the priests three times fill their hands with water, and each time they throw it or scatter it on the earth with a reverent prayer to the sun. Rogerius' Brahman informant told him that this rite was performed because there were many mountains in that place where the sun rose and the sun had to pass through a narrow defile in which demons lurked to prevent the sunrise. Thus in ages past some Brahmans had splashed water toward the sun, which uttered such a loud clang that the demons were terrified and took to their heels.[50] Rogerius' description, accounting a mythological source for the rite, is interesting for the example of synesthesia: the sprinkled sun resounds.[51]

Because none but the Brahmans were allowed to, or indeed could, read the sacred Sanskrit books, Hindu worshipers were instructed

48. Hamilton, p. 317.
49. Olearius, *Travels*, p. 30.
50. Rogers, *Offne Thür*, pp. 154-155.
51. Pythagoras probably identified the intervals between the heavenly bodies with the musical intervals he had discovered, the fourth, the fifth, and the octave; as Burnet observes, "sphere" as applied to the heavenly bodies is an anachronism (p. 110), for they were thought to be fiery wheels. The resounding sun in the Brahmanic legend suggests such a concept: a flat, round, gong-like sun; the image is reminiscent, too, of the opening line of the "Prolog in Himmel" in Goethe's *Faust I:* "Die Sonne tönt nach alter Weise."

about the deeds of their gods by the Brahmans in the temples. Mandelslo witnessed such a meeting: "[In their temples] . . . there are reed [*sic*] certain Legends, the people standing about the *Braman*, who sits down in the midst of them, having his mouth cover'd with a linnen cloath."[52] However, he offers no explanation for the covered mouth, nor does he realize the significance of such a public reading, apparently not understanding that the populace had no other direct source for mythological tales.

When Rogerius requests his Brahman informant for clarification of the fact that a Hindu deity is said to have a wife, he receives the following metaphysical explanation: Padmanâbha denied that their God had a wife such as men on earth have, for in his essence their God was neither male nor female nor human, and no one could know his form. Therefore he had assumed a form and created a wife and the earth, and this in the manner of men. The old heathens, said Padmanâbha, had believed that their gods were *utriusque naturae*, that is, hermaphroditic, and that in the sexual act they were now male and now female, and as the latter could give birth.[53] In one of the Hindu heavens, says Rogerius, there is intercourse between the sexes. The Hindus have a Hell also, called *Jammalocon*, where punishment is ordained for certain terrible sins done upon the earth. Some miscreants are released from Hell after they have spent the time there exacted for their sins, whereupon they return to this world and enter one body or another. Some never escape.[54]

The teleological aspect of metempsychosis is mentioned by both Rogerius and Mandelslo. Rogerius says that it is the opinion of all that human souls go from one body to another, into humans as well as dumb animals, even into plants. Each finds his place according to his deeds.[55] How the transmigration of souls is equated with the works of the person is told in great detail by Mandelslo:

They hold the immortality of the Soul, but believe with all, that, at its departure out of the first body, it transmigrates into that of some other Creature; and affirm, that the Soul of a good-natur'd and docible person, is translated into the body of a Pidgeon, or Chicken; that of a cruel and

52. Olearius, *Travels*, p. 69.
53. Rogers, *Offne Thür*, pp. 236-237.
54. *Ibid.*, pp. 455, 450-451.
55. *Ibid.*, p. 447.

wicked man, into that of a Crocodile, a Lyon, or a Tigre; that of a crafty man, into that of a Fox; that of a Glutton, into . . . a Swine; that of a Treacherous person into . . . a Serpent, &c. Before they are admitted to the enjoyment of a beatitude purely Spiritual.[56]

Mandelslo mentions several versions of metempsychosis, the idea being held diversely by different sects: "The *Benjans* . . . believe with Pythagoras, that the souls of departed persons retreat into beans: an opinion which is very common . . . among the Heathens of the Indies." Again:

[The apes] multiply extreamly, by reason the *Benjans* . . . believe the *Metempsychosis*, or transmigration of souls, and permit not the killing of beasts, and these much less than any other, because they have some resemblance of man, and are perswaded that the merriest and best humour'd souls after their departure out of the body, retire into these creatures.

Here Mandelslo seems to offer an explanation for the much-admired trait of the Hindus, that they kill no beast nor any living thing, not because of any feeling of humanity or sympathy for a lesser being but rather out of a religious conviction. Apes thus are safe from destruction at human hands. Even the deadly crocodile can bask on the sand in safety, first because it harbors a human soul, but also because "the *Benjans* . . . believe that the souls of those who are . . . devour'd by these creatures, are immediately admitted into Paradise [and thus they] take no cours to destroy them." Furthermore, not only the mighty crocodile is safe (though his security is twofold), but even the lowly fly and other insects are accorded human protection: "I came in the evening to Serguntra, but it was so late, that the *Benjans*, who burn no candles for fear that Flies and such other Insects might be destroyed thereby, would not open their shops,"[57] which seemed a great inconvenience to Mandelslo.

In his travels through India, Mandelslo observed and reported with a generally unprejudiced attitude, often enough, however, from the viewpoint of a European in a heathen land. The sketchy information he supplies concerning various Hindu sects is mostly from hearsay. Rogerius, who maintains the impartial attitude of a scholar, sought information from those who were most intimately acquainted with Hindu lore, the Brahmans themselves, who risked expulsion

56. Olearius, *Travels*, p. 68.
57. *Ibid.*, pp. 9, 33-34, 35, 43.

from their caste to provide him with material. Not only is Rogerius more reliable, he is also more thorough: he lists the ten incarnations of Vishnu, though he is able to relate the history of only five.[58]

Perhaps Rogerius' most noteworthy accomplishment, however, is his presentation of the first Sanskrit text, albeit a paraphrase, to come to Western eyes. No age apparently loses its taste for moral maxims, and of those supplied by Bhartrihari, many of which Herder later reworked and published (*Zerstreute Blätter*, IV), let the following be a sample:

Time is a player at dice, a gambler: day and night are the dice, and the world the board. Mankind is the stake, and Time plays.

And even to Bhartrihari, the world was a stage and "Der Mensch . . . wie ein Tantzer." And why does mankind look in vain for God, when God is in him?

My heart! . . . Thou seekest everywhere, but why is it that thou findest not that God who dwells in thine own heart?

And what maintains the universe, and what is the goal of it all?

Brahma is like a potter; grief is his wheel; his heart is the clay, his labor the stock which drives the wheel. What He further has in mind, I do not know.[59]

German readers by 1750 had learned much about India. From the ancient writings of Greek historians something was known of the fabled land, its monsters, its strange customs, and its inexplicable philosophical and religious affinities with the Western world, but nothing was known of its literature. Fable collections and literary treatments of the epic of Alexander contributed little information about India proper. Seventeenth-century novels offered spurious or superficial Indic backgrounds.[60] Though there was a host of travelers after Portuguese and Dutch explorers opened wedges in India, travelers whose journeys to the East turned into tomes, the

58. Rogers, *Offne Thür*, pp. 251-266.
59. *Ibid.*, pp. 482, 485, 492, 533.
60. Immensely popular (ten editions between 1689 and 1766) because of sensational, sanguinary battles, human sacrifice, and the pomp of exotic ceremonies was the *Asiatische Banise* by Heinrich Anselm von Ziegler und Kliphausen. Heroic-galant in the tradition of the *Amadis-Roman*, Ziegler's novel was much imitated, furnishing even an opera (J. Becceau, 1710) and a dramatic tragedy (Friedrich Wilhelm Grimm, 1733). The villain Chaumigrem appears later as a figure in the puppet theater of Goethe's young Wilhelm Meister. Ziegler dealt freely with his sources; the most

principal sources were the accounts of Baldeus, Bernier, Mandelslo, and Rogerius. From these noteworthy observers it was learned that the great subcontinent of India was peopled, not with savage aborigines, though there existed strange, even repulsive sects, but with a civilized, even a cultured race. In a pleasant countryside, so favored by nature's abundance that it was likened to the Garden of Eden,[61] the purity of white contrasted pleasantly with the green luxuriance of vegetation. The people, whose hierarchy of priests enjoyed the exclusive privilege of being able to read the prosody of the holy books, received instruction on the origin of things; they were admonished to observe principles of right moral conduct. The rites of the Brahmans indicated that their system of religious worship was very old. A belief in metempsychosis, already familiar to Europeans through Pythagoras, was found to be flourishing in India, minutely defined and deeply interwoven into the canopy of religion and of great influence upon everyday living. The body of legend, the extent of which was hardly recognized by the early travelers, was a token of an ancient society. A host of new ideas began to seep into the intellect of Europe, and the tongues of Europe tasted strange and exotic words, among them: Ganges.

---

frequently cited is Rogerius. In the novel Bhartrihari furnishes the name of "Bartrouherri," the Moorish commander of Chaumigrem's field pieces; see Henrich Anshelm von Zigler und Kliphausen [sic], *Asiatische Banise oder blutiges doch muthiges Pegu* (Leipzig, 1707), in *Deutsche National-Litteratur*, ed. Joseph Kürschner (Berlin, n.d.), XXXVII, 285. Another novel with a faintly Indic background in the flamboyant style and manner of Ziegler's *Asiatische Banise*, and provoked by its success, was *Der asiatische Onogambo* (Hamburg, 1673) by Everhard Guerner Happel. The excrescent subtitle sums up the work's grandiose ambitions and its limitations: "Darin Der jetzt-regierende grosse Sinesische Käyser Xunchius. Als ein umbschweiffender Ritter vorgestellet, nächst dessen und anderer Asiatischer Printzen Liebes-Geschichten und ritterlichen Thaten, auch alle in Asien gelegene Königreiche, sampt deren Beschaffenheiten, Ordnung ihrer Regenten, und deren vornehmsten Thaten kürtzlich mit eingefürt werden."

61. It is doubtful whether Olearius is correct in assuming that Mandelslo speaks of Ceylon in saying that "Maffaeus wie auch Paulus Venetus (lib 3 c 22) schreiben auch . . . dass man darvor halte / es haben unsere erste Eltern ihren Sitz allhier gehabt / und sey in dieser Gegend das Paradiss gewesen"; see Olearius, *Reisebeschreibung* [1658 ed. of Mandelslo], p. 146. The site of the Garden of Eden in India is generally laid in Kashmir; see François Bernier, *Voyages* (2 vols.; Amsterdam, 1699), II, 277: "De tout ce que je viens de dire on peut assez conjecturer que je suis un peu charmé de Kachemire, & que je pretens qu'il n'y a peut-être rien au monde de pareil ny de si beau pour un petit Royaume . . . & ce n'est pas sans quelque raison que les Mogols l'appellent le Paradis Terrestre des Indes."

2. *Les Brames sont les maîtres de Pythagore, les instituteurs de la Grèce, et par elle de l'Europe entière.* —BAILLY

Although the number of volumes of travel literature concerning India was sizable before 1750, examples of this literary genre increased mightily between 1750 and 1800. They were a generally widespread and favorite reading matter in the second half of the eighteenth century. Collections of books of travel began to appear as early as 1747,[1] and by 1780 there were six multi-volumed collections available.[2] A number of periodicals of the era, too, carried either reports about or excerpts from travel books. The collections contained mainly reprints of older accounts of travels, but concurrently there appeared from the pens of contemporary travelers a multitude of journals, histories, narratives, memoirs, and communications, some not dependable and some most authoritative. It was in these books that the Romantic mythical image of India had its inception, for from them were culled the opinions and assumptions and beliefs which, when gathered and sorted and combined by theorists who were compelled by an attitude of philosophical humanism and bursting with a longing for primal verities, resulted in the development of that mythical image.

From the plethora of travel books and treatises on India which appeared in this half century, the following are representative of a host of minor works: Gerbett, Gatterer, who calls the Hindus the gentlest of people,[3] Niebuhr, who describes Indian pagodas and provides numerous pictures of Indian sculptures,[4] Rochon, Stavorinus, and Boyd.[5] Reinhold Forster (1729-1798) translated several books on India and published two collections of travel narratives, one with Matthias Sprengel (1746-1803).[6] Sprengel himself later

---

1. Schwabe, *Allgemeine Historie.*
2. Grundmann, pp. 17-18, and p. 18, n. 1.
3. Johann Christoph Gatterer, *Allgemeine historische Bibliothek* (16 vols.; Halle, 1767-1771), VI, 233 f.
4. Carsten Niebuhr, *Reise nach Arabien* (3 vols.; Copenhagen, 1774-1778), II, 32 ff.
5. For the works of authors not supplied in footnotes, see Bibliography.
6. Reinhold Forster and M. C. Sprengel, eds., *Beiträge zur Völker- und Länderkunde* (14 vols.; Leipzig, 1781-1784, 1786-1790). Forster was co-editor of only three

published a selection of geographical and statistical reports about newly discovered lands and their inhabitants.[7] Jean Bernoulli (1744-1807) also brought out a three-volume compilation about India.[8]

The persuasion that India was the source of all wisdom had prevailed for centuries. John Z. Holwell (1711-1798), a former governor of Bengal and a survivor of the famed Black Hole of Calcutta, gives an account of his favorable impression of the religious and moral precepts of India. Because of his acquaintance with one of the holy books of the Hindus (the Sanskrit *Satapatha-brâhmana*, called the *Chartah Bhade* in Holwell's adaptation),[9] he believed he discerned a great influence of Indic culture upon other lands in ancient times. The more familiar he became with the Sanskrit work, the more clearly he claimed to see that the mythology as well as the cosmogony of the Egyptians, the Greeks, and the Romans was borrowed from the teachings of the Brahmans contained in the *Satapatha-brâhmana*. Even the extreme rituals of Hindu worship and the classification of Indic gods found their way West, although extremely falsified and truncated.[10]

Another statement concerning India as the originator of knowledge came from Alexander Dow (d. 1779), who spent some time in military service with the East India Company as a colonel, and who translated Firishtah's history of Hindustan in 1768. He prefaces his translation of the Persian historian with a "Dissertation Concerning the Customs, Manners, Language, Religion and Philosophy of the Hindoos," in which he makes the understatement that the "Brahmans of the East possessed in ancient times, some reputation

volumes (to 1783); the remainder were edited by Sprengel alone. See also Reinhold Forster, trans. and ed., *Magazin von merkwürdigen neuen Reisebeschreibungen* (16 vols.; Berlin, 1790-1798).

7. M. C. Sprengel, *Auswahl der besten ausländischen geographischen und statistischen Nachrichten zur Aufklärung der Völker- und Länderkunde* (14 parts in 7 vols.; Halle, 1794-1800).

8. Jean Bernoulli, ed., *Description historique et géographique de l'Inde* (3 vols.; Berlin, 1786-1789). Volume 3, Part 2, dated 1789, is a translation of *Des Pater Josef Tiefenthaller's . . . historisch-geographische Beschreibung von Hindustan*, first published in Berlin, 1785-1788.

9. J. Z. Holwell, *Merkwürdige historische Nachrichten von Hindostan und Bengalen*, trans. J. F. Kleucker (Leipzig, 1778), pp. 266 f. Since Holwell states that he did not have time to learn Sanskrit, his *Chartah Bhade* was not taken directly from the original. Grundmann (p. 71) states that Holwell's source, the *Satapatha-brâhmana*, was later lost.

10. Holwell, p. 275.

for knowledge."[11] The French translator of this work affirms in the preface more comprehensively the probability that the Persians, the Egyptians, the Greeks themselves, and perhaps the Chinese originally received their wisdom from Hindustan.[12] The same idea was advanced in 1775 by Voltaire (1694-1778), in a letter to the astronomer Jean Sylvain Bailly (1736-1793), in which he said that he finally was convinced that astronomy, astrology, and metempsychosis had come to the West from the Ganges.[13] Bailly himself, although he believed that the Persians, the Chinese, and the Indians had all descended from a common ancestral people, nevertheless wrote that the Brahmans were the masters of Pythagoras, the tutors of the Greeks and, through them, of all Europe. He called the wisdom of India sage and sublime.[14] William Macintosh, in 1782, adds further to this picture of the sublimity and the antiquity of Indian knowledge and its influence on the West: "All history points to India as the mother of science and art. This country was anciently so renowned for knowledge and wisdom, that the philosophers of Greece did not disdain to travel thither for their improvement."[15]

Between 1768 and 1781 Pierre de Sonnerat (1749-1814), a learned student of the French botanist Philibert Commerson, made several trips to the East Indies and to India. In his account of these voyages he writes that many people came to the Hindus to borrow the elements of their wisdom, and that Pythagoras left Greece to study under the Brahmans, regarded then as the most enlightened of men. Sonnerat, too, places the inception of wisdom in India when he writes that India, in all its splendor, gave religions and laws to all other peoples, and that Egypt and Greece were indebted to India for all their fables and their sapience.[16]

11. Alexander Dow, trans., *The History of Hindostan* [from the Persian of Firishtah, Muhammad Kāsim ibn Hindū Shāh] (3rd ed.; 3 vols.; Dublin, 1792), I, xix. In the "Dissertation" Dow relates his own impressions of the customs and culture of India and gives also a partial translation of a *sastra* of the Vedas.
12. Alexander Dow, *Dissertation sur les mœurs, les usages, le langage, la religion et la philosophie des Hindous*, trans. M. B. . . (Paris, 1769), p. xiv.
13. Jean Sylvain Bailly, *Lettres sur l'origine des sciences et sur celle des peuples de l'Asie adressées à M. Voltaire* (Paris-London, 1777), pp. 1 ff.
14. *Ibid.*, p. 51.
15. Macintosh, I, 310.
16. M. [Pierre de] Sonnerat, *Voyage aux Indes Orientales* (2 vols.; Paris, 1782),

The German translators of English, French, and Italian travel literature often could not refrain from either appending an investigation of their own—a miscellany of foreign lore they themselves had collected—or else commenting with approval or disapproval in footnotes upon the work at hand. Such a translator was Christian Dohm (1751-1820), who translated the narrative of Edward Ives (d. 1786) into German in 1774. Dohm was perhaps the first to think of India in terms of the cradle of humanity. In a footnote to Ives he observes that the production of coco palms and other trees and plants occurred naturally and did not have to be achieved by artifice and inventiveness. He wonders if this fact should not support the very probable hypothesis, founded on other grounds, that India was the true fatherland, the cradle of the human race.[17] Farther on in the volume he elucidates in more detail, saying that the requirements of life, food, shelter, and clothing were simply gifts of nature in India and did not have to be attained through labor and ingenuity as in less mild regions of the earth. He uses this reason to reinforce his thesis that India appeared to have first nourished human culture, and he finds that the historical proofs for the antiquity of the Indians and their philosophy receive new weight from this physical principle. He suggests that it is a priori presumable that the human mind occupied itself earliest with objects of metaphysical speculation in such regions where human activities were already sustained with enough for physical needs. He asserts that this was particularly so in South Asia, especially in India, which in this respect had advantages over China.[18]

At the end of this passage Dohm apologizes for the digression and asks his readers for ideas relative to the thesis he proposes. He seems to believe that he is the first to suggest that India may be the very birthplace of civilization. Dohm states that the chief source for his supplementary remarks was Holwell, and doubtless it was from this author that he took the theory that geographical location, the whole

---

I, 3-4. This author, who laced his first-hand observations with anecdotes culled from Rogerius, supplied Goethe with the sources for two Indic-colored works: "Der Gott und die Bajadere" and "Paria."

17. Edward Ives, *Reisen nach Indien und Persien*, trans. Christian Willhelm Dohm (2 vols.; Leipzig, 1774), I, 100-101. Dohm was later the author of *Geschichte der Engländer und Franzosen im östlichen Indien* (Leipzig, 1776).

18. Ives, *Reisen*, I, in Dohm's "Zusätze des Übersetzers," pp. 41-42.

milieu of a bountiful nature and climate, affects the way of life and the mode of thought of a people,[19] although such a theory had been implied earlier, in 1756, by Voltaire in his *Essai sur les mœurs et l'esprit des nations*, where, speaking of India, he states that mankind gathered as a matter of course in its delightful climate.[20]

Louis Marie Degrandpré (1761-1846), a French voyager with scholarly pretensions, disputed Voltaire's implication that India was the original home of humankind, and was bold enough to say in his travel narrative that he dared to presume the *Ezur Veda*, supposedly written before the conquests of Alexander, had not been written in Bengal at all. He said further that, were it not for the respect he had for the ashes of the man, he would have the audacity to oppose the opinion of a great author who had not hesitated to declare that India, toward the Ganges, was the land in which mankind first assembled in social groups.[21]

Dohm, in another footnote to Ives, conjectures that the heat of the climate dried up all violent, dissolute passions among the Indians. Nature, which gratified all his needs effortlessly, prevented the Indian from being mischievous and deceitful, and he became so only when unnatural despotism deprived him of the gifts of nature. Dohm further believes that the philosophy of India and its religion is an outgrowth of a simple culture in a state of harmony with a beneficent nature, not the result of subjective speculation. The philosophical ideas are symbols with a rich content—perhaps more original than those of any other people—inspired more by nature and self-reflection than by political priests or lawgivers.[22] Sonnerat, as well, remarks on the effect of climate upon the intellectual development of a people, saying that it is certainly true that the first sparks of reason burned brilliantly in those climes because intellectual faculties do not develop except where physical needs are quelled. Several times he points to the agreement of Indian mythol-

19. Holwell, p. 317.
20. François Voltaire, *Oeuvres complètes*, ed. Louis Moland, (52 vols.; Paris, 1877-1885), XI, 49.
21. B. [sic, L.] Degrandpré, *Reise nach Indien und Arabien in den Jahren 1789 und 1790* (Berlin, 1803), p. 196. He refers here to Voltaire's conjecture in the *Essai sur les mœurs* that the Indians in the region of the Ganges were perhaps the most ancient people assembled in tribes (*Oeuvres*, XI, 49). Actually, Degrandpré's suspicions later were confirmed, for the *Ezur Veda* was a fraud. Voltaire also called India the cradle of all the arts (*Oeuvres*, XI, 158).
22. Ives, I, 375, 342.

ogy and religious dogmas with those of all the Asiatic peoples. This
similarity was for him indisputable proof that all the Eastern religions had a common source in India, presumably the birthplace of
all nations.[23]

Travel narrators and commentators in the latter half of the eighteenth century shared the common belief that India was very ancient. The translator of the French edition of Dow says that the
philosophical wisdom one finds in the *sastras*, the purity of their
dogmas concerning the unity, the attributes, and the providence of
God, concerning the immateriality and immortality of the soul, the
liberty of man, the punishments and requitals to come, the most
important questions of theology and metaphysics which one finds
discussed there, all of this presupposes a very advanced stage of
society, reason perfected by long experience, an immense progress
in the march of the human spirit, and consequently a preceding
antiquity of a prodigious length.[24] Dow himself says "there are many
hundred volumes in prose in the Shanscrita language, which treat of
the ancient Indian, [and] the author . . . has great reason to believe,
that the Hindoos carry their authentic history farther back into
antiquity, than any other nation now existing."[25] Sonnerat believes
that all peoples go back to a real or a fabulous origin, but declares
the origin of the Hindus was lost in the night of time, and that
among the Indians could be found the vestiges of a most distant
antiquity.[26]

Robertson, in his disquisition on India, predicates his own theory
of the great age of their culture on the antiquity of Indian commerce, which he holds to be evidence of a highly civilized society.
He finds further proof in government, citing the vast kingdoms
encountered by the Greeks of Alexander's expeditionary forces.[27]
The conception of India as the very source of civilization, as the
nation where human culture first was bred, contributed in great
measure to the formation of the Romantic mythical image of India.

The curious mixture of primitivism (for the Indians were not a
mechanical society) and sublime culture (but they had developed
the arts to a high degree) was in the possession of a people who

23. Sonnerat, I, 3.
24. Dow, *Dissertation*, pp. xii-xiii.
25. Dow, *History*, I, iv.
26. Sonnerat, I, 2-3.
27. Robertson, pp. 257, 262-263.

were appraised differently by the various observers. Holwell, representative of a minority, reveals a sharply critical opinion of the people of India. He announces that the Hindus, taken as a whole, are as spoiled, crafty, superstitious, quarrelsome, and malicious a people as any in the known world, if not worse, especially the common swarm of Brahmans.[28] This view might perhaps be explained in Holwell's case by his incarceration in the Black Hole and no doubt by the fact that his relations as a governor with foreign subjects were not conducive to pleasant experiences.

Guillaume le Gentil de la Galaisière (d. 1792), who traveled to India in 1761 to observe the transit of Venus and who stayed almost two years at Pondichéry, delineates a more flattering picture of the Hindu. He describes especially the natives of the coast of Coromandel (a part of India frequented often by Europeans because of European settlements there). The Indians are quite handsome and well-formed, he reports, noticing particularly their black, lively, soulful eyes. He reiterates that India is the most accommodating and charming land under the sun, and that it is inhabited by the gentlest and most obliging of peoples.[29]

Macintosh, always favorable in his estimate of every phase of Indian life and culture, says:

Their persons are straight and elegant, their limbs finely proportioned, their fingers long and tapering, their countenances open and pleasant, and their features exhibit the most delicate lines of beauty in the females, and in the males a kind of manly softness. Their walk and gait, as well as their whole deportment, is in the highest degree graceful.[30]

The temperament of the Indian conformed to the ease of his life in the midst of the bounteous nature which impressed most travelers. Ives says that the Indians are a very quiet and harmless kind of people who would insult no one.[31] Macintosh comments with enthusiasm: "The tranquillity of their minds, even in the most trying circumstances, is expressed by a constant smile that sits gracefully on their placid countenances," and he goes on to say that "the

28. Holwell, pp. 313 f.
29. Guillaume [Joseph] le Gentil [de la Galaisière], *Reisen in den indischen Meeren 1761-69*, in Vols. II and IV of *Neue Sammlung von Reisebeschreibungen* (Hamburg, 1781), IV, 324, 398. The original work was *Voyage dans les mers de l'Inde* (2 vols.; Paris, 1779-1781).
30. Macintosh, I, 321-322.
31. Ives, I, 86.

Hindoos are naturally the most inoffensive of all mortals." He comments at greater length on the skill of their imitative talents as
artisans and their intrepidity of spirit:

In Asia, particularly in India, both on this side and beyond the Ganges,
there is a scrupulous tenacity of ancient customs and manners. . . . In
arts [of imitation] the Hindoos are so dextrous, that the original model
is not to be distinguished from the new production. . . . For works of
imitation, their nature seems peculiarly fitted, by that patient perseverance which so eminently distinguishes them. . . . And with all this
perseverance and straining of attention, they preserve an evenness of
spirits.[32]

Sonnerat, describing the inhabitants of the Coromandel coast,
says that they are black, both tall and well-made, but weak, lax, and
effeminate. He says their natures incline to joy and gaiety, and that
they love games, dancing, spectacles, and music.[33] Pierre-Marie-
François Pagés (1748-1793), in his *Voyages autour du monde 1767-
1776* (Paris, 1782), praises the simple, innocent customs of the
Indians, their orderly and quiet way of living, and is inclined to
credit their abstinence from eating meat and highly spiced foods
for their striking gentleness of spirit.[34]

A Carmelite monk, Paulinus a Sancto Bartholomaeo (an Aus-
trian, born Johann Philipp Wesdin, 1748-1806), who was among
the earliest to devote himself to the study of India and Sanskrit,[35]
is astonished at how one people differs from another. The Indians
are agile, nimble, and weak, but are polite and obliging. They act
after reflection, love moderation, and lead a very decent life. The
Arabians, on the other hand, are clumsy, coarse, robust, and loyal,
but seldom take regard of reason and propriety.[36]

32. Macintosh, I, 301-302, 332.
33. Sonnerat, I, 27.
34. Grundmann, p. 67.
35. Ernst Windisch, in his *Geschichte der Sanskrit-Philologie* (Strassburg, 1917),
lists on pp. 19-20 the following Germans who were the first from that land to study
Sanskrit: the Jesuits Heinrich Roth, who studied Sanskrit on his travels in India from
1650 to 1660, Athanasius Kircher, who in 1667 published Sanskrit material received
from Roth, and Johannes Ernst Hanxleden (in India from 1699 until his death in
1732), who was the first European to write a Sanskrit grammar. Paulinus was in India
from 1776 to 1789 and toward the end of the century published in Rome a grammar
and a treatise on Brahmaism.
36. Paulinus a Sancto Bartholomaeo, *Reise nach Ostindien*, trans. Reinhold Forster, in *Magazin von merkwürdigen neuen Reisebeschreibungen*, XV (Berlin, 1798),
p. 133.

Macintosh, in his boundless ardor for the Indian, would place him above the European:

In refinement and ease [the Hindus] are superior to any people to the westward of them. In politeness and address, in gracefulness of deportment, and speech, an Indian is as much superior to a Frenchman of fashion, as a French courtier is to a Dutch burgo-master of *Dort*. . . . The *Hindoos*, especially those of the higher Castes, are in their demeanor easy and unconstrained . . . but their ease and freedom is reserved, modest, and respectful. . . . An Indian [is polite] because he respects you.[37]

The moderation of the Hindus was noticed by Ives, who says that they are very temperate in eating and drinking, and seldom use strong liquor except as medication. His translator, Dohm, also has a favorable picture of the Indian, whom he calls good-natured, calm, moderate, and comparable to the ever-pure Indian sky. In yet another footnote to Ives, Dohm praises the moral sense of the Hindu, which is ingrained in him by the teachings of the Vedas through the Brahmans. He says that their moral teachings are immense and broad; their morality is not exactly prescribed, not hypercritical, but noble and honorable. Their morals and customs are not capricious and devisive, but conciliatory and patient.[38] Macintosh, also, has praise for Indian morality in the tradition of the Brahmans, saying that "their moral principles were the most sublime that could be imagined."[39]

The high code of moral conduct, however, was damaged by the influx of Europeans, who brought greed and spoliation to the gentle, inoffensive Hindu. Ives says that somewhat deeper inland the people were also said to be very honorable and upright, and that on the coast they presumably knew nothing of deceit until they learned it from European traders. His translator and commentator Dohm, also, mentions the ruinous example of foreigners.[40] Reinhold Forster, who provides many footnotes for the German edition of Paulinus' *Reise*, also cannot refrain from mentioning the deleterious influence of the Mohammedan and the European on the Hindu. He accuses the Muslim princes of being the first to bring misery to

37. Macintosh, I, 320-321.
38. Ives, I, 86, 375-376.
39. Macintosh, I, 311.
40. Ives, I, 86, 375.

the formerly happy lands, and says that what the Mohammedans began the Europeans finished, bringing with them as soldiers the refuse of all nations.[41]

Paulinus himself calls attention to the intelligence of the Indians exhibited in their aptitude for language. He relates that from time to time several young Indians came to him, some of them heathen, some converted to Christianity, some speaking French quite well, others, who had received instruction from the Jesuits, knowing Latin. Thus he decided that the Indians had aptitudes for scholarly pursuits, and that their Indic dialects uncommonly facilitated their mastering of European languages.[42] Degrandpré is also cognizant of the ease with which the Brahmans learned languages, saying that it was marvelous, and further that they all spoke and wrote French, English, Portuguese, Arabic, the Malabar dialect, and their holy language, which no one not belonging to their caste knew.[43] Macintosh is very impressed that education does not seem limited to a select group, but that

even the inferior classes are taught reading, writing, and arithmetic: the youth are taught, not within doors, but in the open air; and it is a singular, but not unpleasing spectacle, to behold, in every village, a venerable old man, reclined on a terraced plain, teaching a number of surrounding boys, who regard him with the utmost reverence and attention, like a shepherd feeding his flock. In those simple seminaries . . . the gentle and tractable sons of the Hindoos are not only prepared for the business, but instructed in the duties of life; a profound veneration for the object or objects of religious worship; a reverence of their parents; respect for their seniors; justice and humanity towards all men, but a particular affection for those of their own Caste.

Concerning the language spoken by the Hindus, Macintosh is full of admiration: "The Hindoo language is beautiful, expressive, and nervous. In reading and speaking, the Hindoos are very musical. . . . There is a dead language, understood only by . . . the priests, called the *Sancrit* language, in which their sacred volumes are written."[44]

The commentators emphasize that the keepers of the holy language, in which were preserved all of India's treasures of knowledge,

41. Paulinus, *Reise*, p. 66, n.
42. *Ibid.*, pp. 17-18.
43. Degrandpré, p. 70.
44. Macintosh, I, 324-325.

were most unwilling to divulge their mysteries or to instruct the Europeans in Sanskrit; not even fellow Hindus might be taught to read the holy texts, for the Brahmans through the centuries had reserved this privilege for themselves. Dow says: "The Bedas are, by the Brahmins, held so sacred, that they permit no other sect to read them. . . . The Brahmins themselves are bound by such strong ties of religion, to confine those writings to their own tribe, that were any of them known to read them to others, he would be immediately excommunicated." He also mentions that "these books not only treat of religious and moral duties, but of every branch of philosophical science." Dow himself received instruction in Sanskrit but found it very difficult to learn, hard to pronounce, and so complex that when the time came for him to leave India he had not learned it thoroughly.[45]

Dohm, again in his appendix to Ives, remarks that the Brahmans accept no converts to their religion, chiefly because they do not wish to reveal Sanskrit, the vehicle of their knowledge and religion. It is well known, he says, that the Brahmans accept no proselytes and hand their teachings on only to their descendants and never, except with the greatest of resistance, instruct foreigners.[46] Degrandpré writes that the Brahmans are little communicative. It is a tenet of their religion, he says, to withhold the knowledge of their language and their books from all the world.[47] But Robertson records that Europeans have, only after hundreds of years of direct intercourse with India, just now begun to win the confidence of Brahmans:

That all the science and literature possessed by the Brahmins, were contained in books written in a language, understood by a few only of the most learned among them, is a fact which has long been known; and all the Europeans settled in India during three centuries, have complained that the Brahmins obstinately refused to instruct any person in this language. But at length, by address, mild treatment, and a persuasion, that the earnestness with which instruction was solicited, proceeded not from any intention of turning their religion into derision, but from a desire of acquiring a perfect knowledge of their sciences and literature, their scruples have been overcome. Several British gentlemen are now

45. Dow, *History*, I, xxi-xxii, xxvii-xxviii.
46. Ives, I, in Dohm's "Zusätze," p. 33; Bernier also points out (in *Voyages*, II, 138) that the faith of the Brahmans was not universal, that God meant it only for them, and that for this reason they accepted no foreigners in their religion.
47. Degrandpré, p. 162.

completely masters of the Sanskreet language. The mysterious veil, formerly deemed impenetrable, is removed.[48]

The remarkable stability of the social system in India rested on the division of the populace into castes, a segregation promulgated in the holy books. And the only interpreters of the sacred writings, the Brahmans, had maintained their immutable supremacy in the caste hierarchy in part because of the tenacity with which they held to their privileged position as wardens of the ancient, hallowed language. Specifically, Degrandpré says that if anything could keep the Brahman on his exalted pedestal it was the secrecy which they spread over their primeval tongue, their mysteries, their holy books, and over the wisdom involved. And more than anything, perhaps, was the privilege they insisted upon of attending to the altars themselves. The fact that some English scholars had succeeded in learning Sanskrit and in translating various works found in that ancient tongue seemed to indicate to Degrandpré that the Brahmans were now in danger of losing their high and select position, if, indeed, they had not falsified the material they supplied to translators, thereby observing the religious injunction not to reveal the mysteries of their religion or the cryptic language in which it and their other knowledge was couched.[49]

Paulinus is awed by the fact that the Sanskrit books, containing the wealth of Indian wisdom, were written in verse, and that even their astronomy, art of medicine, and history were divided into cantos.[50] This observation did not go unnoticed by Romantic theorists, who trumpeted a universal poetry, the poetic expression of all wisdom.

Macintosh lauds the ancient tradition of Brahman purity:

It appears, from the concurring testimony of ancient writers, that the Brahmins of India, about two thousand years ago, lived innocent, pure, and austere lives, abstaining from wine and animal food; and, as much as possible, from all sensual enjoyment. They . . . endeavoured to shelter their feeble virtue by retirement in caves and woods, where they subsisted on the spontaneous productions of the earth.

48. Robertson, p. 287.
49. Degrandpré, pp. 70, 163-164.
50. Paulinus, *Reise*, p. 371.

He deems it no compliment to his contemporaries that the Brahmans are no longer appreciated as well as they had been in the ancient past. He believes that, although the Brahmans as a social and ethical group may have become decadent, their philosophy has maintained its original "pure and excellent" virtues.[51] Dohm would place the burden of degeneration upon foreign depravities. He purposely says nothing regarding the religious concepts of India because previously travelers had usually mixed up everything: the profound philosophy of the Brahmans with the silliest superstitions of the rabble, pure concepts which had originated in India with absurd ideas which had crept in from abroad.[52]

Dow excoriates European travelers for casting aspersions upon a religion and a philosophy they failed to investigate in an effort to understand its strange ways.[53] Macintosh stoutly defends the Hindu against charges of idolatry:

Thus far only the Gentoos are idolators, that in worshipping the great God of the universe, they place before their bodily eyes, for the information of their minds, such representations as are calculated to recall, in a vivid manner, to their imaginations, those attributes which they believe that Almighty being only to possess.[54]

And Sonnerat, also, disavows the charge of idolatry and gives a succinct description of the Supreme Being worshiped by the Indians. He denies that the Hindu wisemen are idolators, for they only invent tales which the Brahmans recite to maintain the faith of the people. They worship a supreme and infinite Being, and when asked how they would depict God, they reply without hesitation that He is as difficult to depict as the voice which leaves the mouth or the sound of a bell. Such phenomena can only be heard, just as God can be felt without being defined or depicted in a perceptible form.[55]

In his translation of a *sastra* of the Vedas, Dow presents a dialogue in which Narud (Reason) speaks with Brimha (the Wisdom of the Divinity) and seeks to realize a conception of God:

NARUD: What shall we think of God?

51. Macintosh, I, 311, 314, 317-318.
52. Ives, I, Dohm's "Zusätze," pp. 51-52.
53. Dow, *History*, I, xx.
54. Macintosh, I, 320.
55. Sonnerat, I, 6.

BRIMHA: Being immaterial, he is above all conception; being invisible, he can have no form; but, from what we behold in his works, we may conclude that he is eternal, omnipotent, knowing all things, and present every where.[56]

Even Paulinus, the Carmelite monk, is aware of the essence of the Hindu deity, for he avers that the Indians believe in a single, true God who has the fundament of His existence in Himself and lives from eternity to eternity.[57]

Thus the sketchy knowledge which Europeans had before 1750 concerning India was extended and enlarged by the multitude of travel books and commentaries, printed singly or in many collections, in the last half of the eighteenth century. These accounts are chiefly subjective and written in an uncritical manner with a highly affirmative praise of India and the Hindu. A curious mixture of fact, fiction, and opinion offers the source for the development of the mythical image of India refracted by German Romanticists.

India was looked upon as the source of all human wisdom. Through long centuries the ancient culture which had developed in the very cradle of humanity, the land of the Ganges, had brought forth a great array of natural sciences and a complex system of religion whose influence was extended to all the Western world through the Greeks. The great antiquity of the Brahmans, whose historical beginnings were lost in the ages, attested the immemorial character of the Hindu religion and of the language which had preserved the tenets of that religion for millenia. The high development of ancient Indian culture was proved by the cryptic prosody of its religious scriptures and the hoary ruins of its pagodas and their fantastic sculptures. No other people on earth seemed so old, and certainly no other people revealed a culture whose sublimity in arts and the sciences and philosophy was so ancient.

The contemporary Hindu was pictured as an unspoiled child of nature, whose simple and gentle spirit risked depravity by less cultivated Europeans. His moral sense, imbued into him for centuries, was broad and admirable. He was moderate in his sensual enjoyments and gifted with an inborn intelligence. These exalted people were not idolators, but worshiped a God whose essence in meta-

56. Dow, *History*, I, xxxvii.
57. Paulinus, *Reise*, p. 326.

physical terms was not unlike the familiar God of Christianity.

All these attributes of India and the Hindu needed but the stamp of authenticity to initiate the development of a mythical image, and this stamp was supplied by the first Sanskrit translators.

> *3. In the course of five years, the curiosity of the public has been gratified by two publications as singular as they were unexpected. . . . One is a translation . . . of an Episode from the* Mahabarat, *an Epic poem. . . . The other is* Sacontala, *a dramatic poem.* —ROBERTSON

More than one hundred years passed between the first and second renditions of a major Sanskrit work into a language of Europe. Bhartrihari's *Maxims*, the first Sanskrit text to be reproduced in a European tongue (1651), was paraphrased into Dutch through Portuguese, later published in German (two editions) and in French. Holwell, in 1764, published in his historical essay a partial translation of the *Satapatha-brâhmana*, but not directly from the Sanskrit. Concerning Dow's translation, in 1768, of a *sastra* from the Vedas, Robertson says that it was "not made . . . from the Sanskreet, but taken from the mouth of a Brahmin, who explained the Shaster in Persian, or in the vulgar language of Bengal."[1] Nathaniel Halhed (1751-1830), the first Englishman to acquire a knowledge of Sanskrit,[2] had not yet become proficient in the language when he translated a code of Hindu law from a Persian rendering of the Sanskrit text in 1776.[3]

The publication of the *Yajur Veda* in French in 1778 (translated into German in 1779) is important for its influence on the thought of the time, in particular upon Voltaire. A portion had been translated into German in 1742, though not directly from the Sanskrit; the French edition purported to be the entire book. It was later

---

1. Robertson, p. 359.
2. *Ibid.*, p. 355.
3. Nathaniel Brassey Halhed, trans., *A Code of Gentoo Laws, or, Ordinations of the Pundits* (London, 1776); German ed., *Gesetzbuch der Gentoos*, trans. Rudolf Erich Raspe (Hamburg, 1778).

proved to be a rather deft piece of propaganda instigated by Jesuits in the seventeenth century, ostensibly by a priest named Roberto do Nobili.[4] Voltaire had access to the work before 1756 in manuscript, because he lauds it in his *Essai sur les mœurs et l'esprit des nations*, where he writes that a happy accident had procured for the library in Paris an ancient book of the Brahmans, entitled the "Cormo-Veda," written before Alexander's expedition into India and containing a program of all the ancient Brahmanic rituals. Voltaire admits that the manuscript, translated by a Brahman, is not really the Veda itself, but is a resumé of the rituals contained in that code. He then boasts that the French can be congratulated for having such a knowledge of the most ancient writings in existence.[5]

Méridas Poullé's (1721-1796) translation of a Tamil version of the *Bhagavatapurana*, published in 1788, would not qualify as a direct translation from Sanskrit, but it nevertheless added still more to the information that was accumulating in Europe about Indian culture.[6]

It was in England that the first translations directly from Sanskrit appeared. Robertson wrote, in 1790, that Charles Wilkins' (1749-1836) translation of the *Bhagavad-Gita* was from the *Mahabharata*, a work held "in high estimation among the Hindoos [and] composed, according to their account, by Kreeshna Dwypayen Veias, the most eminent of all their Brahmins, above 3000 years before the Christian aera." He noted further that the drama *Sakuntala*, translated by Sir William Jones (1746-1794), was written "about a century before the birth of Christ." Robertson's gross error in dating the two works is an instance of the universal confusion which prevailed in his day in regard to assigning specific dates to Indic relics.

4. *L'Ezour Vedam ou Ancien Commentaire du Vedam, contenant l'exposition des opinions religieuses et philosophiques des Indiens*. Traduit de Samscretan par un Brame (Yverdon, 1778). German ed., *Ezour-Vedam, oder die Geschichte, Religion und Philosophie der Indier*, trans. J. Ith (Leipzig, [1779]). For the history of this fraudulent work, see Friedrich von Adelung, *An Historical Sketch of Sanscrit Literature* (Oxford, 1832), pp. 75-76.

5. Voltaire, *Oeuvres*, XI, 52.

6. Méridas Poullé, trans. *Bagavadam ou Doctrine Divine* (Paris, 1788). Poullé, whose transliterated name is Mariyadāsa Piḷḷai, was a Christian convert and petty government official in Malabar, who first translated this extract of the Sanskrit work in 1769 with only tolerable faithfulness; see Adelung, pp. 89-90. One scholar claims Poullé revised the original effort in 1793-1795 and has published this revised manuscript; see *Le Bhâgavata*, trans. Meridas Poullé, ed. Père H. Hosten (Pondichéry, 1921), Société de l'Histoire de l'Inde Française, IV, 1.

Robertson mentions also Wilkins' *Heetopades,* "a series of connected fables, interspersed with moral, prudential, and political maxims. . . . At length, these fables made their way into Europe, and have been circulated there with additions and alterations under the names of Pilpay and Esop."[7]

Aside from minor translations of a few poems and land-grant documents, these were the only translations of Sanskrit writings extant in 1790. It was from the translators' comments and remarks in notes and prefaces to these works that the mythical image of India acquired, not a new dimension, but rather confirmation. The works themselves were less influential for the development of the mythical image, but rather sustained that image with ideas and symbols rooted in a real past.

Concerning the Hindu division of the duration of the world into four eras, the first of which was the age of gold, Jones says, in his essay "On the Chronology of the Hindus" (1788): "From the materials with which we are at present supplied, we may establish as indubitable the two following propositions; that the 3 *first* ages of the Hindus are chiefly mythological . . . and, that the fourth, or historical age, cannot be carried farther back than about two thousand years before Christ."[8] Jones is here very conservative in his estimation of the historical age of the Hindus; other writers assume 3,000 or even 4,000 years. Halhed was of the opinion that "the World does not now contain Annals of more indisputable Antiquity than those delivered down by the ancient Bramins."[9]

Poullé, in the foreword to the *Bagavadam,* comments upon the great age of Indic architectural relics. He says that the superb monuments, astonishing for their boldness and the immensity of the labor which produced them, made to endure the onslaught of centuries, were abandoned long ago. But one admires the images which the various sects still venerate. At the feet of some can be seen inscriptions in characters unknown today. The most hasty glance suffices, according to Poullé, to attest to the antiquity of the canonical writings of the people and the legends which are consecrated there.[10]

7. Robertson, pp. 288, 356-357.
8. Sir William Jones, *Works* (6 vols.; London, 1799), I, 309.
9. Halhed, p. xliv.
10. Poullé, p. xxxii.

Jones offers further support for the antiquity of the culture of the Hindus when, in his article "On the Antiquity of the Indian Zodiack," he writes:

I engage to support an opinion . . . that the *Indian* division of the Zodiack was not borrowed from the *Greeks* or *Arabs*, but, having been known in this country from time immemorial, and being the same in part with that used by other nations of the old *Hindu* race, was probably invented by the first progenitors of that race before their dispersion. . . . Since the solar division of [the zodiac] in *India* is the same in substance with that used in *Greece*, we may reasonably conclude, that both Greeks and Hindus received it from an older nation . . . from whom both . . . had a common descent.[11]

Connections betwees the Greeks and the Hindus had been pointed out earlier in general terms—Jones, in his essay "On the Gods of Greece, Italy and India" (1784), compares each mythological figure of India with its corresponding figure in Greece and Rome; but he does not risk making a statement about the chronology of their origin.

The slowness with which scholars were learning Sanskrit is mentioned by Poullé. He writes that various works, reputedly preceptive and inspired, were composed in Sanskrit, which he says was known only imperfectly and by a small number of scholars.[12] A few years earlier Halhed had been eager to learn Sanskrit, but despite persuasion on his part and support by his government, he could not induce the Brahmans to instruct him in the language (although he did learn it later) and was obliged to translate his code of Hindu laws from Persian.[13] But now the mystery had been divulged, and scholars such as Wilkins and Jones, soon to be followed by others, were hard at work translating. Charles Wilkins, in a note to his *Heetopades*, reveals that his Brahman informant and teacher made the following reply when he was upbraided for unveiling the holy secrets to a foreigner:

A wise man is worthy to be advised; but an ignorant one never. When the learned Pandit under whom the translator studied the Sanskreet language at their holy city of Banaris, used to be reproached by other Brahmans for communicating the key of their divine mysteries to foreign-

11. Jones, I, 333-334.
12. Poullé, p. xxix.
13. Halhed, p. xxxvi.

ers, he constantly silenced them by repeating this hemistich in the original.[14]

The influence of natural phenomena as a source for mythology was noted by Jones, who lists four roots of mythology:

I. Historical, or natural, truth . . . perverted into fable . . . hence beacons or volcanoes became one-eyed giants and monsters vomiting flames.

II. . . . a wild admiration of the heavenly bodies . . . the sun, and the far extended adoration of the elements and the powers of nature.

III. . . . divinities . . . created solely by the magick of poetry; whose essential business it is, to personify the most abstract notions, and to place a nymph or a genius in every grove and almost in every flower.

IV. The metaphors and allegories of moralists and metaphysicians.

The presence of natural forces is evident in almost every mythological figure in Hindu lore. In his treatise "On the Musical Modes of the Hindus" (1784), Jones remarks: "In the literature of the *Hindus* all nature is animated and personified; every fine art is declared to have been revealed from heaven; and all knowledge, divine and human, is traced to its source in the Védas." Concerning the forces of nature represented allegorically as Hindu deities, Jones says, in his introduction to *Sacontala*:

The deities introduced in the Fatal Ring are clearly allegorical personages. Maríchi, the first production of Bráhma, or the Creative Power, signifies light, that subtil fluid which was created before its reservoir, the sun, as water was created before the sea; Casyapa, the offspring of Maríchi, seems to be a personification of infinite space, comprehending innumerable worlds; and his children by Aditi, or his active power (unless Aditi mean the primeval day, and Diti, his other wife, the night) are Indra, or the visible firmament, and the twelve Adityas, or suns, presiding over as many months.

The allegorical function of natural forces in symbolic form is extended even to the realm of music. The ingenuity with which the Hindu made a harmonious mingling of music and subjective emotional response is much admired by Jones:

By appropriating a different mode to each of the different seasons, the artists of *India* connected certain strains with certain ideas. . . . Yet

14. Charles Wilkins, trans., *The Heetopades of Veeshnoo-Sarma* (Bath, 1787), p. 319, n. 125.

farther: since the lunar year, by which festivals and superstitious duties are constantly regulated, proceeds concurrently with the solar year, to which the seasons are necessarily referred, *devotion* comes also to the aid of musick, and all the *powers* of nature, which are allegorically worshipped as gods and goddesses on their several holidays, contribute to the influence of song on minds naturally susceptible of religious emotions.[15]

The Hindu conception of God is treated in Poullé's preface to the *Bagavadam*. According to him, the Indians were divided into two principal orthodox sects, each of which maintained itself with difficulty. Sharing the main points of the doctrine, they differed in some distinctions and legal observances, and for one Siva was the Supreme Being, while for the other the Supreme Being was Vishnu. The main point of uniform belief was that God is infinite, eternal, ineffable, and One, who manifests His triple essence under the names of Brahma, Vishnu, and Siva in His acts of creation, preservation, and destruction. The sect of Vishnu teaches, according to the *Bagavadam*, that the infinite God cannot be separated from the universe, which is essentially one with Him, for Vishnu is in everything and everything is in him. Picturing this all-pervading deity in yet another way, Poullé continues that God is infinitely smaller than an atom and also infinitely larger than the whole universe. Vishnu himself says once in the *Bagavadam* that the form of the perceptible and imperceptible universe is his image. In the manner that the grandeur of space is the greatest of the five elements, he is the element which encompasses everything. The most subtle thing is the soul, he says, and that is he. Nothing is more invincible than will, he says, and that also is he. Further, Vishnu is quoted as declaring that among utterances he is truth, among voices he is the resolution to kill nothing that lives.[16]

The English geographer Alexander Dalrymple (1737-1808), in his introduction to Wilkins' *Sakoontala*, also comments upon the Hindu trinity:

It may not be amiss to say a few words concerning the *Mythology* of the *Hindoos*: It is their Doctrine that Brahma [neuter], the Eternal Essence, for Its *efficient purpose*, is composed of a *Triple-Personification; Brahma,* the Creator! *Veeshnoo*, The Preserver! and *Seeva*, The Destroyer! or

15. Jones, I, 230-231, 424; VI, 207; and I, 429-430.
16. Poullé, pp. xii-xiii, 30, 49, 311-312.

rather, The Changer of Things! for *annihilation* is no part of their Faith; on the contrary, they believe in a *pre-existant* state, and think that the effect of procreation, is not *actually* to *produce*, but to produce under a new form: and they believe that all forms shall continue changing, until by progressive purification, they are re-absorbed into the Eternal Essence.[17]

The metaphysical conception among the Hindus of a trinity immanent in one supreme deity had been noted before, but now it was lent the authority of an actual translation from Sanskrit.

Early travelers to India thought the Hindus had no written law; but they observed that the Hindus were lawful and dispensed justice and punishment. Robertson writes that the Hindus "determined every controverted point, by recollecting what had been formerly decided." He notes further that interest in Hindu law had been expressed in earlier centuries, for Abul Fazel, the vizier of the sixteenth-century monarch of Hindustan, Akber VI, published "a brief compendium of Hindoo jurisprudence in the Ayeen Akbery, which may be considered as the first genuine communication of its principles to persons of a different religion." Robertson was convinced of the great age of Hindu law, citing the fact of its existence in Sanskrit, a language for ages no longer spoken, and understood only by the learned Brahmans.[18]

Halhed translated his *Code of Gentoo Laws* from a Persian rendering done by a group of pundits who assembled the laws for him direct from Sanskrit sources. He considers the work to be unique, a compilation of laws made public by the sanction of officials, and a refutation of the common European belief that the Hindus had none but religious regulations. He praises the code and states that the laws

contain the genuine Sentiments of a great and flourishing People, at a Time when it was impossible for them to have any Connexion or Communication with the European World, upon Subjects in which all Mankind have a common Interest. . . . They abound with Maxims of general Policy and Justice, which no Particularity of Manners, or Diversity of Religious Opinions can alter. . . . They become useful References for a Number of National and local Distinctions in our own Sacred Writings,

17. Charles Wilkins, trans., *The Story of Dooshwanta and Sakoontala* (London, 1795), pp. vi-vii.
18. Robertson, pp. 271, 273-274.

and . . . the several Powers of the Mind, in the gradual Progress of Civilization, may by judicious Comparisons from hence be investigated almost to their first Principles.

In Halhed's opinion the great antiquity of the laws is clear, since they "seem calculated for the crude Conceptions of an almost illiterate People upon their first Civilization."[19] Jones believes the laws were codified at least 3,000 years ago.[20] The fact that Hindu law had the sanction of religion, with the tenets of which the legal structure was interwoven, impressed Halhed.[21] His translation was supplemented in later years by Jones's own translation from the Sanscrit of the basic legal code of the Hindus.[22]

The Hindus were a poetic people. Jones praises their poetry: "The Sanscrit Prosody is easy and beautiful: the learned will find in it almost all the measures of the *Greeks*; and it is remarkable, that the language of the *Bráhmans* runs very naturally into *Sapphicks*, *Alcaicks*, and *Iambicks*." An evocation of music is found in their lyrics, in the sense that music calls forth a certain emotional response by means of modes, for "the *Hindu* poets never fail to change the *metre*, which is their *mode*, according to the change of subject or sentiment in the same piece." One species of their poetry, says Jones, "consists almost wholly of a mystical religious allegory, though it seems on a transient view to contain only the sentiments of a wild and voluptuous libertinism."[23] Jones finds the Hindus were accomplished poets who rendered into poetic form their religion, their philosophy, and their epic history. He mentions that they also produced odes, such as the one by the Sanscrit poet Jayadeva, which relates the ten avatars of Vishnu.

In drama, too, the Hindus were competent in early times. Jones believed the Hindus had dramas 2,000 years old. In his preface to *Sacontala*, Jones enlarges upon Hindu drama:

Dramatick poetry must have been immemorially ancient in the Indian empire. . . . By whomsoever or in whatever age this species of entertainment was invented . . . it was carried to great perfection in its kind . . . in the first century before Christ . . . at a time when the Britons were as

19. Halhed, pp. x, lxxiii-lv.
20. Jones, I, 326.
21. Halhed, p. xv.
22. Sir William Jones, *Institutes of Hindoo Law, or the Ordinances of Menu* (Calcutta, 1794).
23. Jones, I, 359, 441, 445.

unlettered and unpolished as the army of Hanumat [satyrs or mountaineers who participated in a great Hindu battle].

Jones was particularly struck by the fact that Hindu drama employed verse when the dialogue was heightened or exalted, and prose when it was unceremonious and intimate:

Men of rank and learning are represented speaking pure Sanskrit, and the women Prácrit, which is little more than the language of the Bráhmans melted down by a delicate articulation to the softness of Italian; while the low persons of the drama speak the vulgar dialects of the several provinces which they are supposed to inhabit.[24]

The *Gita-Govinda*, a pastoral drama by Jayadeva, is translated tastefully by Jones, that is, "omitting only those passages, which are too luxuriant and too bold for an European taste." It has as its subject the love of Krishna (an avatar of Vishnu) and Radha, that is, the love of the preserving and benevolent power (Krishna) for atonement, pacification, or satisfaction—allegorically the soul of man (Radha).[25]

Many of the fables in Wilkins' translation of the *Heetopades of Veeshnoo-Sarma* had made their way to Europe centuries before Wilkins rendered them into English from Sanskrit (1787). In his preface he says:

The following translation . . . is a faithful portrait of a beautiful work, which . . . is the Sanskreet original of those celebrated fables, which after passing through most of the Oriental languages . . . at length were introduced to the knowledge of the European world with a title importing them to have been originally written by Pilpay, or Bidpai, an ancient Brahman; two names of which, as far as my enquiries have extended, the Brahmans of the present times are totally ignorant. Sir William Jones says: ". . . the fables of *Veeshnoo-Sarma*, whom we ridiculously call Pilpay, are the most beautiful, if not the most ancient collection of Apologues in the world."[26]

Wilkins then, from Jones, James Fraser, and other sources, follows the long and intricate peregrinations of the fables through many tongues and finally into the literature of Europe.

The *Bagavadam* (1788) is described in the preface by Poullé as offering an outline of divine and human wisdom of the ancient peni-

24. *Ibid.*, I, 264; VI, 204-206.
25. *Ibid.*, I, 462.
26. Wilkins, *Heetopades*, pp. vii-viii.

tents and venerated sages of India. A canonical book, it was made to regulate the faith for the worshipers of Vishnu. It reveals their belief in a Supreme Being and depicts his various incarnations, some reputed to be of major importance, others adventitious; it describes the creation (or unfolding), the preservation, and the destruction of the universe; it tells of their faith in metempsychosis, in the source of all things, and in the mythological and mystic life of subordinate gods, the giants, and the illustrious men of ages past. Finally, Poullé says, the work presents a shortened table of the various cults and lists ways of rendering God propitious, indicating those which are preferable. It establishes constantly the unity of God under the name of Vishnu, and His supremacy under the attribute of preserving Providence.[27]

Charles Wilkins' translation of the *Bhagvat-Geeta* was the first of a Sanskrit work to be made directly into a European language (1785).[28] In the "Advertisement" to the original edition one finds: "The antiquity of the original, and the veneration in which it hath been held for so many ages, by a very considerable portion of the human race, must render it one of the greatest curiosities ever presented to the literary world." In an epistle prefaced to the book, Warren Hastings, the governor-general of India at the time, comments upon the age and authorship of the poem:

It is an episodical extract from the "Mahabharat," a most voluminous poem, affirmed to have been written upwards of four thousand years ago, by Kreeshna Dwypayen Veiâs, a learned Brahmin; to whom is also attributed the compilation of "The Four Vêdes, or Bêdes," the only existing original scriptures of the religion of Brahmâ; and the composition of all the Poorâns, which are to this day taught in their schools, and venerated as poems of divine inspiration. . . . He must at all events, claim the merit of having first reduced the gross and scattered tenets of their former faith into a scientific and allegorical system.

The principal design of the dialogues given in the *Bhagavad-Gita*, says Wilkins, was "to unite all the prevailing modes of worship . . . his design was to bring about the downfall of Polytheism." Wilkins remarks also that "the text is but imperfectly understood by the most learned Brahmans of the present times,"[29] which reveals the

27. Poullé, pp. xvi-xvii.
28. Robertson, p. 354.
29. Charles Wilkins, trans., *The Bhagvat-Geeta, or Dialogues of Kreeshna and Arjoon* (London, 1785), pp. 5, 19-20.

difficulty of the esoteric dialogue, for the real understanding of which a thorough acquaintance with every phase of the Hindu religion and philosophy is required. Wilkins' translation of the great Hindu philosophical epic (printed in 1785) was the only one available (except for extracts of it made by Herder in the fourth collection of *Zerstreute Blätter* [1792], and a French translation in 1787) until 1802 when Friedrich Majer, an indefatigable scholar of Indic mythology and an eager translator of Jones's versions of the *Mohamudgara* and Jayadeva's *Gita-Govinda,* published his German translation, taking Wilkins as his source.[30]

William Jones's translation of *Sacontala* (1789) had a more immediate reception in Germany, Georg Forster's version appearing two years after Jones's work. In the preface to his translation, Jones remarks: "Latin . . . bears so great a resemblance to Sanscrit, that it is more convenient than any modern language for a scrupulous interlineary version."[31] Actually, Jones translated Kalidasa's drama into Latin and then into English. The play found quick acclaim in Germany in Forster's translation.

Wilkins published, in 1795, a prose translation of the *Mahabharata* episode used by Kalidasa for his source of *Sakuntala.* Although the characters are supposed to be historical (having lived, according to Jones, 1200 B.C.), the intervention of gods in the action, and the curious, almost anthropomorphic depiction of plants and animals, caused Dalrymple, anxious for a sympathetic reception by contemporary readers, to remark in the preface to the book:

It has been, in remote Ages, the uniform opinion of all Nations of the Human Race, that there existed an immediate Intercourse with *Supernatural Beings*: sometimes through the invisible agency of *Fairies,* of *Visions* and *Dreams*; sometimes by the open agency of *Spiritual Beings,* appearing for the purposes of Judgment or Mercy: . . . in modern times . . . the Supposition is readily admitted, under the designation of *Imagery,* and the personification of *qualities* and *attributes,* called Allegory.[32]

With the publication of works translated directly from Sanskrit, the sources for the Romantic mythical image of India were complete. The great antiquity of the culture of India, its law, its arts,

30. Friedrich Majer, trans., "Der Bhaguat-Geeta," in *Asiatisches Magazin,* ed. Julius Klaproth [pseud., Louis de L'Or, Wilhelm Lauterbach] (2 vols.; Weimar, 1802), I and II.
31. Jones, VI, 204.
32. Wilkins, *Sakoontala,* pp. i, iii-iv.

its literature, was given new credence by Halhed, Jones, Wilkins, and Poullé. The great barrier to a final understanding of that ancient culture was now removed, for European scholars now received the help of Brahmans in learning Sanskrit. Jones, in his comparative study of the gods of India and those of Greece and Rome, offered a speculation on mythology and its connection with natural phenomena. Nature, personified and humanized, became an essential ingredient in the striking harmony found in Hindu culture among the branches of wisdom and the arts: philosophy, history, poetry, mythology, music, law, religion, and nature were blended and intermingled into a melodious unison expressing human knowledge and human yearning to know perfection in the essence of God.

Here were the sources, scattered and incoherent, from which Herder developed an ideal, mythical image which furnished inspiration and became an object of longing for the Early Romanticists in Germany.

II. The Delineation of the Image

Wo Sakuntala lebt mit ihrem entschwundenen Knaben,
   wo Duschmanta sie neu, neu von den Göttern empfängt,
Sei mir gegrüsst, o heiliges Land, und du Führer der Töne,
   Stimme des Herzens, erheb' oft mich im Aether dahin.[1]

The lines above, in which Johann Gottfried Herder (1744-1803) refers to the chief figures in the Sanskrit play *Sakuntala,* identify India as a holy land for which he yearns. These lines might serve as a motto to characterize his attitude toward India, an attitude of extreme reverence and adulation which resulted finally in the formulation of a mythical image, whose development can be traced in the fancy of Herder.

1. Herder references are to volume and page of his *Sämtliche Werke,* ed. Bernhard Suphan (33 vols.; Leipzig, 1877-1913); lines from a poem found in the *Nachlass,* XXIX, 665-666.

All his life Herder was a voracious reader. In Königsberg, where he studied under two great minds of his age, Johann Georg Hamann (1730-1788) and Immanuel Kant (1724-1804), he was spurred on to read in the natural sciences and the humanities. There is no doubt that he was influenced by Kant's geographical and anthropological studies and by Hamann's *Kreuzzüge des Philologen* (1762) in many of the ideas which later made their appearance in his *Abhandlung über den Ursprung der Sprache* (1770) and *Ideen zur Philosophie der Geschichte der Menschheit* (1785-1787). The last-named work is particularly valuable in the development of the mythical image of India.

Herder was an original and sometimes even a daring thinker, despite his large dependence upon others as sources for ideas, and despite his claim that he was no scholar but merely had a great talent for the fertile rephrasing of the ideas of others.[2] This is largely an accurate estimate of himself, but it does not take into account the talent he possessed for imbuing his writings with breathless enthusiasm and convincing persuasion. It was perhaps these qualities which brought him a large and appreciative audience. He was certainly no scholar in the modern sense: he was not always accurate; he wrote subjectively; he did not always credit his sources. But he was supremely gifted in gathering together and refashioning the ideas of others in such a manner as to stimulate thought and opinion. Through such stimulation did the Romantic image of India find general acceptance among the Early Romanticists in Germany.

The sources from which Herder shaped a mythical image of India were travel books, essays, and the early translations of Sanskrit works. He became acquainted in his youth with the massive travel literature of his age. His first essays contain reports and quotations from travel books (I, 17, 48, 49), and into this inexhaustible fountain of impressions and opinions and ideas he dipped to the end of his life.

Herder very early turned his probing, speculative gaze toward the East. In the essay *Abhandlung über den Ursprung der Sprache* (1770) he considers the Orient as the site where language first developed (V, 72). He points to the Oriental alphabets as prototypes of the alphabets of the West (V, 139), and he states that the gram-

2. Grundmann, p. 3.

mar of the Greeks was naturally better than that of the Oriental tongues because it was descended from them (V, 143). Fourteen years later, in his *Ideen zur Philosophie der Geschichte der Menschheit*, Herder abides by the same opinion, saying that the oldest cultivated languages are to be found in Asia, and that Asia had a script in the oldest times (XIII, 407-408).

In *Auch eine Philosophie der Geschichte zur Bildung der Menschheit* (1774), in which he proposes his theory of the four ages of mankind, Herder places the childhood of the human race in the Orient and eulogizes the Orient as God's chosen land (V, 483). He suggests a comparison of the Orient and Egypt to support his thesis (V, 488). He finds the religion of the Orient the oldest and considers the religion of the Norse a relic of the Orient given Nordic form (V, 497). In Greece the holy veil of the religion of the Orient was removed and became a beautifully spun-out fable, the dream of youths and the plaint of maidens. Oriental wisdom was simply pleasant chatter (V, 417). Herder exclaims in exultation: "Dort *Morgenland!* die *Wiege* des Menschengeschlechts, Menschlicher *Neigungen* und aller Religion" (V, 562). Dohm may have preceded Herder in calling India the cradle of mankind. His translation of Ives appeared perhaps previous to Herder's *Auch eine Philosophie*, which saw print in June, 1774 (V, 594). However, one must not assume that Herder's phrase is almost verbatim from Dohm. Voltaire preceded them both in applying a similar phrase to India in 1756. But in the *Ideen* Herder stoutly claims rhetorically that all the peoples of Europe originated in India (XIII, 406).

Herder, after Voltaire, would locate the area of the inception of human culture near the Ganges (V, 487), a region which was the primordial garden where the first flicker of human wisdom was nourished. He claims that the land of gold and precious stones mentioned by Moses could hardly be any other than India; all India considers the meandering holy Ganges the river of Paradise (XIII, 432). Again and again, in his discussions of the Brahmans, the caste system of India, its religion, mythology, literature, and arts, Herder remarks upon the great antiquity necessary for the development of such a complex, varied, and enduring culture. No human antiquity could be older than the cradle of its origin.

The view of India held by Herder is not altogether uncritical. He does not admire every facet of the Hindu personality, spirit, and philosophy. As did Goethe much later, he deplores the treatment accorded pariahs (XIV, 30).[3] The Hindu seems to him to lack sympathy and to give in too easily to destiny (XIV, 31). The resignation of the Hindu to his fate disturbs Herder, but the tumultuous emotion which intersperses the passive resignation almost seems to justify such a surrender to fate (XIV, 39). The Hindu practice of *suttee* is incomprehensible to him (XIII, 325), and he echoes Hamilton's explanation for the widow-burning ritual: that Hindu women, angry about the infidelities of their husbands, used to poison them. To combat the practice, it was ordained that widows should be burned with their husbands. However, Herder holds the practice to be the consequence of the belief in metempsychosis, according to which a widow who dies on the funeral pyre of her husband achieves thereby direct admittance to Heaven for them both, saving them from transmigration into another existence. Despite his censure Herder admits in the end that the custom has been ennobled by the Brahmans (XIV, 31). But his avowed dislike of a few features of Hindu life is far surpassed by his favorable impression of the whole.

3. The Europe of forty years later still complained about the lot of the pariah. Independent of the drama of Casimir Delavignes, Le Paria (1821), which Goethe recommended as a "beautifully conceived, well executed play" (Johann Wolfgang von Goethe, *Werke* [141 vols.; (Weimar, 1887-1912)], I, 41, *ii*, 100-102; Goethe citations are to this edition, given parenthetically as division, volume [and, when necessary, small Roman italics for part], and page), the one-act *Paria* by Michael Beer appeared in 1823, also praised by Goethe and given a careful production in Weimar (IV, 39, 45). Neither of the works is cast in the frame of the mythical image, of course, nor is the poetic trilogy by Goethe, "Paria," which came into print early in 1824. In a letter to K. F. Reinhard of July 5, 1824, as well as in an earlier conversation with Eckermann on November 10, 1823, Goethe remarks that he had let the theme ripen in him for forty years until it was cleansed of all impurities (letter, IV, 38, 187; conversation with Eckermann in Flodoard Freiherr von Biedermann, ed., *Goethes Gespräche, Gesamtausgabe* [4 vols.; (Leipzig, 1910)], III, 39). Goethe's source was Sonnerat (I, 205-206). The actual legend is framed by two poems, a prayer of supplication and a prayer of gratitude by a pariah. In the first the lowly pariah begs for a sign of divine recognition, and in the last acknowledges the message of the legend. The legend itself is a clarification of innocence and guilt, a metaphysical explanation of the cleft between body and spirit, sublime and base desires in Goethean terms and in a highly condensed poetic form. See also Paul T. Hoffmann, "Der indische und der deutsche Geist von Herder bis zur Romantik." Dissertation, Tübingen, 1915, pp. 30-35. Thomas Mann, in *Die vertauschten Köpfe* (Stockholm, 1940), transforms the legend brilliantly in an ingenious amalgamation of Sonnerat's narration, Goethe's poetic treatment, and a version told in an essay by Heinrich Zimmer ("Die indische Weltmutter," in *Eranos-Jahrbuch 1938*, ed. Olga Fröbe-Kapteyn [Zürich, 1939], p. 179).

The modern Hindu, as Herder describes him, seems to be a creature of innocence; he is childlike, kind, graceful, and beautiful. In his estimation of the Hindu, Herder reveals for the most part an idealistic approval and admiration. After Bernier, he speaks of the inhabitants of Kashmir as though they basked in the Garden of Eden. He says they are considered to be the most intelligent and gifted of the peoples of India, adept alike at poetry and science, trade and art. The males are well-built, and the women often paragons of beauty (XIII, 221). The opinions of Herder regarding the Hindus themselves, expressed in no less laudatory terms, are found in the *Ideen*. Published before Sanskrit translations appeared, the *Ideen* has as its source largely the travel narrative by William Macintosh, whom Herder sometimes quotes directly in part. He shares Macintosh's unbridled admiration of the Hindus when he says that the Hindus are the gentlest of the races of men, and that they dislike doing injury to any living creature. Their figure, he says, is erect, slim, and handsome, their limbs of fine proportions, their fingers long and delicate, their faces open and pleasing. The features of Hindu women reveal the tenderest lines of beauty, and those of Hindu men disclose a virile but mild disposition (XIII, 222). Herder speaks further of the purity of their senses, unspoiled by intoxicating beverages; he praises with a quiet exaltation their guileless hearts thriving under the propitious blessings of their homeland (XIII, 293). He finds that the Hindus are graceful, peaceful, unblemished, innocent, and that they maintain a tranquil and democratic pedagogy (XIV, 29). What wonders of art may be expected from the Hindus, asks Herder, since they are, especially in the higher castes, a well-educated, musical people. One should be aware, he says, that the Hindus are the only folk on earth who have raised erotic pleasures to the level of a beautiful, even a religious, art (XVI, 71). Herder characterizes the Hindu as being endowed with superlative gifts of spirit, body, and mind. It is a portrait of a noble people enjoying a highly developed culture and living in an idyllic land.

These mild, gentle, and peaceful people naturally fell victim to the spoliation and oppression of rougher, more warlike nations. In the garden of nature that is India, the first society of mankind was formed; but it was destined to fall prey to the greed of others (XIV, 32). Time, Muslims, missionaries, and gluttonous Europeans have together destroyed, damned, and despised much of India's art (XIV, 73-74). Testimony that Herder's sympathies lay with the Hindu, not with the European, is evident. The European, who might have looked in awe upon this beautiful land, the site of ancient peace, goodness, and gentleness, does not emerge very favorably when compared with the Hindu. It is undeniable, says Herder, that the Brahmans have inculcated into their people a meekness, courteousness, moderation, and modesty such that in comparison Europeans often appear to be unclean, drunken, and raving (XIV, 28-29). Even as late as 1802, in the *Gespräche über die Bekehrung der Indier durch unsre Europäischen Christen*, he castigates the missionaries for the harm they have perpetrated in India. He does not oppose the conversion of Hindus to Christianity; on the contrary, he is of the opinion that they deserve inclusion in the faith and that their very nature makes them fit subjects for conversion (XXIII, 497). But the Christian missionaries have not approached the task of conversion with the spirit of sympathy and understanding which the minutely developed culture of the Hindu deserves. The admirable tales of mythology and the essential truths of Hindu philosophy have been misconstrued by those who would convert this pliant and agreeable people. The missionaries have done great harm: they were foolish and were neither tolerant nor compassionate; they lacked judgment and were unperceiving. Herder adjures the European thus: "Christen, ihr habt viel zu vergüten, viel zu versöhnen" (XXIII, 505). In later years, when he recommends *Sakontala* to his readers, Herder cautions them: "Lesen [Sie] das Buch; aber nicht Europäisch, d.i. um etwa nur den Ausgang zu wissen, mit flüchtiger Neugierde, sondern Indisch, mit feinaufmerkender Ueberlegung, Ruhe und Sorgfalt" (XVI, 88). To Herder *indisch* becomes an adjective with desirable connotations, while *europäisch* is an unsavory token.

Herder expresses a recurrent interest in metempsychosis because, although the theory is not new to Europe, he now has before him the land where the belief is most firmly held and where it has exerted a great influence upon a way of life. But he cannot reconcile himself to approval of the belief in the Hindu sense, and finally he restates it in Western terms. To the Hindu, metempsychosis meant a rebirth, as an atonement for sins or moral failings, into an animal or

even a plant. Once reborn, the soul would have another opportunity
to atone for the sin by good works or devotion and, finally, to
achieve reunion with the world-spirit, the essence that is God. Herder blames this belief for the unenviable place of the pariah in the
Hindu social structure. It was thought that the pariah deserved his
fate for delinquencies in a previous life (XIV, 30). Herder continues that the doctrine has had other unpleasant consequences, such
as the arousal of a false sympathy for all living things, which simul-
taneously lessened true empathy for the miseries of man, for unfor-
tunates who were believed to be sinners burdened with earlier evil
acts or to be men tested under the hand of a fate which would reward their virtue in a future existence (XIV, 30-31).

In the first collection of *Zerstreute Blätter* (1785) Herder presents a discussion of metempsychosis in three dialogues between
Charikles, who takes a sympathetic view, and Theages, who takes
a negative stand. Here, as an explanation for the source of the belief, he focuses on metempsychosis his conception of a cultural stage
comparable to childhood, saying that the doctrine was a primitive
expression of penance. Charikles asks why the doctrine has been
prevalent so long, and Theages replies that it was the childhood of
the world, the infancy of man's wisdom about human destiny that
saw the development of metempsychosis. Among the Egyptians,
the Brahmans, and perhaps even in the case of Pythagoras himself,
the transmigration of souls was penance in a perceptive, moral fancy.
The wisdom of the oldest nations was nurtured among the priests.
When the doctrine became established, it was able to relieve many
common people of vices and accustom others to virtues. When one
looks at the fate of animals with the eyes of an Indian or an Egyptian, Theages says, when one observes with the quiet compassion of
a childlike world co-existent with animals, one would prefer to be a
white elephant rather than a pig (XV, 297-298). But the world, no
longer in its childhood, was now too sophisticated to believe in metempsychosis. According to Theages, incarnation in an animal form
might be penance in the eyes of God, but it would never result in a
spiritual or moral improvement in the soul of man, because in the
body of an animal that very attribute which could improve the soul
would have been taken away (XV, 299). Theages continues that
the fable of metempsychosis is not for mankind at the present time,

for he should not be given an opportunity to recover the dignity and perfection of the soul that he has lost through neglect; no such thing was ever ordained by God. Theages would prefer other beliefs in regard to the state of existence after death. More beautiful in the mind at the moment of death is the assemblage of ancestors among the Orientals, the Elysium of the Greeks, the Valhalla of the Norse —these are more attractive than the ox and the cow who wait for the soul of the moribund mortal (XV, 299-300). Charikles, much enlightened by the discussion, concludes with an adaptation of the theory of metempsychosis, elevating it to the distinction of a metaphysical idea with a more sublime, though unknown, goal: "Reinigung des Herzens, Veredlung der Seele mit allen ihren Trieben und Begierden, das dünkt mich, ist die wahre Palingenesie dieses Lebens, nach der uns gewiss eine fröhliche, höhere, aber uns unbekannte Metempsychose bevorsteht" (XV, 303).

With the appearance of Sanskrit translations in England and with the publication of Forster's German version of *Sakuntala*, Herder learned more about the philosophy of India and revised his speculations about the origin of metempsychosis. In the essay *Denkmale der Vorwelt*, printed in the fourth collection of *Zerstreute Blätter* (1792), he says that metempsychosis was inherent in the philosophical system developed by the Brahmans, and that the burning of the dead may have contributed to the formation of the belief (XVI, 78-79). He also ascribes to metempsychosis the failure of Indic culture to apply its sculptural talents to ideal representations of the human body. The body was considered to be a congress of elements which upon its dissolution returned to their source, to their immersion in an encompassing All (XVI, 82). By the time the sixth collection of *Zerstreute Blätter* was published in 1797, Herder had delved even deeper into Hindu philosophy, and in *Palingenesie* he speculates again on the origin of metempsychosis, his attention now directed solely to the phenomenal belief among the Hindus. One effect of such a belief is exaggerated sympathy and compassion for animals, a fancy increased by the personification of animals in fables (XVI, 345-346). The character and natural milieu of the Hindus contributed to the refinement of the belief into a modus vivendi by the Brahmans. Without passion, but tender in sentiment, sundered from fermented wine, animal flesh, and other intemperance, accustomed to cleanliness, and at home almost in the open in a mild climate, the Hindus feel less confined and not in conflict but in consonance with the elements, with the subtle life-soul which permeates all things. All creatures and plants are malleable forms into which the universal soul is poured, and it can inspirit any animate container. The world of the Hindu, writes Herder, is a stream of facile metamorphoses. The preserving godhead, Vishnu, often transformed himself, and the philosophy as well as the moral foundation of the Hindu aims at destroying the madness of separability and adopting a condition in which there is no causative variability. Such an arrangement made a pleasant dream of metempsychosis (XVI, 347). For a people living close to nature, imbued with a reverence for and a self-identification with the basic elements, metempsychosis could offer a reassurance with regard to the unknown. But Herder cannot accept the belief as a way to attain absolution for sins; he cries out: "Hinweg . . . mit der Seelenwanderung, als einer Büssungshypothese!" (XVI, 349).

Concluding his speculations on metempsychosis, Herder says that the belief was inherent in the religious philosophy of the Hindus and denies that this sublime philosophy was engendered by a belief in metempsychosis. The spirit of the Enlightenment asserts itself in Herder when he says that metempsychosis was a delusion of the senses while the fundamental tenet of Hindu philosophy was a verity founded on the rational conception of the unity of the universe. An inclination to follow the idea of metempsychosis was caused by a compassion for all living things (XVI, 359); however, fancies of this kind are not philosophy but a sentient delusion of sentient man (XVI, 363). Metempsychosis is inherent in the conception of a unity of creation developed from such impressions. Herder enlarges upon the idea of creation wrought by the conception of a single world soul. The symbolic form of creation has for a sentient people great vividness and a rich allegorical sense, for every creature remains indestructible in essence as long as it exists. However, the roles change easily as soon as the vessel containing the soul is broken. Even amidst the greatest reality of the world, *maja*—illusion—can be found. The life-soul which flowed into the shape of an animal can also, in the great order of things, organize a human being, and if the sequence of events requires, the opposite may happen. The soul simply changes its habitation; it always plays its role and has its functions; however only in the finer powers—mind, reflection, memory—and out of their co-operation is the noblest power achieved—conscience. Herder calls on Hindu mythology for an analogue: everything is an eternally incubated egg, as Brahma once appeared to be. Thought and movement divided Brahma and the egg, and those qualities continue to be effective in a firmly determined standard of measure. The gauge consists of awareness and the five senses, the circular limit of all transformations, of all aspects (XVI, 364-365). Then, approaching his conclusion, Herder says that it was only the philosophy of the perceptive eye, the sense of sight, which convinced the Hindu that just as the parts of the body return to their elements, the quickening soul also returns to the great source, the world-soul (XVI, 366). Herder's conclusion regarding metempsychosis absolves Hindu philosophy from folly. It was not the belief in palingenesis which produced that sublime ethic which is embodied in the teachings of the Brahmans and in the *Bhagavad-Gita*, and which deserves the respect of the West. It was rather the great basic premise: one in all, and all into one. All men are for a short time quickened by one world spirit, and all men should use this short interval, each according to his powers, most nobly with reflection and with good conscience. Men should be led by reason, not by delusion and aversion; truth, not error, should govern mankind (XVI, 367). Thus Herder's lengthy reflections upon metempsychosis end with the clarion call of the Enlightenment emphasized. He finds the metaphysical essence of the belief true and would support this truth as he interprets it.

The Brahman, who stands at the pinnacle of the social and intellectual order of the Hindus, is given much attention by Herder. Like the people he served and ruled, the Brahman's origin, lost in antiquity, is given a mythological explanation. He is said to have sprung from the head of the creative aspect of the Hindu trinity, Brahma, while the other castes sprang from inferior organs (XIV, 25). The oldest schools of the Brahmans were on the Ganges, says Herder (in further support of the great river as the point of origin of the culture), and spread from there (XIV, 26-27). Even though it is said that the Brahmans came from the north, north of the Ganges, north of India, the culture is evidently so old *in* India that

Herder cannot be concerned with attempting to trace its further antiquity (XVI, 66). As a class the Brahmans have retained much of the original purity and excellence of their ancestors (XIII, 294). The Brahman has kept his high status by refusing to reveal the mysteries of his religion, by keeping for himself the right to learn Sanskrit and thus study the holy writings and the books of ancient wisdom (XIV, 26). The endurance and immutability and solidity of Hindu culture is due to the Brahman. The very existence of a caste system, a permanent feature of Hindu society, with the Brahman at its peak, has contributed to the unchanging structure of the social order. The natural effect of the overwhelming superiority of the Brahman with regard to the cultivation of morals, virtues, religious precepts, art, and a way of life among the Hindus has been enormous (XIV, 29). It was the Brahman who actually governed, since the government of Hindu India was based on the *Laws of Menu*, which were interpreted and explained by the Brahman. It was the Brahman who led the Hindu upon virtuous paths, inculcating in him the faith revealed in the sacred books. It is in the Brahman that the lofty conception of God has maintained its purity, whereas long centuries have contaminated the idea among the common people (XIV, 29). The Brahman, the keeper of religion and law, the depository of wisdom of medicine, astronomy, mathematics, and other sciences, taught the youth and thus propagated his wisdom through succeeding generations. He preserved and related the national epics and the tales of mythological heroes. Concerning the place of the Brahman as a molder of philosophy, Herder says (evidently after Dohm) that the path to a humanistic philosophy is more efficacious through moderation of sensual enjoyments than through a thousand artificial abstractions (XIII, 294). The very essence of Hindu culture centered in the Brahman.

The religion of India, whose followers are supremely tolerant even amidst the intolerance of Mohammedans and Christians, is the noblest of the whole Orient, Herder says: more scholarly, more human, more advantageous. The pantheistic conception of the Hindu Godhead seems to him to be parallel to the Christian idea, and well-stated in the metaphysical language of Hindu philosophy: "Das Erste *und einzige Wesen*, das . . . Brehm, die Selbständigkeit, ist, hat die Indische Philosophie in einer so entfernten Höhe, zugleich aber auch in einer so innigen Nähe mit uns vorzustellen gesucht, dass sie von beiden Seiten schwerlich übertroffen werden möchte" (XVI, 79). This God, Who pervades all things, into Whom the souls of mankind finally return, immanent in every creature and every object, cannot be worshiped in any representational form, for He is formless. Herder lets a Brahman speak: "Was Sonne und Licht der sichtbaren Welt sind, das ist der unsichtbaren, der Verstandeswelt *Gott* und die *Wahrheit* . . . die vom Wesen der Wesen kommt" (XXIII, 499). Thus the essential nature of the God of the Hindus, Who cannot be described or perceived by human senses, requires that symbols, the noblest and most primary, be used to depict His attributes. The Hindu trinity serves to symbolize the omnipotent aspects of their God. These symbols, the foundation of Hindu mythology, and their offspring and accomplishments represent to the Hindu the principles of his religion. The Hindu trinity—Brahma, Vishnu, and Siva; the creator, the preserver, and the destroyer-propagator—symbolizes the three essential cosmic forces at work in the universe. As a Hindu might, Herder explains the system of this trinity very sensitively with the image of a flower:

Eine schaffende, erhaltende und zerstörende Kraft war die Grundlage dieses Systems. . . . Jede Blume lehrt uns dieses System, (die Indier liebten die Blumen) und was jene lehrten, bestätigen die Blumen des Himmels, Sonnensysteme, Milchstrassen, alle Theile des Universums: Schöpfung, Erhaltung und Untergang sind die drei Punkte ihrer grossen oder kleinen Epoche. . . . Auch das war schön bei diesem Poem des Weltalls, dass die *Fortpflanzung* der Wesen ein Mittelpunkt der Vereinigung aller drei Kräfte ward, die einander begegnen, einander aufzuheben scheinen, und eben dadurch die Kette der Natur weiterhin gliedern. Fruchtbarkeit zerstört die Blume; und doch streben zu dieser Blüthe alle ihre Kräfte; was sie zerstöret, erhält die Schöpfung. (XVI, 78)

It is significant here, where Herder points out the Hindu love for flowers, that the symbol of a flower becomes in essence eventually the symbol of cosmology.

Herder believes that the first faint stirrings of religion were to be found in the worship of natural phenomena, in reverence to nature and awe before its revelations (XIII, 304-305). He notes that the religion of the Brahmans, who supposedly entered India from the north, fixed its first mythological residence in the mountainous paradise of Northern India (XVI, 71). The mythology of a people has its roots in nature. Herder speaks of the "Blumenphantasie der Indier, die, wie sie selbst, die wohllüstigste Ruhe des Paradieses hauchet" (XIII, 307). Their gods bathe in seas of milk and sugar; their goddesses live in the cups of sweet-smelling flowers upon cooling ponds (XIII, 307). Herder points out that he considers the mythology of India older than that of any other land. The sagas of Europeans and Africans are nothing more than strayed fragments of young legends in comparison with the gigantic structure of old cosmogonies in India (XIII, 412). He looks upon the mythology of the Hindus as first, childlike attempts to arrange objects systematically in ideas or images, to apprehend the spirit of whatever exists or happens, to express their sentiments about such objects or events, and through custom, song, story, and tradition not only to confirm "this little treasure of human abstraction" but also to commend it to their descendants (XXVI, 491). He also sees something of the ancient history of India in Hindu mythology; of all the wisdoms of man, only history seems to be lacking in India (XIII, 415-416). In describing the personages in the pantheon of India's mythology, Herder chooses representations found in Hindu art. Although he does not ignore altogether the more fearful depictions of Hindu mythical figures, he emphasizes the beauties and the humanistic symbols of wisdom of these gods and goddesses (XVI, 69-70).

The shape of Indic art was determined, says Herder, by the religion of the Hindu, by his conception of God. The symbolic aspects of the triad God, the sub-deities, and the lower orders of mythological creatures are depicted in the plastic arts, immortalized by Hindu sculptors and architects centuries ago. Herder believes that in the history of humankind the art of India will remain forever as a monument of a philosophical system which could perhaps have come into being only on the banks of the Ganges, and which also seems to be immortal (XVI, 77). The antiquity of Hindu culture is evident in its arts. Herder points out the fabulous Hindu temples, in his essay on *Denkmale der Vorwelt* in the fourth collection of *Zerstreute Blätter* (1792), and gives a perceptive critique of the sculpture and architecture of India, noting factors which have delimited the conception and execution of these arts. To him a monument can be a voice from another age (XVI, 56), and he sees in the plastic arts a representation of the development of a people's culture; where history fails, he would trace the story of a people in its sagas when they are supported and reinforced by monuments (XVI, 57-58). Herder remarks how little is known about Hindu art, the symbolism of its figures, the meaning of its inscriptions. From what is known, however, he concludes that the form and purpose of this art was local and national in character, no matter where the religion of India may have had its beginnings (XVI, 67-68). Obviously, most of the monuments of India were inspired by religion, for the sculptured figures represent the major and minor gods and goddesses. The dearth of information about Hindu art causes him to presume, from what he knows of the factors which encourage and influence artistic productions, that contemporary Hindu art, in a period of the history of that culture when it is under the subjugation of foreign powers, hints of the glorious examples of art it must have executed when it flourished in sovereign splendor in ages past (XVI, 71). These conjectures lead Herder into an almost ecstatic hope that the models of classic Greek art may be found in India.

In his critique Herder does not neglect the negative aspects of Hindu art. He considers the chief detriment to that art to have been its very source, the religion itself and the features of that religion. The symbolic concepts of the gods remained symbols in the art, thereby powerfully limiting plastic representation (XVI, 74). The monstrosity of some depictions of Hindu gods, which so revulsed Goethe,[4] Herder explains upon the basis of the symbolism which

4. Goethe's inclination to seek beauty in the classic perfection of harmonious form caused him to find the grotesque formlessness of Indic art abhorrent. He was not led by an idealistic appraisal of the Indic image to attempt a synthesis of art and religion. He could not justify Indic depictions of Hindu gods. Even though as a boy he was entertained by the antic adventures of the ape-hero Hanumant related in Oliver Dapper's travel narrative (see Bibliography), the boyhood attitude (see *Dichtung und Wahrheit*, I, 28, 144) had become one of severe aesthetic condemnation in the man:

> Auf ewig hab ich sie vertrieben,
> Vielköpfige Götter trifft mein Bann,
> So Wischnu, Kama, Brahma, Schiven,
> Sogar den Affen Hannemann. (Zahme Xenien,
> I, 3, 257)

The Indic temples, and with them the religion of the Hindus, are castigated by the aroused poet:

was inherent in Hinduism (XVI, 76). Taken as a whole, however, his investigation of Hindu art ends with the expression of a longing for the lost state of innocent childhood amidst the blessings of a benevolent nature. These longings were to strike a sympathetic response in the heart of the Romanticist as an aspect of the mythical image.

In the *Ideen* (1784), published before the first direct translations of Sanskrit works appeared in England, Herder expresses an interest in Oriental literature and notes its divine simplicity and dignity (XIII, 410). When translations of India's Sanskrit poetic literature

---

> Auch diese will ich nicht verschonen,
> Die tollen Höhl-Exkavationen,
> Das düstre Troglodyten-Gewühl,
> Mit Schnauz und Rüssel ein albern Spiel;
> Verrückte Zierat-Brauerei,
> Es ist eine saubre Bauerei.
> Nehme sie niemand zum Exempel,
> Die Elefanten- und Fratzen-Tempel.
> Mit heiligen Grillen treiben sie Spott,
> Man fühlt weder Natur noch Gott. (Zahme Xenien,
> I, 3, 256)

The feeling of repulsion even became one of horror when he was confronted with Indic religious art:

> Nicht jeder kann alles ertragen:
> Der weicht diesem, der jenem aus;
> Warum soll ich nicht sagen:
> Die indischen Göttern, die sind mir ein Graus?
> (Zahme Xenien, I, 3, 256)

Goethe is simply incapable of accepting absurd animal forms or hideous contortions in human shape as representations of divinities:

> Und so will ich, ein- für allemal,
> Keine Bestien in dem Götter-Saal!
> Die leidigen Elefanten-Rüssel,
> Das umgeschlungene Schlangen-Genüssel,
> Tief Ur-Schildkröt' im Welten-Sumpf,
> Viel Königs-Köpf' auf *einem* Rumpf,
> Die müssen uns zur Verzweiflung bringen,
> Wird sie nicht reiner Ost verschlingen.
> (Zahme Xenien, I, 3, 251)

In a letter written on April 20, 1815, to C. J. H. Windischmann he says: "Let me admit that those of us who were raised on Homer, who gave ourselves body and soul to Greek sculpture as the most proper embodiment of divinity for mankind, that we, I say, enter only with a kind of dread into those limitless halls where misshapen creatures crowd upon us and deformed shapes float off and disappear" (IV, 25, 274-275; author's translation). This feeling he sums up in the lines:

began to be published, Herder fulfilled an old longing to see the writings of the Hindus. In 1792, in his letters "Ueber ein morgen-ländisches Drama," when the treasures of Hindu literature have been glimpsed by him in *Sakontala* and other works, Herder notes that the oldest and most beautiful fables are, as is well known, of Hindu origin, and that the fine spirit of fantasy of the Hindu is abundantly revealed in Indic mythology (XVI, 91). Much of Hindu literature has a sententious character: the fables and maxims all point up a moral and are essentially didactic in nature. Herder, basically a product of the rational thought of the Enlightenment, found the gnomic trait of Sanskrit literature appealing to his own didactic predisposition. It is not surprising that, with the aid of Georg Forster (1754-1794), the German translator of *Sakuntala*, he should have availed himself of the translations which were ap-pearing in England. Forster possessed a copy of Wilkins' translation of the fable collection *Hitopadesa* (an excerpt of the *Panchatantra*) and Herder asked to see it. Forster sent it to him with a letter offer-

---

Gott hat den Menschen gemacht
Nach seinem Bilde;
Dann kam er selbst herab,
Mensch, lieb und milde.

Barbaren hatten versucht
Sich Götter zu machen;
Allein sie sahen verflucht
Garstiger als Drachen.

Wer wollte Schand und Spott
Nun weiter steuern?
Verwandelte sich Gott
Zu Ungeheuren? (Zahme Xenien, I, 3, 250)

Goethe's attack upon Indic art and religion in the *West-Östliche Divan* (I, 7, 217) caused Friedrich Schlegel to write his brother August Wilhelm Schlegel on November 13, 1819: "What do you say about Goethe's Divan? Are you going to let him, an outsider, get away with imprudently vilifying everything Indic?" (Oskar Walzel, ed., *Friedrich Schlegels Briefe an seinen Bruder August Wilhelm* [Berlin, 1890], p. 631; author's translation). The defense of India in the review of the *Divan* by the Orien-talist J. G. L. Kosegarten (*Haller Allgemeine Literaturzeitung*, 1819, Nos. 286, 287) caused Goethe to answer him on December 30, 1819 (IV, 32, 137): "We owe so much to the good Indians that it probably was fair to defend them against my dis-pleasure. . . . May good fortune soon lead me back into this realm, whereupon I shall take the liberty of requesting your reliable company." Thus not without a note of ironic, if friendly, sarcasm does Goethe hold fast to his position. Friedrich Schlegel places him outside the circle of judicious admirers of India, and in fact Goethe's very nature could not accept the drastic art forms of Hindu sculpture, nor the gods repre-sented, nor the religion which was thus symbolically manifested. See also Paul T. Hoff-mann, pp. 26-27, 44-45.

ing him also the Wilkins version of the *Bhagavad-Gita*.[5] It was in
these works and in Rogerius' Bhartrihari maxims that Herder sought
inspiration and delved for ideas, and from these works that he translated and refashioned the musings into didactic poems. A large number appeared in the fourth collection of *Zerstreute Blätter* under the
title of "Gedanken einiger Bramanen" (XXVI, 406-416) and others
were scattered among his works (XXVI, 417-433).

In the foreword to the fourth collection of *Zerstreute Blätter*
Herder asks his readers to approach the "Gedanken einiger Bramanen" without prejudice for or against them. He continues: "Wo
Ihnen in diesen der Geruch einer zu starken Würze vorkommt, da
denken Sie, er ist von einer Indischen Pflanze" (XXVI, 310). In
Herder's versions of Indic thought the strong odor became a capti-
vating aroma, as may be seen in the judgments of two of his contemporaries. On May 20, 1792, J. G. Eichhorn (1752-1827), a biblical scholar and Orientalist at Göttingen, wrote to Herder: "Sie leis-
ten der Asiatischen Literatur einen Dienst, den ihr noch niemand
geleistet hat, dass Sie mit unnachahmlicher Kunst unserer Zeit und
Welt alles näher bringen, ohne den Asiatischen Geist zu mindern,
und dadurch Liebe zu ihm erwecken." And Karl Ludwig von Knebel
(1744-1834), a classical translator at Weimar, wrote to him, upon
the publication of "Gedanken einiger Bramanen": "Es sind wahre
Indische Steine."[6]

A clean manuscript copy of a perhaps unfinished essay on the
mythology of the Hindus is testimony to Herder's avid interest in
that feature of Indic literature and of his early familiarity with the
maxims of Bhartrihari, for as examples of Indic thought he has
copied fifty-three maxims which must have held particular fascination for him.[7] Bhartrihari is represented in Herder's published works
with seventeen epigrams in sixteen of the "Gedanken einiger Bramanen" (one verse combining thoughts from two of the Sanskrit
poet's aphorisms; see No. 41, XXVI, 415) and with four aphorisms
in three selections from the ninth and one selection from the tenth
part in Herder's *Sämtliche Werke* (XXVI, 425, 427, 431, 433). The
motifs of the Bhartrihari maxims all concern moral or ethical ideas,

5. Paul T. Hoffmann, p. 10.
6. Heinrich Düntzer and F. G. von Herder, eds., *Von und an Herder. Ungedruckte Briefe aus Herders Nachlass* (3 vols.; Leipzig, 1861), II, 302-303; III, 80.
7. Herder, *Werke*, XXVI, note to pp. 406 ff. on pp. 491-492.

and Herder reshaped the original sources to fit his own poetic ability and adapted them to his own point of view. In his adaptation of Bhartrihari, Herder most often retains the same idea of a maxim; frequently, however, he selects one or two of several ideas, changes the sequence of thought or metaphor, refines, polishes, expands, or even shortens the images to shape them into his own subjective interpretation.

The epigrammatic lyrics of Bhartrihari were published in a Sanskrit edition (with a Latin translation) by Peter von Bohlen (1796-1840), professor of Oriental languages in Königsberg, in 1833.[8] It is notable that two years later, in his metric translation of the gnomic poems into German, Von Bohlen retained four of Herder's adaptations of the poet,[9] a gesture complimentary not only to Herder but to his immediate source, Rogerius, as well. As has been noted, Rogerius published only two of the three *śatakas* by Bhartrihari, the second and the third (to be cited, after Rogerius' numeration by series, chapter, and verse—for example, Bthr. 1.4.5.). The genius of Herder's spirit, which revealed itself in the empathy with which he was able to project his sensitive awareness and grasp the essence of an idea—an alien idea, clothed clumsily in the phrases of a sequence of three translations—can be shown in the four instances where Von Bohlen, translating directly from the Sanskrit, found Herder's renderings admirable enough to be retained.

The stiff and almost archaic prose paraphrase of Rogerius does not, of course, capture the lyric quality of Bhartrihari. The following lines, although they contain the seed of poetic metaphors, are couched in prosaic phrases of almost pedestrian quality:

> Wann du mit Bösen / Mittelmässigen /
> und Guten / Freundschaft machest / so wird
> es solcher Gestalt zugehen / als wie mit
> einem Tröpflein Regenwassers; denn fällt
> solches auf ein gluendes Eisen / so wird es
> nicht mehr zu finden seyn; fällt es dann auf
> ein Krug-blumen-blat / so wird es scheinen
> als ein Perlein: Fällt es aber / zu bequemer
> Zeit / in eine Auster / so wird es in der
> That ein Perlein werden. (Bthr. 2.6.8.)

8. Peter von Bohlen, ed., *Bhartriharis Sententiae* (Berlin, 1833).
9. Peter von Bohlen, trans., *Die Sprüche des Bhartriharis* (Hamburg, 1835), note to No. 50, p. 184.

In Herder's rendering the aphorism becomes advice given warmly; the illustrative metaphors are no longer in a future time, but are given in terms of an experienced narrative past.

> Sohn, die Freundschaft mit den Bösen,
> mit Gleichgültigen und Guten
> sei dir ja nicht Einerlei!
>
> Ein Tropfe Regenwasser
> fiel auf ein glühend Eisen,
> und war nicht mehr.
>
> Er fiel auf eine Blume
> und glänzt' als eine Perle,
> und blieb ein Tröpfchen Thau.
>
> Er sank in eine Muschel
> zur Segenreichen Stunde
> und ward zur Perle selbst.   (XXVI, 406)

Rogerius' missionary calling explains the sometimes prophetic biblical cast to his renderings (though they lack the finer simplicity of the language of the Bible):

> Gleichwie es mit dem Schatten der
> Sonne beschaffen / im Aufgang derselbigen;
> also wird es sich auch verhalten mit
> derjenigen Freundschaft / die man mit den
> Bösen macht. Aber die Freundschaft mit
> den Frommen wird seyn / als der Schatten /
> welchen die Sonne gibt / wann sie nach
> dem Untergang wandert.   (Bthr. 2.5.9.)

Herder's version in unrhymed tetrameter, though it contains the same thought, is phrased in concise terms more appealing to the imagination:

> Wie der Schatte früh am Morgen
> ist die Freundschaft mit den Bösen;
> Stund' auf Stunde nimmt sie ab.
> Aber Freundschaft mit den Guten
> wächst wie der Abendschatte,
> bis des Lebens Sonne sinkt.   (XXVI, 407)

The last line is a thought of the durable qualities of a good friendship, appended by Herder to reinforce the image of the long postmeridian shadow which grows ever longer until it vanishes into twilight. Here a shadow merges with darkness imbued with a sense of eternal comradeship.

Herder's genial ability to reduce a prosy thought to its essential epigrammatic idea is seen in the following comparison. Rogerius says:

> Gleich wie die Flamm von einem Licht /
> indem es umgekehrt / eben so wol stets über
> sich glimmet: Also auch ein Mensch / der
> auffrichtigen Hertzens ist / wiewol ihm
> irgend ein Unfall begegnet / so wird er doch
> von seinem guten Fürhaben nicht abwendig
> gemacht werden. (Bthr. 2.8.7)

Herder reduces the image to its essential idea in a couplet:

> So wie die Flamme des Lichts auch umgewendet hinaufstralt;
> so vom Schicksal gebeugt, strebet der Gute empor. (XXVI, 412)

Both Rogerius and Herder avoid an elegiac mood in a verse containing a Brahmanical farewell to the world. Rogerius renders the solicitation of the elements in a fervent voice, but then becomes less forceful in his address:

> O / Mutter / die Erde! O / Vatter /
> der Wind! O / Freund / das Feuer! O /
> Verwandschafft / das Wasser! O / Himmel /
> der Bruder! auf das allerfreundlichste
> bezeige ich euch alle Ehrerbietung; denn
> weil ich mit euch wol gelebet hab / erhalte
> ich nun die Seeligkeit: Ich will euch aber
> gern alle verlassen / und nach dem Himmel
> zugehen. (Bthr. 1.10.10)

Herder entitles his version "Abschied des Einsiedlers," thus explaining the familial and friendly relationship between the speaker and the elements: no other acquaintance had he. Herder makes of the piece a solemn and impassioned farewell as a conclusion to his "Gedanken einiger Bramanen":

> Erde, du meine Mutter, und du mein Vater, der Lufthauch,
> und du Feuer, mein Freund, du mein Verwandter, der Strom,
> Und mein Bruder, der Himmel, ich sag' euch allen mit Ehrfurcht
> freundlichen Dank. Mit euch hab' ich hienieden gelebt,

Und geh jetzt zur anderen Welt, euch gerne verlassend;
   Lebt wohl, Bruder und Freund, Vater und Mutter, lebt wohl![10]

(XXVI, 416)

These examples may suffice to illustrate Herder's happy aptitude for striking through the entanglement of Rogerius' too formal grammar and verbiage and plumbing the ethos of the Sanskrit thought by a kind of extrasensory empathy.

On May 17, 1791, Forster had sent Herder his *Sakontala*. Six months later Herder acknowledged Forster's enthusiastic letter, revealing a zealous attitude toward the play.[11] Herder did not hesitate to recommend the drama to his friends and acquaintances, and he set about at once to publish a critical evaluation of the work. As he specified to Forster, the appraising remarks concerning *Sakontala*, entitled "Ueber ein morgenländisches Drama," appeared in the fourth collection of the *Zerstreute Blätter* in 1792. As a motto Herder prints Goethe's quatrain titled "Sakontala":

Willst du die Blüthen des frühen, die Früchte des späteren Jahres,
   Willst du, was reizt und entzückt, willst du, was sättigt und nährt,
Willst du den Himmel, die Erde mit Einem Namen begreifen,
   Nenn ich, Sakontala, dich, und so ist Alles gesagt.[12]

10. This valedictory has a curious history: it was chosen as an epitaph by a suicide; see the section on Karoline von Günderode.

11. Paul T. Hoffmann, pp. 9-10.

12. Herder, *Werke*, XVI, 85; see also Goethe, *Werke*, I, 4, 122. The repugnance which never left Goethe in regard to India's art and mythology did not extend to the literature. As the distichs indicate, he was delighted with the incomparable creation of the Hindu maiden Sakuntala. In a letter to the French Orientalist Antoine-Léon de Chézy of October 9, 1830, thanking him for a de luxe edition of the drama, Goethe wrote: "The first time I became aware of this unfathomable work [shortly after the publication of Georg Forster's translation in 1791], it aroused such an enthusiasm in me, attracted me so much, that I did not cease studying it, indeed, even felt impelled to the impossible task of adapting it for the German stage, even though only inadequately. Through this admittedly fruitless endeavor I became so intimately acquainted with this highly treasured work, it determined such an epoch in the course of my life, it became so much a part of me, that for thirty years I have not looked at the English or the German [version]. . . . Only now do I grasp the extravagant impression that this work exerted upon me. Here the poet appears to us in his highest role, as a representative of the natural state, of the finest way of life, of the purest moral striving, of the most dignified majesty and the most earnest contemplation of God: at the same time, however, he remains lord and master of his creation; he can dare common and ridiculous opposites which nevertheless must be considered as necessary links in the whole organism" (IV, 47, 284-285; author's translation). Goethe not only always held the drama in high esteem; the technical structure of the play also was of influence upon him. The "Vorspiel auf dem Theater" of *Faust*, written in 1797, was prompted by Kalidasa's introductory scene to *Sakuntala*, a traditional device employed by many

Herder never spoke more rapturously of anything native to India
than he speaks of *Sakontala*. The Indic studies of Herder found
their peak in his devotion to this play, his *indische Blume*. In this
drama he finds the ideal he has sought: innocence and unity with
nature, the marvelous treated as ordinary, tangible incidence, a supreme harmony of the arts. He exclaims: "*Sakontala* heisst mein
Drama: ein Indisches Schauspiel, von Kalidas gedichtet, von W.
Jones herbeigeschafft, und ins Englische, aus dieser Sprache von G.
Forster ins Deutsche so gut übersetzt, dass es sich fast besser als das
Englische Original lieset. Säumen Sie nicht zum Genuss dieser uner-
warteten Blume zu gelangen" (XVI, 84-85). In the play he finds all
his humanistic longings granted a poetic existence. He discovers a
more attractive presentation of Hindu beliefs here than in any religious treatise (XVI, 91). He speaks with admiration of the characterization and of the hues of the drama in diction, simile, and
metaphor, denoting the subtle colorations of mood and meaning
which identify it with the sublime land of its origin (XVI, 102-104).
In 1803, the year of his death, Herder wrote a preface for the second
edition of Forster's translation. In it he expresses the amazement
and unexpected delight the Hindu drama brought (XXIV, 576), he
lauds Forster's lexicon to the play (XXIV, 576-577), and he apostrophizes the idea of India revealed in the play (XXIV, 578). He
continues:

Indic dramatists. One scholar, W. Sauer ("Sakuntala, Goethe und Schiller. Einflüsse
der Sakuntala auf Goethes Faustprolog . . . ," in *Korrespondenzenblatt für die
Gelehrten- und Realschulen Württembergs*, XL [1893], 297-304), believes that the
nandi or prayer which precedes the unfolding of the drama was transformed by Goethe
into the "Prolog im Himmel" of *Faust*. Whether this be so or not, it is undeniable
that Goethe modeled his "Vorspiel" on Kalidasa's. He does allow the poet to appear
on the stage, whereas the Indic dramatist restricts the poet to mere mention by the
director and the actor. Goethe's reaction to the play was wholesome and honest
admiration, not beguilement by a mythical image.

Still another work of Kalidasa enchanted Goethe in later years, prompted by the
meteorological theories of the Englishman, Luke Howard. It was Howard who classi-
fied cloud formations, and thus gave form to what had seemed the epitome of formlessness. In a letter to Ottilie von Pogwisch of March 27, 1817 (IV, 28, 37) Goethe
mentions an Indic treasure which had come to his notice in English. The reference
is to Horace Wilson's translation of Kalidasa's *Meghaduta* (*The Megha Duta or
Cloud Messenger*, trans. Horace Wilson [Calcutta, 1814]). In the poem "Howards
Ehrengedächtnis" (I, 3, 98; II, 12, 40), which Goethe sent to friends in England in
1821, he contrasts and balances the playful wantonness and arbitrary creations of the
Hindu god Kamarupa with the scientific determinism and formulations of Howard.
Again, amidst his own delight, Goethe molds the Indic source to his own will, not in
the manner of a mythical ideal. See also Paul T. Hoffmann, pp. 28-30, 35-36, 38-42.

Uebrigens ist *Sakontala* . . . ein *Drama*, wie irgend Eins es seyn mag . . .
die zarteste Schicksalsfabel. . . . Die Sprache ist geschmückt, Blumen-
reich und nie doch übertrieben, das Betragen der Personen und Stände
gegen einander, seyn sie Götter oder Menschen, ist so anständig und
artig, dass in allem Diesem das Stück seines Gleichen suchen dürfte in
allen Sprachen, unter allen Nationen. Auch die eingemischten Stimmen
der Musik, die Züge der Malerei, des Schmuckes, des Scherzes sind eben
so original als zierlich, die Begriffe der Religion endlich, zumal in den
Wohnungen des Paradieses, sind (wer darfs läugnen) selbst paradiesisch.
(XXIV, 580)

He eulogizes the figure of Sakuntala, comparing this "child of nature" with a flower unfolding its innocence in a holy retreat (XXIV,
578).

Herder calls *Sakontala* an epic drama (XVI, 100), but cautions
his readers to take it up with a sympathetic mind, in an Indic sense;
here his chief concern is that the readers of the play, perhaps still
engulfed in the rationalism of the Enlightenment, might be dis-
turbed by the marvelous aspects of the drama, the interaction of
men and gods, and the personifications of nature (XVI, 96). He
gives his attention to the enchantment that the illusion of the marvelous lends to the play, and finds in it the peace of the gods (XXIV,
578-579).

Later, the Romanticists perceived the mythical image in their
perusal of the essays of Herder, of his poems and the play, and of
the articles and disquisitions aroused through a universal interest in
India. The chief contributor to the development of this image, and
to its enshrinement as the epitome of Romantic longing, was Herder. India was an ancient land watered by a holy river, the Ganges,
the river of Paradise, which came to symbolize for the Romanticists
the idyllic existence they saw reflected in Hindu culture. A protean
spirit served and guarded by a superior class of holy men, implanted
into every denizen of that land a simplicity and peace of soul which
made for balanced virtues and ease of living. It was a land where
poetry permeated every aspect of human wisdom, creating a sublime
harmony of all knowledge. Here philosophy was one with religion,
and a Universal Spirit was immanent in every creature and in every
creation of nature. A mellow kinship pervaded all things. A marvelous magic was the companion of ordinary reality. Here, truly, was
aesthetic perfection, and here one could find perfect contentment.
This was the kernel of the mythical image of India.

III. The Scrutiny of the Image

1. Welche neue Quelle von Poesie könnte uns aus Indien fliessen.
—FRIEDRICH SCHLEGEL

The Translators

The first glimpse that German readers got of Georg Forster's translation of *Sakontala* was in Schiller's *Thalia* in 1791, where, before the publication of the entire play in book form that same year, there appeared the love scenes between Sakuntala and Dushmanta from the first and third acts.[1] Schiller found embodied in the character of Sakuntala his ideal of beautiful femininity. In a letter to Wilhelm von Humboldt of December 17, 1795, he places Sakuntala

1. *Thalia,* Heft 10, 1791, pp. 72-88; not the second and third acts, as Paul T. Hoffmann states, p. 40, n. 3.

above the feminine characters of Greek drama, endorsing the universal acclaim which *Sakontala* found in Germany.[2]

Not since Rogerius' collection of maxims by Bhartrihari, translated into German in 1663, had there appeared in Germany a Sanskrit work. Herder had rendered some Sanskrit aphorisms in his works, but *Sakontala*, in Forster's translation from the English version (1789) by Sir William Jones, was the first complete example of Sanskrit literature to be published in Germany.[3] Jones, whose edition of the drama contained no notes and only a short preface, perhaps expected his English readers to have become familiar with Hindu mythology and with life in India through the publications of the Asiatic Society of Calcutta, of which he was president. To be sure, German readers knew something of India and its inhabitants from travel books and from Herder, but they knew almost nothing about the mythology of India. Forster, in presenting *Sakontala*, was unveiling an ancient and exciting culture, and he wished his readers to be hospitable to the new ideas and to become informed about the mythological richness of that culture. Therefore, he appended to his translation a voluminous lexical commentary, compiled from English sources, on names of persons, plants, deities, and certain religious rites, hoping to make it possible for the German reader to orient himself in the idyllic and exotic world of the drama and thus be able to appreciate it fully (IX, 314 ff.).

In his foreword Forster recommends Indic literature as represented by *Sakontala* for the simple relationship the Hindu, in a childlike and unspoiled state, has with nature. The modern European, living in a highly civilized culture, he says, has lost this intimate identification of himself with nature. He reminds his reader that, disposed by scientific refinement in skills and customs to an artificially gauged and rationalized way of life, the European could easily lose sight of an ingenuous feeling for nature, if he did not still encounter it in less sophisticated peoples. For this reason, says Forster, the European cannot remain indifferent to the literature of India. A new field, an admirably beautiful trait of human character is opened to the sensibilities and imaginations of the peoples of

2. Paul T. Hoffmann, p. 40.
3. Georg Forster, *Sakontala oder der entscheidende Ring*, in *Sämmtliche Schriften* (9 vols.; Leipzig, 1843), IX. Parenthetical Forster references are to this edition.

Europe (IX, 167). He recalls the universality of human emotions, and hopes that the European will offer the same hospitality to this gentle Hindu stranger that is practiced religiously in India (IX, 168).

Since his *Sakontala* is the translation of a translation, Forster cautions the reader that it has undoubtedly lost something of its vitality (IX, 315). Especially does he seem to regret having to render in prose a work which originally was written mainly in verse. The verse meter gave the play a rhythmic coloration which reflected the progression of the action; but even Jones did not attempt to reproduce this contrapuntal art of the original Sanskrit (IX, 316). Several lyric verses are interpolated in the drama by Kalidasa as songs or declarations of love, but Forster was forced to follow Jones in the main and departed from his source in rendering only a few short lyric passages in the prologue and in the body of the play (IX, 340).

The central character of the drama, after whom it is named, is Sakuntala, the daughter of a celestial nymph and an earthly prince. She has grown up in a paradise-like grove under the fatherly care and guidance of the Brahman hermit Kanna. Considered to be his daughter, she bestows loving care upon the flowers and animals sheltered by the grove and offers hospitality to any stranger who wanders by. In the absence of Kanna one day, Dushmanta, the emperor of India, happens upon the grove while hunting, and falls in love with Sakuntala. They pledge their vows in a Hindu marriage rite, and he gives her a ring as a token of his love, and then returns to his palace. Later, while Sakuntala is resting, she fails to observe the rule of hospitality to a Brahman, Durwasa, who lays a curse upon her. He thunders that the one about whom she has been lost in thought, to whom her heart clings while a God-fearing man asks in vain for the rights of welcome, that one will have forgotten her when she sees him again, just as a sobered man forgets the words he spoke in his intoxication (IX, 230). Shaken by the malediction, Sakuntala prepares to follow Dushmanta and takes farewell of her foster father Kanna, her friends, and the blossoms and plants and animals she has cared for so tenderly. Even the dryads of the grove gather to bid her farewell. In a prophecy by Kanna she learns that she is to become the mother of a great king, and with dread and hope she sets out for Dushmanta's palace accompanied by Gautami—an old woman—and two Brahmans. On the way, as she dips water from a pond to bathe her face, she unwittingly loses the ring. When she gains admittance to Dushmanta at the palace, he, whose memory of her has been obliterated by the curse of Durwasa, will not admit having known her previously. No amount of persuasion or gentle remonstrance by Sakuntala avails. Dushmanta refuses to recognize this serene and poised woman, who carries the child of another, no matter how beautiful she may be (IX, 256). However, he orders that she be given asylum in his halls until the baby is born. As she is led to her quarters, her mother, Menaka, spirits her away to the abode of Kasyapa and Aditi, Hindu divinities, the parents of the ruler of the heavens, Indra. The lost ring finds its way to Dushmanta by a fisherman and when he sees it his memory returns and he is overcome with anguish for having rejected Sakuntala's entreaties. Indra sends for Dushmanta to wage war against evil demons, and having accomplished this task the Hindu monarch is borne in Indra's chariot to the divine abode of the gods, where he is reunited with Sakuntala and his son Serwademana; he then returns rejoicing with them to his kingdom.

Forster praises the characterization of Sakuntala lavishly. All the female characters, he says, have the greatest simplicity, and the heroine, Sakuntala, is fascinating by reason of her simple, childlike naïveté, the delicacy of her impassioned feelings, and the total absence of all presumptuous intention in what she does, says, or thinks. The excessive susceptibility of her constitution to the heat of the climate gives her a charming destitution which the courteous Hindu respects, for the code of the Brahmans requires the most correct regard for the lesser strength of the other sex. Her love for plants and animals, her belief in omens, her heated indignation, the involuntary expressions of her inclinations, her frank love, her placid life, and her devotion at parting are inherent, natural emotions, nothing acquired, nothing dinned into her, nothing artificial or foreign to her nature. This beautifully strung instrument, says Forster, sounds harmoniously at the lightest or the most violent touch (IX, 349-350). This rapturous creature lives in the grove under the protection of Kanna and in the closest harmony with a personified nature. Forster emphasizes that the childlike imagination of the Hindu personified all of nature, even the plants; the animating powers of the trees were divine creatures, as among the Greeks. Very closely connected with this belief is the sanctity and inviolability of the woods and groves in which those men favored by God reside (IX, 330). Sakuntala has the affections of a sister for the plants she waters. Upon her departure from the grove she embraces and takes a tender farewell of a favorite flower:

> O strahlendste der schlängelnden Pflanzen! empfange meine Umar-mung! Erwidre sie mit deinen biegsamen Zweigen! Von diesem Tage an, gross wie die Entfernung ist, die mich von dir trennt, bin ich dein im-merdar!—O geliebter Vater, sieh diese Pflanze an, wie mein anderes Ich.
> (IX, 240)

Sakuntala is also concerned for the well-being of an animal friend:

> Mein Vater! Du siehst die Antelopenkuh, die dort wegen der Bürde, womit sie trächtig ist, so langsam sich fortbewegt; wenn sie dieser Bürde los sein wird, sende mir, ich bitte dich, eine gütige Botschaft, mit der Nachricht ihres Wohlseins.—Vergiss es nicht. (IX, 241)

Her farewell to a fawn is full of pathos:

> Was weinst du, zärtliches Geschöpf, für mich, die unsern gemein-schaftlichen Wohnort verlassen muss? Wie ich dein pflegte, da du deine Mutter bald nach deiner Geburt verlorest, so wird mein Pflegevater, wenn wir scheiden, dich hüten mit sorgsamer Wartung. Kehre zurück, armes Geschöpf, zurück—wir müssen scheiden! (IX, 241)

This rhapsodical harmony of nature and human beings could not but appeal to the senses of the Romantic poet, who fostered a re-awakened sympathy for nature.

Outside the heavenly palace of Kasyapa, Dushmanta is transfixed by the figure of a yogi, whose strict contemplation has, in its im-mobility, almost fused him with nature. Commenting upon this phenomenon, Forster remarks that the yogi, as he is depicted by the poet of *Sakuntala*, is the epitome of austerity in seclusion. He says rapturously that "das Bild ist wirklich schön in seiner Riesengrösse" (IX, 333). The yogi is described by Matali, the charioteer of Indra:

> du [siehst] einen frommen Jogi unbeweglich stehen und sein dickes sträubiges Haar halten . . . die Augen auf die Sonnenscheibe gerichtet. Gib Acht: sein Leib ist halb bedeckt mit einem Termitengebäude von Thon; eine Schlangenhaut vertritt die Stelle der priesterlichen Schnur und gürtet zum Theil seine Lenden; viele knotige Pflanzen umwinden

und verwunden seinen Hals, und ringsum verbergen die Vogelnester seine Schultern. (IX, 297)

This wonder is only one example of the marvelous magic of the play, and the vivid portrait implanted this yogi in the Romantic mind as the ideal of the ascetic Hindu.

The realms of the lesser divinities and of men are entwined. The dryads of the grove eagerly prepare Sakuntala's gown for her departure, as one of Kanna's pupils relates:

plötzlich erschienen die Nymphen des Waldes und erhoben ihre Hände, die mit jungen Blättern wetteifern an Weichheit und Schöne. Einige webten ein Unterkleid, glänzend wie der Mond, zur Vorbedeutung ihrer Glückseligkeit: eine andere drückte aus den Lakscha-saft, um ihre Füsse köstlich roth zu färben; die übrigen waren beschäftigt mit Verfertigung des glänzendsten Schmucks, und alle mit eifrigem Bemühen schütteten ihre Gaben über uns aus. (IX, 237)

When she leaves, Sakuntala bids farewell to each dryad.

The Emperor Dushmanta, in the service of Indra to do battle for him against enemy demons, is carried to the residence of Kasyapa through the spaces of the heavens in the chariot of Indra, atop clouds pregnant with rain. He is astonished at the sight of the earth beneath him:

Erstaunende Aussicht! Noch so fern, dass die tiefen Gründe sich mit den Berggipfeln vermischen, die Bäume ihre astreichen Schultern emporstrekken, doch unbelaubt zu sein scheinen, die Flüsse wie glänzende Fäden sich schlängeln, unbemerkbar ihre Fluthen. (IX, 296)

Here the prosaic world of the grove and of the palace, enchanting in itself, mixes with the miraculous world of the divine immortals who soar through the heavens.

In *Sakuntala* appears the form of the sacred flower which plays such an important role in Hindu mythology, the blue lotus. Forster remarks that the lotus must have attracted the Indians because of its exceptional beauty and size. Its blossoms glow with manifold nuances of color, especially its corolla with a red shimmer. Its delicate blue petals are like fans. Also, Forster says significantly, the lotus must have been important to the Indians because nowhere is the articulation of the plant more clearly visible in the seed itself. He continues that it is the flower of night, the timid flower which

is alarmed by the light of day and frightened by the stars. It opens
and is fragrant only to the moon, and sinks its head under the rays
of the sun (IX, 340-341). The blue lotus petal is mentioned by
Dushmanta (IX, 180).

The following verses from the prologue of the play symbolize the
Hindu's conception of the Godhead revealed in nature:

> Wasser war des Schöpfers erstes Werk;
> Feu'r empfängt die Gaben
> anbefohlen im Gesetz:
> heilig ist die Opferweihe!
>   Zeiten misst das Himmelslichterpaar
> und des Schalles Führer,
> zarter Aether füllt das All!
> Erd' ist des Gebärens Mutter;
>   Leben alles Athmenden ist Luft!
> So in acht Gestalten
> sichtbar, nähr' und segn' euch Gott,
> I s s a, der Naturverwandler!   (IX, 171)

Forster says that this lovely verse-monument to an ancient Indic
concept is of inestimable value for the investigator of religious ideas
and of the various paths of fantasy among the primeval peoples of
Asia. By Issa, which signifies "ruler," the Hindus meant the eternal
forces of nature through which everything exists, which preserve
everything, which supplant that which has been dissolved and refashioned into another shape: in a manner of speaking, it is fate or
destiny. The Godhead is visible to man in eight forms, says Forster:
in water, in fire, in the offering, in the sun and moon, in the ether,
in the earth, and in the air. This is a beautiful concept, he feels, but
it is even more remarkable that Hindu priests dared to hypothesize
divine power in the *ghi*, the purified butter poured as an offering
on the temple flame (IX, 333-334). In the metaphysical system of
the Hindu there is a revelation of God that stands in direct connection with the elemental forces of nature; most astonishing is the
fact that even the holy offering is symbolic of the essence of the
Universal Spirit.

Forster, although admirably successful and adroit in his translation, bemoans the lack of a Sanskrit dictionary, which would be an
invaluable aid in the study of the literature of India (IX, 314). He
hints also at the ultimate, inescapable result of Romantic interest

in that literature, remarking about Sanskrit (after Jones) that it is more perfect than Greek and richer in expression than Latin. In addition, Sanskrit has achieved a far greater philosophical polish and refinement than either and, at the same time, has an admirable agreement with both which cannot be by chance and which no philologist can investigate without becoming firmly convinced that all three are derived from a common source, presumably no longer extant (IX, 351). Thus Forster calls the reader's attention to the interrelationship that was felt to exist among the three languages, and he hints at the final consequence, the development of the science of comparative linguistics.

Before his untimely death, at 40 in 1794, Forster was instrumental in bringing other information about India within the circle of German readership. Although he did not present another Sanskrit work, in the *Neue Beyträge zur Länder- und Völkerkunde* he published, with M. C. Sprengel, a number of essays and informative articles on India.[4] He also translated *Thomas Howels Tagebuch seiner Reise nach Indien,* which appeared in Reinhold Forster's and M. C. Sprengel's *Beiträge* in 1791. The next year he himself published William Robertson's work on India in a translation by Dorothea Margarethe Liebeskind (1765-1822?).[5]

The first volume of the publication of Sir William Jones's Asiatic Society, the *Asiatick Researches* (Calcutta, 1788), with its wealth of essays on Hindu culture, was translated by the mythologist Johann Friedrich Kleuker (1749-1827) with Johannes Fick and published in 1795.[6] The Hindu code of laws translated by Jones in 1794 was put into German in 1797 by Johann Christian Hüttner (1766-1847), a traveler to China in 1793-1794 and after 1809 an interpreter in the British foreign office in London.[7]

4. Georg Forster and M. C. Sprengel, eds., *Neue Beyträge zur Länder- und Völkerkunde* (8 vols.; Leipzig, 1790-1793), XIII. Among the essays: "Neueste Bemerkungen über die Sieks in Hindostan, und ihre Religionsgebräuche," translated from an essay in the *Asiatick Researches* by Wilkins, III; "Ueber die Gottesurtheile unter den Hindus," by Ali Abrahim Khan, president of the magistracy at Benares, III.

5. [Dorothea Margarethe Liebeskind, trans.], W. *Robertson's historische Untersuchung über die Kenntnisse der Alten von Indien* (Berlin, 1792).

6. J. F. Kleuker and Johannes Fick, trans., *Abhandlungen über die Geschichte und Alterthümer der Künste, Wissenschaften . . . Asiens* (Riga, 1795). Kleuker was also the translator of the Orientalist Abraham Anquetil-Duperron (1731-1805) and of Holwell.

7. Johann Christian Hüttner, trans., *Hindus-Gesetzbuch* (Weimar, 1797).

A most important contribution to the further understanding of Hindu religion and mythology in Germany was the publication in 1797 of Paulinus a Sancto Bartholomaeo's *Darstellung der Brahmanisch-Indischen Götterlehre*, a translation of his *Systema Brahmanicum* (Rome, 1791).[8] Paulinus, who described his impressions of the Hindus in a travel narration (discussed in Part I above) resided on the Malabar coast as a missionary from 1776 to 1789. Although he was severely criticized by later scholars who questioned his knowledge of Sanskrit and denounced him as coarse and offensive for the spite and hostility which he exhibited toward English and French Sanskrit researchers,[9] he is generally broad-minded, considering the cloth he wore, in his detailed explanation of many Hindu religious rites and festivals in the *Götterlehre*, weaving into his discourse many points concerning the mythology, cosmology, and religion of the Hindus.

Paulinus would trace the origin of Hindu philosophy and mythology to an almost mystical confluence of history and astronomy. He claims that from the order, majesty, system, ruling power, wisdom, and the allegorical force and sanctity of the spirits, especially the evil spirits, can be derived not only the philosophy of India and its sects, the religious veneration of the planets and the elements, the names of kings, and many of the laws, but also a great part of Indian history and even the Brahmanic religion. He continues that even the realm of earth seems to be adapted to the system of their idea of the heavenly realm (pp. 36-37). He then offers four points as proof of his thesis. First, he writes, the Hindu monarchs are suns and moons in accordance with the practice of applying heavenly bodies to creatures on earth. Secondly, planets are all masculine in gender to Brahmans and represent philosophers, counselors, priests, and contemplative individuals and teachers. Third, the good and evil spirits, or Titans, which are pupils of the planets and constellations among the heavenly hosts, designate good and evil men on earth, and accordingly Indian wars and the history of India are interwoven with the system of heavenly bodies and with allegory. Fourth, their philosophy of mundane matters is intimately connected with astronomy and the system of the cosmos (pp. 37-38).

8. Paulinus a Sancto Bartholomaeo, *Darstellung der Brahmanisch-Indischen Götterlehre* (Gotha, 1797). Parenthetical references are to this edition.

9. Von Adelung, pp. 24-25.

The relationship which he discerns between terrestrial and heavenly affairs proves indisputably to him the great antiquity of the culture of India and is the key to all the arts and writings of the Hindus (p. 38). But even so, Indic history goes back no further than the Flood, he hastens to add.

Paulinus traces the reverence shown the male and female sex organs by Hindu sects to the cosmology depicted in Hindu mythology. The old wise men considered heaven to be the father and the earth the mother, and asserted that everything was created through fire and water, warmth and moistness, and through the reaction and influence of the sun, the moon, the planets, and the other astral bodies upon the earth. Therefore, the Hindus symbolized the earth by the *yoni* or female sex organ, or by the lotus blossom as the first product of the sun and water. The effect of the sun and the planets, however, the Hindus picture symbolically by the *lingam*, the male member or phallus, because those constellations strew semen which is absorbed by the earth from which the *lingam* sprouts and is brought forth by the influence of warmth and moisture. Paulinus comments that this is the reason the Hindus attribute the introduction of the *lingam* as a religious symbol to Siva, the personification of sun and fire (p. 50). However, despite the Indian indulgence in extravagant worship of the sex symbols on certain festival days dedicated to an array of gods and goddesses, the people are generally decorous, modest, and serious (p. 172).

In general Paulinus praises the devotion of the Hindu to his gods. It is the monk's opinion that the religion of India is indigenous to that land. One should be convinced by the fasts, ritual bathing, pilgrimages, and quests that the origin of Indian idolatry was to be sought locally and not in Egypt, Scythia, or Siberia, nor among the Hebrews. History in India, the mythology, mysteries, and dogmas had their beginnings on the subcontinent and crept from the cradle there. Almost the whole of India's religion, the temples, regions, and streams are inseparably bound together (pp. 62-63). The Carmelite would also attribute to India the source of folk superstitions found in every part of the world (p. 79).

The bad influences exerted by Europeans upon the gentle behavior of the Hindus is remarked upon by Paulinus, especially in regard to the violent European thirst for gold. An anecdote about the King of Travancor is told. Upon being reprimanded by a European for the severity with which he exacted the payment of a tax, the king replied: "You yourself taught me stringency and atrocity in government" (p. 210, actually p. 204). The Brahman order of Samanen, holy men who withdraw from society and live in the woods, is really the source of the charming depictions of forest dwellers frequently met in Indic writings (p. 74). Kanna was undoubtedly one of these. He is revered deeply as a man of great piety and perceptive wisdom by those who serve him and learn from him in the hermitage grove. As a contrast Paulinus mentions the caste of pariahs, the outcasts of the Hindu social order, who perform the most menial labors and are distinguished principally by the fact that, unlike the Brahmans, they partake of the meat of animals (p. 230).

One Hindu symbol of particular interest is the wheel of Vishnu, the *ciacram*, which serves the double purpose of a dreadful weapon and a preserving force (p. 103). Another interesting, but by no means exclusively Hindu, symbol is the weighing of evil deeds against the soul of the dead in a scale. Jama is the subdeity who, in the service of Siva, administers reward and punishment. He is represented in this office surrounded by genie: upon one side the soul of the dead is weighed against evil deeds in a scale, one pan containing the soul, the other the evil deeds; upon the other side of Jama other genie tally up the good and evil deeds in piles of white and black balls. Below the god the souls of the evil are subjected to horrors equal to later Western mythopoeists: they are boiled in cauldrons, roasted on spits, fried in pans, and impaled on forks (p. 161).

In a further effort to establish an analogy with the Christian religion Paulinus calls the reader's attention to the report of the Brahmanical conception of death given by the Greek historian and well-traveled geographer Strabo (*ca.* 63 B.C.—A.D. 21), who relates that the Brahmans consider death a birth of the human soul into another life, the genuine existence (p. 26).

Despite his caviling with contemporary Sanskrit scholars, and despite his transparent intent to subordinate the religion of the Hindus to Christianity, Paulinus attempts scrupulously to disclose the diversities of Brahmaism. He is frank in his admiration of many traits of character in the Hindu, speculative about the immense age of the culture, and almost unique among the commentators in his judicious estimate of the erotic elements in Hindu worship.

The first organ to state German Romantic principles was the periodical published in Berlin from 1798 to 1800 by August Wilhelm and Friedrich Schlegel, the *Athenäum*. In this publication the theorists of the Romantic Movement outline the principles which were to guide the creative minds of the Romantic poets, although in some particulars they were anticipated by the poets. India is not neglected in the formulation of the theories of Romantic poetry.

In an essay on "Die Sprachen," in the form of a dialogue, Wilhelm Schlegel offers Sanskrit as an example of a language in which the powers of observation in a people are in harmony with the degree of receptivity. The language, whose name means *perfect*, is lent grace. God himself invented the written characters, Wilhelm Schlegel says.[10]

Herder's metaphorical comparison of the historical ages of the world to the ages of man found an excited salutation among the Romanticists. In an essay "Ueber die natürliche Gleichheit der Menschen," published in the *Athenäum* (1799), the minor Romantic philosopher August Ludwig von Hülsen (1765-1810) describes in a concise paragraph the idyllic existence of a primitive people. Among all the peoples of the earth which trace their origin beyond historical fact, he says, the legend of a primordial golden age is found: a condition of the most intimate concord and love, where peaceable gods wandered among men and where a youthfully beautiful and harmonious life blessed the innocent race (II, 157-158). The golden age mentioned by Von Hülsen is not the exclusive property of the Romantic theorist or the poet: the idea of a golden age of mankind is a common one. Nor is the idea of a golden age applied only to the idyllic scenes of ancient India—it is even more frequently used with reference to the period of the highest attain-

---

10. *Athenäum, eine Zeitschrift*, ed. August Wilhelm Schlegel and Friedrich Schlegel (3 vols.; Berlin, 1798-1800), I, 23. My citations are from the photomechanical reprint in three volumes, with a concluding essay "Athenaeum, Die Geschichte einer Zeitschrift," by Ernst Behler (Darmstadt, 1960). The pagination in the reprint differs from the original in two respects: it is sequential throughout the first volume, whereas the pages of the first two issues comprising the first volume in the original were numbered separately; the last volume corrects the two-page error in the numbering of the original. Further *Athenäum* references are given parenthetically by volume and page of the modern reprint.

ments of the Greeks. But the Romantic spirit manifested itself in a more protean conception of the golden age; the Romanticist looked beyond Greece toward Asia, toward the source of human wisdom, and exalted the childhood of mankind as imagined in India as the most original golden age, where a harmony of religion, philosophy, and literature produced an existence for which the Romantic spirit yearned.

In the "Blütenstaub" fragments published in the *Athenäum* (1799) Novalis says: "Wo Kinder sind, da ist ein goldnes Zeitalter" (I, 101). He expresses a longing for the return of a society where poet and priest were incorporated in one being: "Dichter und Priester waren im Anfang Eins, und nur spätere Zeiten haben sie getrennt. Der ächte Dichter ist aber immer Priester, so wie der ächte Priester immer Dichter geblieben. Und sollte nicht die Zukunft den alten Zustand der Dinge wieder herbeyführen?" (I, 90). The idea of the singularity of a poet-priest is implied in the idea of the unity of poetry and religion. Such a unity was thought to have existed in India, where the religious precepts were stated poetically in the mythology of the Hindu gods. For Novalis mythology not only removes the distinction between the wisdoms of poetry, history, and religion, but even dissolves time itself, in that it contains the past, the present, and the future (I, 102). Essentially, Novalis, in pleading the unity of poetry and religion (= philosophy), in expressing his longing for the return of naïve wisdom, joins Friedrich Schlegel's call for a new mythology.

In the "Ideen," published in the *Athenäum* in 1800, Friedrich Schlegel identifies Novalis with the wisdom of the Orient: "Allen Künstlern gehört jede Lehre vom ewigen Orient. Dich nenne ich statt aller andern" (III, 33). Already, he admits, eyes are turned toward the Orient, and he says that even outwardly the way of life of artists should differ from that of other men, because "sie sind Braminen, eine höhere Kaste, aber nicht durch Geburt sondern durch freye Selbsteinweihung geadelt" (III, 31).

Friedrich Schlegel, in the "Gespräch über die Poesie," also printed in 1800 in the *Athenäum*, states the Romantic credo that mythology and poetry are one and inseparable (III, 96). And it is in this same essay that he finds the occasion to declare that the highest principles of Romanticism are embodied in the Orient. Prophetically, he wishes the treasures of Oriental literature were as accessible as those of Greek and Roman antiquity:[11] "Welche neue Quelle von Poesie könnte uns aus Indien fliessen," he exclaims, and calls upon the Germans, who possess an inborn genius for translation, to replace the brutal and dull English and unveil the sources of the ideal Romanticism. His adjuration is: "Im Orient müssen wir das höchste Romantische suchen" (III, 103). India is not only the land of sensual longing, where a naïve and gentle people live in the closest harmony with nature—it is also the land of intellectual longing, where a unity of wisdom spreads through every phase of knowledge the harmony of poetry, a *Universalpoesie*, a lofty conception of the permeation of a poetic spirit into every utterance of the human soul.

It was in Ludwig Tieck's *Poetisches Journal* that Friedrich Majer, a translator, mythologist, and cultural historian, published his first study of Indic mythology.[12] Other periodicals of the era began to print essays on the literature or mythology of India, or translations (by way of English sources) of Sanskrit poems. The *Göttinger Musenalmanach* of 1801 contains (p. 217) an Indic song. In the *Oster Taschenbuch von Weimar* (1801), Majer wrote again on India, and in 1802 in H. J. Klaproth's *Asiatisches Magazin* he published a translation of Wilkins' *Bhagavad-Gita*, the first in German. In the same periodical he also is represented by an essay on the in-

11. Goethe was repeatedly attracted to Indic literature, though not with the expectancy that it would reveal the source of Romantic poetry. However, despite his interest in it, he always maintained a wary stance. Even as late as 1826, when he wrote a letter on October 22 to Wilhelm von Humboldt, he reveals his guarded acceptance of Indic utterances: "I have by no means an aversion to things Indic," he claims. "But I am afraid of them, because they tug my powers of fantasy into formlessness and the difform, against which I must guard myself more than ever" (IV, 41, 204; author's trans.). Goethe was beyond doubt enticed by the literary creations and repulsed by the sculpture of India, an ambivalence which he confessed in one of the "Zahme Xenien" (I, 3, 251), a sequel to his explicit damnation of the "beasts in the hall of the gods":

> Der Ost hat sie schon längst verschlungen:
> Kalidas und andere sind durchgedrungen;
> Sie haben mit Dichter-Zierlichkeit
> Von Pfaffen und Fratzen uns befreit.
> In Indien möcht ich selber leben,
> Hätt es nur keine Steinhauer gegeben.
> Was will man denn vergnüglicher wissen!
> Sakontala, Nala, die muss man küssen,
> Und Megha-Duta, den Wolkengesandten,
> Wer schickt ihn nicht gerne zu Seelenverwandten!

See also Paul T. Hoffmann, p. 46.

12. *Poetisches Journal*, ed. Ludwig Tieck (Jena, 1800).

carnations of Vishnu and a translation of the *Gita-Govinda* (after
Jones).[13] The dramatic poem, filled to superfluity with blossoming
nature, contains a number of references to blue water lilies[14] and to
the blue petals of the lotus,[15] the mystic flower of Hindu mythology.

In addition to his own verse translation of the *Gita-Govinda*,
which Majer considered inferior, Friedrich von Dalberg (1760-
1812) also translated in 1802 an essay by Sir William Jones, "On
the Musical Modes of the Hindus" (1784).[16] Von Dalberg appends
to his translation of Jones's essay (which takes up only about forty
pages of the volume) a summation of his own studies of Indic music
and that of other Asiatic peoples. His sources include an essay on
Indian music by Sir William Ouseley (1767-1842), the Oriental
scholar, and the travel narratives of Paulinus, Bernier, and Reinhold
Forster.

Von Dalberg is affected by an enthusiasm for India in the Romantic tradition, emphasizing the advantageous climate, the musical structure of the language, the physical attractiveness of the people, and their sensitive intellectual accomplishments. He applies
these characteristics especially to their music and its allied arts. Nature seems to have endowed the beautiful nation of Hindus with a
splendid aptitude for music and its related arts, he says. The rich
fulness of their poetry, their receptiviity to the good and the beautiful would make this apparent, even if it were not known that their
most superior dramatic and lyric poems were intended to be sung,
arrayed in melody (p. ii).

Accepting the opinion of Herder and others that India was the
cradle of humanity, Von Dalberg joins the Early Romantic theorists in citing Asia as the source of science and art, where also the
first knowledge of music was to be sought, since it was in the Orient
that music developed earliest (pp. iii-iv). The development of music
was a gradual process, taken by the Hindus as a gift of the gods who
also were the originators of instruments to play the divine music
(p. 44). The alliance of music and religion is demonstrated by its
being the exclusive property of the priestly caste (p. 46). And fur-

13. *Asiatisches Magazin*, see Bibliography.
14. *Ibid.*, II, 334, 346, 347, 353, 358.
15. *Ibid.*, II, 329, 353, 355, 362.
16. Jones, *Works*, I; see here Friedrich von Dalberg, trans., *Über die Musik der
Indier. Eine Abhandlung des Sir William Jones* (Erfurt, 1802). Parenthetical references are to the edition of Von Dalberg.

ther, this intimate interrelation of religion and art is manifested also in the plastic arts and in mythology (p. 96).

The Hindu, favored by his climate and endowed with a gentle spirit and a lively imagination, personified all the objects of nature and thus, in applying his fantasies to poetry, especially to that poetry assisted by music, he produced a graceful and pleasant genre (p. 87). The personification of objects was extended to embrace also the personification of ideas, particularly, outside the realm of religion, the tones and modes of music. Here again the antiquity of Hindu music is attested, for only a carefree and childlike imagination could have conceived such a theory (p. 86).

Von Dalberg praises the Hindu selection of the *vina*, or Indian lute, as an instrument for the accompaniment of the voice. The delicately strung, softly sounding instrument is the only one mentioned for the voice in the Indian works on music. Von Dalberg believes that it contributed largely to the early perfection of the Indic musical system. And he states particularly that the intimate relation of the Hindu with nature contributed to the selection of a stringed instrument rather than the shrill flute for voice accompaniment (p. 57).

He cites the antiquity of Indic music, not only as an aesthetic art, but as a systematic science (p. iv). But a chief virtue of the Hindu composer was that he did not dwell to an exaggerated degree upon the physics of his art; his object was, rather, to please his listeners and to touch their gently sensitive emotions. The Hindu composer left musical theory to mathematics and physics and was himself principally concerned in artful combinations of song with instruments, gesture, and dance (p. 48).

Bernier and Reinhold Forster are heavily drawn upon by Von Dalberg for his depiction of the inhabitants of Kashmir as being better favored by climate and endowed with more attractive traits than the other peoples of India. He asserts that authorities agree that, of all the regions of India, Kashmir is best suited, by reason of its mild climate, charming landscape, fruitfulness of field, and purity of healthful air, to be the earthly Paradise. The beauty of the land corresponds to that of its inhabitants: they are lighter and paler in color, more attractively endowed with physique, more industrious, more intelligent, and better-natured than other Hindus (p. 98).

As do Herder, Majer, and Friedrich Schlegel, Von Dalberg also bemoans the paucity of translations from Sanskrit, and he reproves Jones mildly for not having been more thorough in the original essay on Hindu music, since the English scholar was favored with a more abundant source material (p. iii). A step toward the betterment of the German position in regard to the availability of Sanskrit sources was soon to be taken with Friedrich Schlegel's sojourn in Paris.

During the summer of 1800 Friedrich Schlegel became acquainted with Majer in Jena, and Josef Körner suggests that it was perhaps through his acquaintance with the mythographer that Friedrich Schlegel received his first impulse to devote time to the study of Sanskrit literature.[17] This need hardly be true, since it was not solely through Majer that Friedrich Schlegel became interested in India. Before 1800, in the *Athenäum*, he had alluded to the Orient as the treasure house of the highest Romantic tendencies, and had expressed his wish to see more examples of Indic literature. However, it may well be that Majer's excitement about India contributed to sustain Friedrich Schlegel's interest. From Paris, to which he journeyed early in 1802, he edited the journal *Europa*. In this periodical (1803-1805) the mythical image of India is given a new voice and the Romantic attitude toward India takes the form of a scientific analysis.

In an essay, "Reise nach Frankreich," Friedrich Schlegel interpolates a poem, written presumably upon his first sight of the Wartburg, the Thuringian castle where Luther took refuge to finish his translation of the New Testament. Friedrich Schlegel casts a poetic glance back into Germany's medieval history and finds the treasures of the Orient wending their way into the valley in the train of returning crusaders:

> Langsam dann im Thal gezogen
> Auf allen Strassen und Wegen
> Orients Reichthum in vollem Triumphe,
>
> . . . .
> Blühende Stein' und farbige Früchte,
> Indiens goldenster Segen.[18]

17. Josef Körner, ed., *Die Brüder Schlegel: Briefe von und an Friedrich und Dorothea Schlegel* (Berlin, 1926), p. 535. Further references to this collection will be given parenthetically by Körner and page.

18. *Europa*, ed. Friedrich Schlegel (2 vols.; Frankfurt a.M., 1803-1805), I, 9. Further *Europa* references are indicated parenthetically by volume and page.

The treasures of India in gold and gems and exotic fruits had long been traditional—but the intellectual treasures are the wonder of the age.

The Romantic image of India finds expression in Friedrich Ast's (1778-1841) essay, "Epochen der griechischen Philosophie." He suggests that there are three periods in the history of human civilization: that of the Hindu, in which the root of religion falls, where nature and love were intimately reciprocal, the period of golden innocence, of undivided religion, philosophy, and art; that of the Greeks, in which nature emerges as the objective entity in itself, and at Athens the state emerges as objective humanity; and finally, the period of the new world, of Christianity, of the Romantic Age, in which spiritual love of the infinite is revealed (II, 64-65). Here is stated the Romantic attitude toward nature and India: it is an idyllic paradise where nature is entwined with love; the emotion and the object are inseparable, each includes the other. In India there was a pure, golden innocence, the innocence of childhood. In India the wisdoms of humankind were unified; any expression of one was of necessity an expression of the others. Ast also relegates Greece to a secondary position in the Romantic conception of the history of the development of the human intellect: India is the first stage, Greece the second. The Romanticist looks beyond Greece to India.

In "Ueber Litteratur, Kunst und Geist des Zeitalters," by August Wilhelm Schlegel, from the Berlin lectures of 1802 printed in part in the *Europa*, a list of events is given which have had a decisive influence upon the shape and form of modern Europe. Foremost he lists the Reformation; the remaining events are either inventions or discoveries, among them the re-discovery of India (II, 76). The Romantic enthusiasm for India, manifested in a consuming interest in the people, the literature, and the language, and transformed into a deep longing for the re-attainment of a legendary and fanciful golden age, was contributory to the influence of India upon the intellect of Europe. Wilhelm Schlegel joins Friedrich Schlegel, Majer, Von Dalberg, and Herder in expressing his wish to see more of the ancient records of India. He expects to find significant information about the history of humankind unfolded when the documents of Indic mythology, history, and literature have been properly understood. He alludes to the progress made in the translation of San-

skrit works by the English (II, 43-44). German efforts in this direction were yet to come.

It was inevitable that the Romantic mythical image of India could
not endure for a long period of time: the tension of an emotion
must finally snap, and the Romantic attitude was an intellectualized
emotion. Considerable influence was exerted by the mythical image
as long as it lasted but, as shall be shown, the effort to make the
image present reality by going to the pristine source, to the Sanskrit,
resulted in its shattering; afterward it glimmered forth only as literary imagery, as an ironic device, and as a symbol of the longing now
acknowledged to be incapable of realization. The fading of the
mythical image began when German effort was applied to the study
of Sanskrit; thus the development of comparative linguistics, a
sequel of that study, is of importance.

Wilhelm Schlegel, in a review of A. F. Bernhardi's *Sprachlehre*
(1801) in the *Europa*, says that the feeling for the individuality
of a language is exhibited by masters of style, but that the gram-
marians have not accomplished the description of a language. An
aid to descriptive grammar, he says, would be the development
of a comparative grammar, or, in modern terms, comparative linguistics. He would first begin with the Oriental languages and then
proceed to those of the West. Of course, he admits, it is easier to
outline such a program than it is to carry it out: "Doch würde
solchergestalt die Philologie immer mehr zur Kunst werden" (II,
203-204). The Romanticist wished to see art revealed in every
science, so Wilhelm Schlegel's wish to raise philology more into
the realm of art is not surprising. He could not have known that the
application of linguistics and philology to the study of Sanskrit was
to seal the dissolution of the Romantic mythical image. Even had
he known, he would not have been stayed, for the goal of every
scientist and of every artist is the pursuit of truth—and the Romantic mythical image of India, for all of the universal verities it reflected, was a figment of diverse imaginations, basically unreal, com-
pounded through centuries of half-knowledge and suddenly focused
into illusory sharpness and brightness and with equal suddenness
eclipsed.

In Paris, Friedrich Schlegel sank into an Oriental atmosphere
among the Sanskrit manuscripts collected by the Bibliothèque Na-

tionale. His first instruction in Sanskrit and his first readings into the manuscripts will be discussed in the following chapter. From the essays in the *Europa* one may cull his statements concerning the realization and the attainment of the mythical image of India, opinions destined to fade swiftly into disillusionment upon his recognition that the image was beyond substantiation. In an essay entitled "Einige Nachrichten über die neuesten Arbeiten der Pariser Philologen," Friedrich Schlegel expresses his opinion about the *Oupnek'hat* of the French Orientalist Abraham Hyacinthe Anquetil-Duperron (1731-1805), whose passion for the languages of the East led to enlistment in 1754 as a private soldier so that he could go to India. Friends secured his discharge and arranged for him to be sent with a salary from the French governor in India. Upon leaving India in the course of the Seven Years' War he brought 180 Oriental manuscripts back to France. He had mastered modern Persian and claimed knowledge of Sanskrit sufficient to translate, although later scholars hotly debated his Sanskrit achievements. In 1771 he published the *Zend-Avesta* and a life of Zoroaster. The *Oupnek'hat*, published in Paris in 1801-1802, is a compilation of copious extracts from the vedic Upanishads, made however from a quite unreliable Persian rendering by Mohammed Darah Shekuh from the seventeenth century.[19] Friedrich Schlegel calls the *Oupnek'hat* a remarkable phenomenon, although he finds it infused with an impenetrable murkiness. He continues: "Was mir übrigens besonders auffiel, war, dass jener Prinz [Mohammed] dem *principium unificationis* nachreiste, also wahrscheinlicher Weise ein indischer Spinozist war" (I, 115). The word *nachreisen* reveals Friedrich Schlegel's own subjective longing to find in India a perfect religion, a longing which was of great influence upon his interest in the study of Sanskrit. The principle of unity here mentioned is a metaphysical conception of the singleness of God's essence, the unity of the substance of God: everything which exists is only a modification of the primordial unity that combines matter and spirit. The Hindu conception of the Supreme Being may be compared to Spinoza's idea, at any event superficially; thus Friedrich Schlegel and the other Early Romanticists felt nothing spectacularly new about Hinduism; rather a

19. Von Adelung, pp. 82-83.

sense of familiarity hovered about what seemed to be the utterances of a more ancient, more naïve Spinoza.

At intervals an intellectual atmosphere, like the positively charged earth in a thunderstorm, primed for the lightning bolt, may be especially receptive to new ideas. At such times the poet and the theorist may present, each in his own language, similar interpretations of a new idea arrived at independently and coincidentally. Such, it seems, may have been the case with the theorist Friedrich Schlegel and certain Romantic poets, above all Novalis and Hölderlin. The Romantic longing for India was not only for a beautiful clime and the carefree ingenuousness of a people living in accord with nature; it encompassed also the unity of human wisdom found in ancient India and preserved to a large extent through the centuries. The unity of religion, philosophy, and art had been sundered in the civilization of the West, and the Romantic spirit longed to synthesize the two disparate attitudes and achieve once again a golden age.

Such a synthesis would be a revolution of the spirit, and the impulse to such a revolution could come only from the Orient, according to Friedrich Schlegel. In the East, where the kernel of united and centralized power is found, the possibility of inspiration, of enthusiasm, can never be effaced beyond a trace because nature itself established there an original and inexhaustible source (I, 36). He recalls the reputation of Asia as the source of all religion and mythology, the principles of life, the cradle of ideas, and he notes wryly that in the West the original conceptions have been formed anew, often past recognition (I, 37). The singularity and unified character of the wisdom of the Orient manifested itself in a multiplicity of arts and sciences in Europe. The separation of poetry and philosophy is a European phenomenon, and the unity of these wisdoms found in India is more forceful and more beautiful. He gives an example of the greater sublimity of religious ideas in India as compared with the manifestations of those ideas in ancient Greece and in Europe: the most spiritual self-annihilation of the Christians, and the most rampant and wildest materialism in the religion of the Greeks are found in Indic archetypes, in their common homeland. The real essence of religion, he says, is to be found at least in part in India. If one considers the lofty sensibility on which the truly universal education of the Hindu is based, a sensibility which is able to embrace everything divine in a divine manner into infinity, then what has been called religion in Europe seems hardly to deserve the name. Friedrich Schlegel would advise him who would see religion to travel to India, where he might be sure of finding at least fragments of that which he would seek in vain in Europe (I, 32-33). There is in Friedrich Schlegel an intensification of religious longing for India, a longing which mirrored a religious crisis in himself.

Thus, in the theoretical statements of the Schlegels in their journals, and in the translators and philosophers represented in independent volumes and in the periodicals, the Romantic mythical image of India finds its projection. Not only is there a nostalgia for the idyllic existence of ancient Hindu culture, where a happy people lived in the closest communion with nature, there is also a longing for the harmony of the arts and sciences as perceived in that culture. Remnants of the primordial religion are to be found in India. The most profound revelation of the human spirit could be attained through a synthesis of the intellectual cultures of the Orient and the West.

2. *Nach dem Morgenlande, an die Ufer des Ganges und Indus, da fühlt unser Gemüt von einem geheimen Zug sich hingezogen.* —GÖRRES

The Mythologists

Ich lebe jetzt ganz in Indien und fühle mich dadurch oft wohltätig der traurigen Gegenwart entrückt. —MAJER

In a reply to a letter from a professor in Halle requesting biographical data in 1851, Schopenhauer wrote:

1813 . . . durch den Krieg verdrängt . . . sah [ich] mich genöthigt mit meiner Abhandlung über den Satz vom Grunde in Jena zu promoviren. Darauf brachte ich den Winter in Weimar zu, wo ich Göthe's nähern Umgang genoss, der so . . . wohlthätig auf mich gewirkt hat. Zugleich führte, unaufgefordert, der Orientalist Friedrich Majer mich in das In-

dische Alterthum ein, welches von wesentlichem Einfluss auf mich gewesen ist.[1]

In many biographical investigations of Schopenhauer which take
note of this single mention of Friedrich Majer (1772-1818), the
"Orientalist" is called "well-known" and even "celebrated." But
despite the influence he exerted on Schopenhauer and on such significant literary contemporaries as Goethe, Clemens Brentano,
Achim von Arnim, and Jean Paul, Majer remains, because of his
natural modesty and awkward social graces, one of the least-known
figures of the age. He is mentioned in none of the standard biographical reference works; at best he is merely listed in some bibliog-
raphies. For ordinary biographical data and more intimate personal
characterization one must rely on Majer's own works and on the
correspondence of his contemporaries.[2]

Friedrich Majer, the son of a pastor, was born in Unterkoskau in
Thuringia. His first university studies, as also his first publications,
were in law and history. He studied law at Jena in 1791, and in the
winter of 1796-1797 was active in Göttingen as a lawyer. Even then
he collected material about India and held weekly lectures before a
small group of friends, for when continuing his studies privately in
Jena and Weimar he had been befriended by Herder, whose student
he became. His new teacher had already idealized ancient India, to
provide the Early Romanticists with a touchstone to draw their
gaze beyond the traditional majesties of Greece. Throughout his
long years of tutorship and service at various courts, Majer constantly kept before him Herder's eclectic compilation of information about the mythology and literature of India, and he collected
books on the subject for his own library.

In Weimar the ingenuous and splendid young man (as Brentano
called him)[3] moved among the most scintillating literary figures of
his time. In the circle of friends at the literary salon of Johanna
Schopenhauer, the mother of the philosopher, Majer was known as
"der mythologische Majer," to distinguish him from "Kunst-Mey-

1. Ludwig Schemann, ed., *Schopenhauer-Briefe. Sammlung meist ungedruckter
oder schwer zugänglicher Briefe von, an und über Schopenhauer* (Leipzig, 1893),
p. 332.
2. *Ibid.*, pp. 440-441.
3. Reinhold Steig, ed., *Achim von Arnim und die ihm nahe standen* (3 vols.;
Stuttgart, 1894-1904), I, 78.

er," the art historian and friend of Goethe, Hans Heinrich Meyer. Because of his curious orthography, and also his single-minded mythological studies, Majer was called a *Magier* ("Wizard") by Goethe.[4] Although as an understanding friend he served as the intermediary between Brentano and Sophie Mereau (later the poet's wife), even in the self-effacing role of the *cavalier servente* (to quote Brentano), Majer could not help talking about his favorite topic, India, to judge from the somewhat exasperated closing lines of a letter from Brentano to Sophie: "Werden Sie ewig in Weimar sitzen bleiben? und Majer, wird er Ihnen von des Gottes verlornen Hammer vordichten und von den indischen Göttern?"[5]

In 1804, as a counselor in the principality of Reuss-Schleiz, Majer became the tutor and companion of the young heir apparent, with whom he resided in the following years in Würzburg and Erlangen. In October, 1804, in a letter to Sophie, now his wife, Brentano alludes to Majer with a mixture of light scorn and sympathetic understanding:

Niemand mehr um, und der Gott Kama ist von mir in seiner himmelblauen Uniform im Isenburgischen Hotel im Hof stehend erblickt worden. Er ist schon ein halbes Jahr mit seinem Zögling in Würzburg und lebt beständig unter der höchsten Noblesse, auch sagte mir Medicus, wie er bereits mehreren Damen als ein sehr tieffühlender junger Mann erschienen sei.[6]

In the reference to Majer as "der Gott Kama," Brentano is mindful of Majer's aid in the courtship of Sophie Mereau, for the Hindu god Kama is the god of love. Despite his azure-blue uniform Majer blended into the intellectual background of his day, an unimportunate figure, gentle and withdrawn, although ever eager to talk about India.

During the time of the Rhine Confederation (1806-1813) Majer found himself in his financial affairs dependent entirely on his literary efforts, and he resided mostly in Weimar. In 1813 he became immersed in politics, wrote a political tract, and in poor health and low spirits isolated himself from his friends and lived his last years in devoted labor on his work on Brahma.

4. Schemann, p. 441.
5. Steig, I, 79.
6. *Ibid.*, I, 118.

He did not altogether escape the official attention of the scholarly world during his life. He was made a member of the Munich Academy of Sciences, and as early as 1796 was praised by the *Göttinger Gelehrten Anzeigen* as a writer who combined a warmth of spirit with a rare modesty,[7] an estimate which quite early took cognizance of the humble and meek demeanor which was to relegate him to long anonymity.

Majer's first efforts as an author were in the field of history, *Geschichte der Ordalien* (1795), but his visionary ambition encompassed more, as in *Zur Kulturgeschichte der Völker* (two volumes, 1798, with a foreword by Herder). He even conceived of a work in the spirit of Herder's *Ideen,* and wrote fragments for a history of the universe, the solar system, the earth, and the human race, a work he entitled *Die Weltalter.* It was to include further an unhypothetically critical and pragmatical genealogy of migratory myths and religious systems.[8] As other spirits of his day, Majer too was broken by the neglect of his contemporaries and by personal misfortune: the fragmented character of his life is reflected in the literary fragments which form the bulk of his work.

As the author of essays on Hindu mythology, translations of Sanskrit works (albeit at second hand), and mythological reference works, Majer became the chief German purveyor of Indic knowledge in his time. His interest in India awakened by Herder, he was in turn to further Indic studies by contributing to the inspiration of Friedrich Schlegel to pursue the study of Sanskrit—the first such scholar in Germany—for the purpose of translating the literature from the original language. It was Majer who introduced Schopenhauer to Indic antiquities, which exerted a basic influence on that philosopher.[9] During his whole life Majer pursued the chimeric mythical image of India, searching beyond the myth for the essential character of ancient India. A Romantic spirit, Majer did not attain his goal of revealing the religion and literature of India, but he never lost sight of it, and because of his pioneering efforts others followed in his path to the source he had sought.

When Friedrich Schlegel voiced a fervent plea in the *Athenäum*

7. Schemann, p. 442.
8. *Ibid.*
9. Paul T. Hoffmann, p. 57.

in 1800 for German translators to turn their genius toward the revelation of the literature of India, he found quick response in his
newly met friend, Majer. Caught up by Herder's happy appraisal of
Indic thought and letters, particularly by his generous reception of
Sakuntala, Majer, in Schlegel's plea, heard support for his own consuming participation in the revelation of Indic culture to Germany.

The projection of the Romantic mythical image of India found
a new agent in Majer, who was indefatigable in his pursuit of Indic
studies, although, like his contemporaries, he was dependent entirely upon the slight amount of material available in translations by
English scholars such as Wilkins and Jones, and the Hindu Méridas
Poullé, who translated from Tamil into French.[10]

Although he gave informal lectures on India to friends in Göttingen as early as 1796,[11] Majer's first published study on Hindu
mythology was "Ueber die mythologischen Dichtungen der Indier,"
printed in Tieck's *Poetisches Journal* in 1800. As a point of departure in the essay, Majer proposes to instruct the reader of *Sakuntala*
in the mythology of India so that the magic of the play may find
appreciation. The novelty of the Hindu milieu and the exoticism of
the Hindu pantheon revealed by Kalidasa enchanted the German
reader, particularly the Romantic spirits who saw embodied in the
play an image of the past for which they yearned. The allusions to
Hindu mythology left the German reader, however, at a disadvan-
tage, despite the copious lexical appendix supplied by the translator;
without a knowledge of Hindu mythology, the reader of *Sakuntala*
was denied a vital dimension of experience in his reading of the
work.

Majer's essay is in the form of an epistle addressed to a girl,
"Alwina," who has read the play and glimpsed in the fey enchantment of it the youthful fantasy of a golden age and the whole character of an ancient people. A new heaven and a new earth lay before
the astonished eye of the reader, who felt transported back into the
appealing and chaotic confusion of childhood years. Majer says
that the mythological literature of a people offers the best source
for an appraisal of the spiritual, even of the physical, characteristics

10. Körner, p. 535.
11. Friedrich Majer, *Brahma, oder die Religion der Indier als Brahmaismus*
(Leipzig, 1818), p. v.

which make for uniqueness. A people's way of thought, judgment, and behavior are reflected in the imagery of its mythology (*Journal*, I, 165-167). At the very outset, however, Majer cautions the reader to avoid a comparison of the amazing figures of the Hindu temple with those of Greece and Rome and Egypt, though this had been done by Jones. He compares the mythological writings of the Hindus to blossoms (a Romantic commonplace with regard to the mythical image) too fragile to flourish easily under other skies; but he suggests that the myths of Greece are perhaps acclimatized descendants of Hindu myths, for he considers the gods of Asia older than the gods of the West (*Journal*, I, 168-170).

Majer finds the religion of India a mixture of reason and fantasy: reason represented by the metaphysical conception of the Highest Being held by the priest-wisemen; fantasy exemplified by the mythological literature in which metaphysical ideas are symbolized in the figures of active and forceful deities (*Journal*, I, 170-171). The Hindu conceived of the Highest Being as having an immanent quality, as being present in all things, as being the originator of all phenomena. God was at the same time the container and the creator of the universe and all its denizens. God is the spirit and the creation, the form of All, its beginning, being, and end. In all creatures of nature God is the noblest part. Millions of forms, races, species, and colors make up the form of God. All spirits and all shapes of being are gathered together in God (*Journal*, I, 173). Majer finds this idea of the Deity the most sublime he knows, and he admires especially the paradox of the proximity and the remoteness of God in this conception (*Journal*, I, 175).

The mother of the mythological tales of the Hindus, says Majer, was the fantasy of a happy childhood. The Hindu idealized and quickened his conception of the triad deity and of every phenomenon of nature about him. He made the elements, the shining sun, the stars of heaven, and animals and plants objects worthy of religious veneration (*Journal*, I, 176-177). Finally, Majer presents examples of Hindu mythology as expressions of the dawn-dreams of humanity, just as a naïve spirit might conceive them. He expresses the wish that the material he offers may in part fulfil the hope of Herder and Friedrich Schlegel to see more of the abundant poetry of India (*Journal*, I, 183-184).

The examples which Majer offers are the history of the creation according to Poullé's *Bagavadam*, the story of creation taken from the preface of the *Laws of Menu*,[12] and the story of the drink of immortality and the victory of the forces of good over the forces of evil in the world (the victory of the gods over the giants). This article was the first in Germany devoted entirely to a study of Hindu mythology.

In the *Oster Taschenbuch von Weimar* (1801), edited by Leopold von Seckendorff-Aberdar, Majer published fragments from the holy writings of the Hindus and an essay on the Hindu conception of the four ages of the world.

In an essay entitled "Die Verkörperungen des Wishnu," published in Klaproth's *Asiatisches Magazin* in 1802, Majer offers his theory that the epic poems of the Hindus incorporate actual historical events of the dim past transformed into poetic fantasies by the retelling of succeeding generations (*Magazin*, I, 117-118). Majer believed that the Hindu myths, especially the tales of the incarnations of Vishnu, furnish the best historical evidence for the incredible age of mankind, and even sources of information about prehistoric events (*Magazin*, I, 119-120).[13] Later, Jean Paul, in his preface to Johann Arnold Kanne's *Erste Urkunden der Geschichte oder allgemeine Mythologie* (1808), observed that India lacked a national history, a lack which disappointed Hegel, who wrote: "Indien hat nicht allein alte Religionsbücher und glänzende Werke der Dichtkunst, sondern auch alte Gesetzbücher... und doch keine Geschichte."[14] In this preface Jean Paul stresses the idea (previously held by Majer) that the history revealed in the writings of India is not to be taken as literal political history but rather as intellectual history. It discloses the primordial story of humankind, a tradition preserved by man's inner destiny. It is, specifically, the account of

12. Nathaniel Halhed's *A Code of Gentoo Laws* (1776) was translated by Rudolf Erich Raspe as *Gesetzbuch der Gentoos* (Hamburg, 1778). The Hindu code of laws was translated for the first time from the Sanskrit into English by Jones in 1794, and it was from this version (used by Majer as a source) that Hüttner published his translation.

13. See also Majer's *Allgemeines Mythologisches Lexicon* (2 vols.; Weimar, 1803-1804), II, 486-487.

14. Georg Wilhelm Friedrich Hegel, "Vorlesungen über die Geschichte der Philosophie" (1805-1831), in *Sämtliche Werke*, ed. Hermann Glockner (23 vols.; Stuttgart, 1927-1929), XVII, 161. Further references in the text are to this edition of Hegel's works, cited as volume and page.

the revelation of God to man.[15] Majer felt that the minds of his time should strive to comprehend the mysterious symbolic conceptions in which the first cultured peoples, in his estimate the Hindus, had recorded their observations about the essence and phenomena of nature (*Magazin*, II, 67-68).

In Majer's theory that the myths of India contain the kernel of the cultural history of that land is found the Romantic urge to combine the sciences and the arts into one sublime poetic phenomenon. Majer thought that miracles could be performed in the heavens and on earth by the sciences. He would mix mythology and physics, for old, almost faded visions of the infancy and dawn of humanity would then rove about in brilliant, luminous form. He would call upon astronomy to join the harmonious fusion of art and science, for the orbits of the planets were the law books of the cosmos, and in the dark of night man can see above him in the broad reaches of space the old history of the universe written in the glowing stars (*Magazin*, I, 118-119; *Lexicon*, II, 486).[16]

A real, but generally ignored, accomplishment of Majer was his translation of Wilkins' version of the *Bhagavad-Gita*, published in the *Magazin*. Majer presents the work as an example of the earliest expression of the Hindu intellect, deserving of the highest respect. As a Romantic enthusiast ever urging the synthesis of the intellectual treasures of the Orient and the Occident, he refers to the analogy between the ideas contained in this ancient philosophical work in its epic frame and the ideas of Plato and Spinoza, as well as those of Jakob Böhme, whose mystic reflections enjoyed a rejuvenation among the Early Romantic theorists and poets (*Magazin*, I, 406-407). Indeed, Warren Hastings, the governor-general of India, says in a letter in Wilkins' edition of the epic (a letter mentioned also by Majer) that he would not hesitate "to pronounce the Geeta a performance of great originality; of a sublimity of conception, reasoning, and diction, almost unequalled; and a single exception, among all the known religions of mankind, of a theology accurately corresponding with that of the Christian dispensation, and most

15. Johann Arnold Kanne, *Erste Urkunden der Geschichte oder allgemeine Mythologie* (2 vols.; Baireuth [*sic*], 1808), I, 13.

16. These utterances are preliminary to similar ones expressed later by the Romantic natural philosopher Gotthilf Heinrich Schubert in his work, *Ansichten von der Nachtseite der Naturwissenschaft* (1808).

powerfully illustrating its fundamental doctrines."[17] Majer's publication of the great metaphysical dialogue between Krishna and Arjuna is not a critical study, but he furnishes additional notes to those appended by Wilkins, in an effort to clarify further the obscure mythological references in the work.

The *Asiatisches Magazin* also contains two other translations of Sanskrit works made from English sources. One, the "Moha Mudgava" (correctly: *Moha Mudgara*), although unsigned, may have been by Majer from the translation of Jones (*Magazin, II*, 265-268).[18] The other is the *Gita-Govinda* of Jayadeva, also translated originally from the Sanskrit by Jones,[19] and here translated into German prose by Majer, who criticizes Jones's rendering of the work and says that it became, in the English translation, an epic idyl, in design quite incomprehensible to the reader (*Magazin, II*, 305). The work had already been translated into German (also taken from Jones's version) by Friedrich von Dalberg,[20] but in a shortened and incongruous lyric scheme. Majer prefaces his translation with the story of Krishna, but he necessarily omits the ode to Vishnu (since Jones also does), which is prefatory to the drama. Majer considers the work a musical play, accompanied in its original form by musical choruses and dances. For the Hindu, he says, drama and music and dance were inseparable, and thus, in a typically Romantic manner, he would find in the synthesis of the three arts the highest example of poesy (*Magazin, II*, 307, 374).

In his *Allgemeines Mythologisches Lexicon* Majer proposed ambitiously to furnish information about the mythologies of all peoples. The first division of the work was to concern the non-classical cultures, that is, Hindu, Chinese, Aztec, Incan, and others; the second division, the mythology of the classical world. He succeeded in publishing the second division in 1810-1814, but because of a disastrous loss of half his notes for the first division, it (published in

17. Wilkins, *Bhagvat-Geeta*, p. 9; see also *Asiatisches Magazin*, I, 415.
18. Jones, *Works*, I, 207-212.
19. *Ibid.*, I, 463-484.
20. Friedrich von Dalberg, trans., *Gita-Govinda* (Erfurt, 1802). Goethe, in a letter to Schiller on February 19, 1802 (IV, 16, 43-44; see also IV, 16, 18) bemoaned also the inadequate translation of Von Dalberg. Jones had omitted what was unsuited for English taste, now Von Dalberg had not only made further omissions for the sake of German sensibilities but had misunderstood very beautiful, innocent passages and mistranslated them. Goethe threatens to retranslate the end of the idyl, which had been spoiled by the "German mildew." See Paul T. Hoffmann, pp. 42-43.

1803-1804) includes only the alphabetical listing A-J.[21] Majer's preparatory reading for the *Lexicon* must have been immense. It is not primarily a reference work on Hindu mythology, yet for entries in this area alone he cites more than forty sources in his footnotes. He also incorporates into the *Lexicon* portions of essays he had written previously for the *Asiatisches Magazin*. His ultimate hope was somehow to link the cultures of the New World with those of the Old, but like so many of his plans it was not to reach fruition.

The Romantic longing for other climes and other ages, in the search for the primeval essence of the Supreme Being and His first revelation to mankind, is revealed by Majer in the preface. He says that a premonition of infinitely important results for all of humankind led him like a guiding star in his tireless endeavor to unveil prehistory through the study of mythology. The motivation which caused Majer to undertake this long look into the far reaches of history seems to have been a kind of mystic religious awe. He writes:

Dann wird jene wunderbare Zeichensprache und geheimnisvolle Symbolik aus den Frühlingstagen des Menschengeschlechts wohl noch mehr enthalten, als einen Inbegriff des Wissenswürdigsten, was die ersten Erfahrungen und Bemerkungen der Urwelt über Erscheinung und Wesen des Unsichtbaren im Sichtbaren der Natur fanden und wähnten: eine *Offenbarung* des Ewigen, deren reine Glorie das geblendete Auge des Sterblichen kaum ertragen wird. Tradition und Weissagung von diesem Unsichtbaren im Sichtbaren sind das Wesentliche aller Religion und Mythologie bei allen Völkern und unter allen Zonen. Merkwürdige Erinnerungen sagen uns, dass es schon einmal nicht mehr unsichtbar für uns war, und wir sollen wieder finden, was wir verloren haben.

(*Lexicon*, I, vii-viii)

Thus Majer's nostalgic search through mythology into the past has as its basis the longing for a metaphysical revelation of an Eternal Being, for the Invisible made visible once again.

To furnish an idea of the sublimity of the Hindu conception of God, Majer cites the writings of the Hindu poet-priests. He quotes *Chartah Bhade*, taken from Holwell. Deeply impressed by the Hindu depiction of the essential attributes of God, Majer says that the Hindu conception was the result of a modest effort of early Oriental wisdom to express the idea of an eternal existence (*Lexicon*, I, 238). In no other place on earth have human beings expressed the truth

21. Körner, pp. 196-197, and p. 535; see also Majer, *Brahma*, p. ix.

and splendor of God more beautifully than in India, says Majer, calling India God's first terrestrial workshop (*Lexicon*, I, 240).

Majer mentions *Sakuntala* as a work of priceless value in understanding the culture of ancient India, and he deplores the rarity of the idyllic hermitage such as sheltered Kanna, the teacher and mentor of the Hindu princess (*Lexicon*, I, 287, 297). In Kanna's grove there was a reciprocal affection between the creatures of nature and humankind. Majer's sentiment is a Romantic expression of longing for the simple morality and idyllic surroundings supposedly enjoyed ages ago by the Hindu.

In the ruins of Illoura, an old city with wondrous temples nearby, Majer finds proof for the antiquity of the culture of India. Contemporary Hindus placed the construction of the temples in prehistoric times shrouded by the veil of mythology. The assumption of great antiquity is further reinforced by the dilapidated condition of the temples, which only long ages could have accomplished. Majer suggests that it might even be doubtful that the great structures had been temples were it not for the cognizance of the enormous influence of the ancient Brahmans, and through them the Hindu religion, upon the people (*Lexicon*, II, 442). In accordance with the Romantic view, Majer's glance goes beyond Greece and seeks the oldest wisdom in India. There he finds the idea of the four ages of the world given in a more complete form and stated convincingly as a basic truth, while in Greece the legend of the four ages seems preserved like the chord of a faint song heard from the distance (*Lexicon*, II, 485).

Majer continued to be a Romantic spirit to the end. He planned a history of the religions of India, but his death terminated the project and the *Brahma* is the only work finished of four he planned. Although he was plagued by personal calamity and sickness in his last years, his longing for India did not decrease. He believed that India could furnish the key to wisdom and all the arts, the essence of religion, and the perfect kinship of man and nature. His nostalgia is revealed in a letter to Friedrich Schlegel in 1816, written long after popular credence in the Herder-inspired mythical image of India had begun to wane:

Ich lebe jetzt ganz in Indien und fühle mich dadurch oft wohltätig der traurigen Gegenwart entrückt. Wäre ich nur aus dem unfreundlichen

Norden, vielleicht würde dann doch die Parze meinen Lebensfaden noch etwas verlängern, dessen Abreissen ich so gar nicht ungern entgegen sehe.[22]

His thread of life was lengthened by only two years, for he died in 1818.

Majer was unaware of his real accomplishments; succeeding scholars and poets, even of modern times, unwittingly owe much to the influence Majer exerted on his contemporaries. He was not especially gifted as an author and only moderately so as a linguist. His activity was generally limited to the compilation of material about Indic literature and mythology and to translations of a few Sanskrit works from English versions. His merit, however, lies in the enthusiasm and the thoroughness with which he gathered and smoothly summarized material concerning the character, customs, language, philosophy, and art of India, and in the modest, yet imposing way in which he warmly drew attention to India, so that the imprint was left ever after on German letters.

> *In der nordischen Sage finden wir Indische*
> *Weichheit wieder.*   —KANNE

Jean Paul, in the preface to Kanne's *Erste Urkunden der Geschichte oder allgemeine Mythologie* (1808), finds it quite proper, as has been mentioned, that the history preserved in India's literature is intellectual rather than political. The archetype of history encountered there is the first and true history: Indic written tradition has stored up the inner destiny of man, his thought, reflection, and musing, which taken together offer a speculative religion, a philosophy in the theory of a godhead according to which nature is the body of the Divine Being and God the soul of the world. Jean Paul accents further the pure and clarified unity, harmony, and indivisibility of religion and myth in India.[23] The union of philosophy and religion was a primary goal of the Romantic spirit, and again and again the Romantic theorists point to the prototype found in India.

Johann Arnold Kanne (1773-1824), who was among the first to recognize the significance of India for the history of religion, thinks of India in the light of the mythical image as a world of childhood— but he finds there an unchildlike incisiveness and humorlessness. He

22. Körner, p. 197.
23. Kanne, I, 13-14.

depreciates the unity of the wisdoms as envisaged by the Romanticists in the mythical image in that he says man achieved his full consciousness only when he lost religion as an essential element of the unity, for only when morality came into conflict with life could the greatest expression of consciousness occur in the development of poetry as an independent art—and the development of poetry in this aspect occurred in Greece, where the Orient met the traditions of the whole world.[24]

The idea that God revealed Himself to man in the word is elucidated in Kanne's *Pantheum* where, in accordance with his theory, mythology is represented as the self-revelation of God. Ancient, primal truth was preserved most purely by the sages of India, Kanne believes; but even they derived their teachings from the wisdom of an archetypal ancestral stock from which faith was handed down to all peoples.[25] The true doctrine was pantheism, the oldest natural philosophy, according to Kanne, who thus disputed Friedrich Schlegel's decisive differentiation between the Indic dogma of emanation and pantheism.[26]

In the *Erste Urkunden* Kanne essays a philological comparison of the Greek and Indic names of gods, striving to show that the culture of Greece came from the Orient. He asserts, too, that the alphabet entered Greece from the East.[27] The influence of India is traced by Kanne even into the culture of the Norse, where he denotes the "gentleness" in the sagas as Indic in nature.[28] But Kanne's philological approach, his subjective attempt to transform the gods of India into the gods of Greece and Scandinavia, and his polemics against Friedrich Schlegel on the subject of pantheism dash the mythical image of India to pieces (coincidentally, and ironically, with Friedrich Schlegel's own disillusionment, which received public expression at the same time), so that only shards remain here and there to reflect the harmonious wonder formerly contained in the image.

Auch unter diese [indischen] Blumen ist ein Gott hinabgestiegen, Himmelsaat ist in den crystallenen See gefallen und es hat

24. *Ibid.*, I, 31.
25. Fritz Strich, *Die Mythologie in der deutschen Literatur von Klopstock bis Wagner* (2 vols.; Halle a. S., 1910), II, 324.
26. *Ibid.*, II, 171.
27. Kanne, II, 616, 637.
28. *Ibid.*, I, 33.

das Gewächs zum Licht hinaufgetrieben, und wie es die Blü-
thenblätter aufgeschlagen, ist das neue Wort hervorgequollen,
und die Pflanzen haben es verstanden, und die Menschen es ih-
nen abgelernt. —GÖRRES

The task of Johann Joseph von Görres (1776-1848) was to exhibit
the unity of faith and knowledge in mythology. Ricarda Huch
quotes his *Glauben und Wissen*, in which he strikes a Goethean
refrain but leads the glance East and not South: "Kennt ihr das
Land, wo die jugendliche Menschheit ihre frohen Kinderjahre
lebte? . . . Nach dem Morgenlande, an die Ufer des Ganges und
Indus, da fühlt unser Gemüt von einem geheimen Zug sich hingezogen."[29] There could be no plainer statement of the Romantic
longing for India.

Görres strikes a familiar refrain: the Orient, along the Ganges
and the Indus, was the primitive homeland of the human race, the
fount of all its legends and poetry. The Godhead had creatively
revealed Himself in the All, and the gods had then in a post-creation
manifested themselves in the holy myths of India, from which the
wandering peoples had carried the divine poem in all directions over
the earth. All man's knowledge rests on these holy traditions, Görres
claims.[30]

In an essay on "Religion in der Geschichte," printed in the third
volume of the *Studien* edited by Karl Daub and Friedrich Creuzer,
Görres says that the mysteries of religion originated in India. Their
essence was poetry and they were the foundation of all the arts.
They hid in themselves the germ of all poetic development; the
drama, the hymn, and the epic grew out of them, as did ethics and
philosophy. Görres asserts that all intellectual development in all
forms goes through art and wisdom and life back into the myths of
Asia and can be understood only in reference to them.[31]

From the lectures which he gave in Heidelberg in 1806 grew
Görres' *Mythengeschichte der asiatischen Welt*, in which his eye
sweeps over such a broad area, the whole mythological world of the
Orient, near and far, that the mythical image of India is almost lost
in a multitude of observations upon the Egyptians, the Greeks, the
Chaldeans, the Persians, Chinese, Israelites, and others. Görres

29. Richarda Huch, *Die Romantik* (2 vols.; Leipzig, 1924), II, 32.
30. Strich, II, 328.
31. *Ibid.*, II, 330.

attempts to follow the mythical figures and the religious ideas common to these cultures, but the confusion almost obliterates the mythical image, although it is in India that he would find the source.

In a true Romantic vein he calls early man the word articulated by the earth, just as the earth is the word of God; in the speech of man the muffled language of the elements is heard. He finds thus, in the history of mythologies, the transformation of the physical world into the organic world, the living world. Mankind, at the dawn of history, wanders as though hypnotized upon the earth, innocent and in harmony with all creation. Unaware of himself, man apprehends the deeper awareness of the earth. His thoughts are dreams (echo of Novalis) in his innermost nerve fibers, but they are true, for they are revelations of nature, which never lies. In his study Görres seeks a record of the culture of the early existence of man, and he finds it expressed most faithfully in the Indic Vedas.[32] In Anquetil's *Oupnek'hat* Görres discovers the real doctrine of the Vedas, in which he is convinced lies the oldest mythological system and the seed of all mythical history.[33]

The source of the world's religions Görres locates in the lavish gardens of the two Indian peninsulas, India and Indo-China, south of the Himalayas; here God was one with nature, and mankind learned of his higher kinship with God from an intimate communion with nature. A god descended, Görres says, and mingled with the flowers. Divine seed fell into the crystal lakes, and the plants were impelled to seek the light. When the blossoming petals opened, the new word emerged, and the plants comprehended it and man learned it from them.[34] This is the language of Romanticism, a mystic projection of the mythical image. The very character of the Hindu religion points to a tropic origin in the distant past, Görres says.[35] Then, from the dawn dream of mankind, he pursues the ancient nature myths to their precipitation in the very oldest Bible, the Vedas, to their rooting and flourishing in the romantic mythical wilderness of the Puranas, multiple in form and riotous in fantasy, to their development as historical poetry in the epics of the

32. Joseph Görres, *Mythengeschichte der asiatischen Welt* (2 vols.; Heidelberg, 1810), I, x-xi.
33. *Ibid.*, I, 129.
34. *Ibid.*, I, 70.
35. *Ibid.*, I, 144.

Ramayana and the *Mahabharata*, and finally to their transformation into the ethics of the *Dharma Śasta*, the laws of Menu.[36]

That the mythology of India was a precursor to that of Greece is advanced by Görres, in that he cites ancient Greek historians who speak of the Brahmans as teaching those principles embodied in Greek philosophy before they found expression in Greece. Even Megasthenes and Aristobolus admit, he says, that everything which the ancient philosophers speculated about on the nature of things had already existed among the Brahmans. And he gives other instances where Greeks were able to give what they considered definite information about certain beliefs held by the Hindus. Among other things Herodotus mentions that the Hindus kill no animals and subsist only on vegetable food. Ctesias describes a holy place venerated under the names of the sun and the moon, where every year the Indians gather in the cooler months. Megasthenes penetrates more deeply into Indic concepts when he comments that the Hindus considered life similar to the state of the embryo right after conception, while death was birth into the true and blissful life for those who had genuine wisdom.[37] Greek mythology fades into the background. Even Jakob Grimm, in a letter to Görres, writes that there was a gentleness and tenderness of feeling in Hindu mythology which was lacking in the mythology of the Greeks. The Greek myths seemed to him much more authentic, but the myths of India were nevertheless more credible.[38]

Görres' work as a history of mythology would be more valuable were there more order to it; he proceeds simply on a chronological basis, taking each culture in turn, but making many excursions outside the realm of his present subject. However, his analogies between Indic and Greek deities illuminate the still discernible form of the mythical image.

> *Endlich war es auch Indien, wo man wahrscheinlich zuerst die ewigen Gesetze der Sittenlehre und des Rechtes gleichsam hervorlockte aus dem Wesen und Verhältnis der Thiere und Pflanzen aus der umgebenden Natur.*   —CREUZER

In the foreword to his *Symbolik und Mythologie der alten Völker* (1810), Friedrich Creuzer (1771-1858) writes that in his study of

36. *Ibid.*, I, 190.
37. *Ibid.*, I, 129-131.
38. Strich, II, 175.

the mythology of the ancients he neither wanted nor would have been able to compose a philosophy of myths, symbols, and tenets of faith, but rather had endeavored to construct a philological-mythological ethnography.[39] If he meant to orientalize the Germans, in the Romantic sense of a synthesis of the Orient and the West, as Ricarda Huch quotes him, "Wir von Orient so sehr isolierte Deutsche müssen auf diese Weise orientalisiert werden—sonst ist nicht zu helfen,"[40] then he chose the wrong methodology, for a purely historical inspection of the mythical image of India removes it from its ideal realm and distorts it by focusing it sharply through the frame of science.

Creuzer, in this work, does not reveal a longing for India. His attitude is rather one of superficial admiration, not the fiery yearning of the Early Romanticists. He cites the customary Greek sources concerning India, beginning with Herodotus and including Ctesias and Arrian.[41] He remarks upon the importance of India as a source for poetry, social culture, morality, and religion, but his tone is moderate and objective.

India was undeniably a great treasure house of literature, and Creuzer joins Herder, Friedrich Schlegel, Von Dalberg, and Majer in expressing the wish for a look at more of the literature of India. The refinement of culture, the separation of classes, the intellectual aspirations of the people, the friendly climate, and the beneficence of nature made the development of drama inevitable. He mentions *Sakuntala* and the qualities of India revealed in the play which draw a special admiration: the ardor and the sensible demeanor of the characters, the profound and graceful feeling for nature and the similarly idealized view of the plant world, the effeminacy of the mild and peaceful nation, then the expression of the fine cosmopolitan tenor and way of life of the monarchs and their courts. He finds the drama is proof of the genteel manner of the kings and the strict division of the castes. It betrays the high form of India's society.[42] Although characteristics of the mythical image are discernible, Creuzer's reasonable and judicious estimate contrasts greatly with the exuberance of Herder and Majer.

39. Friedrich Creuzer, *Symbolik und Mythologie der alten Völker*, in *Deutsche Schriften* (3rd ed.; 4 vols.; Leipzig, 1836-1843), I, xv.
40. Huch, II, 32.
41. Creuzer, I, 361-362.
42. *Ibid.*, I, 374-375.

Creuzer recognizes that India was originally the home of the fable as a vehicle of moral didactics. The ageless laws of moral conduct and justice were drawn from the character and relationships of animals and plants and from nature all about, and they were given the form of the nature fable or apologue.[43] He mentions the engaging originality and humanity of moral theories expressed in Indic literature, such as in the *Bhagavad-Gita*. He says that the Hindu, fortunate in observing nature in ethical matters and able to depict through nature the great moral truths, was eminently successful also in the realm of the theoretical, for through examples in nature he made substantial the greatest religious mysteries.[44]

Creuzer's plan to write a philological-mythological ethnography was in part inspired by his vain and luckless love for Karoline von Günderode—who should write in the vein of *Sakuntala*, he once said in a fervent letter[45]—but his honest quest lacks the gusto of inspiration from the mythical image. Just as his indecisiveness and variability destroyed his love, his over-rationalization and the imposition of his pre-figured plan dimmed the mythical image for him. Clearly, his are not the opinions of a Romanticist lost in the longing contemplation of that idealized India.

3. *Bald werden, die in toter Weisheit schliefen,*
    Die Götter, aufstehn und zu Priestern weihen
    Die Forscher, die vom Quell der Dichtung tranken.
    —AUGUST WILHELM SCHLEGEL

The Philosophers

Nachdem so mein Herz aller Begier nach dem Indischen verschlossen ist, nachdem ich in der That für das Vergängliche gar kein Herz mehr habe, erscheint meinem Auge das Universum in einer verklärten Gestalt. —FICHTE

However great may have been the influence of Johann Gottlieb Fichte (1762-1814) upon the Early Romanticists, his lack of artistic

43. *Ibid.*, I, 375.
44. *Ibid.*, I, 441, 444.
45. Friedrich Creuzer and Karoline von Günderode, *Briefe und Dichtungen*, ed. Erwin Rohde (Heidelberg, 1896), p. 86.

and historic sense is probably the main reason he fails to take admitted cognizance of the mythical image of India. The theoretical flights of his philosophical inquiries were too lofty to afford him an opportunity to observe the historical and literary penetration of India into German letters through the imaginative longing of the Early Romanticists. His development of the thought process of a thesis, antithesis, and synthesis swayed all thinkers after him; his postulation of a non-ego in opposition to an ego, in order that the ego might become active, removed the human spirit from philosophical isolation and made nature an object which, reconciled with mind, could bring about the fusion of the real and the ideal. But nature, a non-ego to Fichte, was a means to an end: posited as a non-ego, it made the ego capable of action and self-recognition. However, the non-ego of nature is not personified—it does not intrude upon the property of the ego. Fichte does not share the Romantic adulation of nature.

Nevertheless, what seems to be an echo of Hindu philosophy is here and there to be heard in Fichte's works. Particularly in the *Bestimmung des Menschen* (1800) can one discern shades of influence, very likely unrealized by Fichte himself: a yogi-like concentration upon the removal of all feeling for the physical world and its transitory manifestations yields a perception of the essence of God. Here he writes that after his heart had been shut off from all mundane desire, indeed after he had no more heart for the transitory, then the universe appeared to him in a transfigured form. The dead, burdensome mass which filled up space had disappeared, and in its place flowed, lapped, and rushed the eternal stream of life and vigor and deed—of primordial life, of the life of the infinite God: for, he cries ecstatically, all life is God's life, and only the religious visionary can penetrate the realm of beauty. In such a trance-like intuition of an immanent spirit of God, he apprehends an affinity with everything around him. He says that he feels akin to God. Everything is animate and inspirited and watches him with bright spirit-eyes and speaks in spirit-tones to his heart. He seems to envision himself, multifariously divided and separated, in all shapes about him; as the morning sun is reflected gleaming at itself abundantly from a thousand dewdrops, so does he seem to beam upon himself from all the forms about him which have received his fragmented self.[1] Such a mystic effusion is very reminiscent of the yogi's ascetic and rapturous immersion in the All.

The immanence of God in all creation is not, to Fichte, evidence of a cycle, evidence of an emanant God (that is, a God who has His Being in Himself and who reveals his attributes in various emanations which finally return to their source), but rather a continual approach to completion in an undeviating line which proceeds into infinity. In objects which appear to others as dead matter Fichte sees an eternal life and pulse, in tactile and spiritual nature. He sees that very life mount constantly higher and grow and become transfigured as a more spiritual expression of itself. The universe is to him no longer, as it once was, the circle which doubles back upon itself, the game which is incessantly repeated, that monster which devours itself in order to give birth to itself again. The universe has rather become etherealized and bears the proper stamp of the Spirit: constant advance to the more Perfect in a straight line which leads into infinity.[2] It is easy to see here a quickening of all inanimate nature and its elevation to an intellectual sublimity undreamed of—but this is not the mythical image of India. Fichte perhaps helped make the cognizance of certain aspects of the image possible (for example, a paradoxical self-identification with nature), but he did not himself observe or celebrate the literary or social attributes of the image, nor perceive in himself a longing for India.

> *Auf dem Wege der abgezogensten Selbstbeschauung, das Universum zu finden war das Geschäft des uralten morgenländischen Mystizismus.* —SCHLEIERMACHER

In his *Reden über die Religion* (1799) Friedrich Schleiermacher (1768-1834) edges toward a projection of the mythical image, but he achieves, and this in spite of himself, only a faint glimmer. He expresses approval of the conception of the universe as a totality, a unity in multiplicity, as a manifestation of religion.[3] This view seems to lean toward the Hindu idea of an immanent Supreme Being present in all forms and yet containing all forms, but no-

1. Johann Gottlieb Fichte, *Die Bestimmung des Menschen,* in *Sämmtliche Werke,* ed. J. H. Fichte (11 vols.; Berlin, 1845-1846), II, 315.

2. *Ibid.,* II, 317.

3. Friedrich Schleiermacher, *Reden über die Religion an die Gebildeten unter ihren Verächtern,* in *Werke, Auswahl in vier Bänden,* ed. Dr. Otto Braun and Prof. D. Joh. Bauer (4 vols.; Leipzig, 1911), IV, 287.

where does Schleiermacher mention India or Hinduism (or Brahmaism), although in voicing the same idea again he refers to mystics of the East. He writes, in what appears to be an allusion to yogi absorption, that the discovery of the universe on the path of the most abstract introspection was the occupation of Oriental mysticism, which with admirable audacity linked the infinitely large directly to the infinitely small and found everything right on the edge of the void.[4] But this is a measured admiration of a macro-microcosmic view of the universe, and not an enthusiastic affirmation or manifestation of longing. He even displays censure toward one aspect of the mythical image, that of the harmony of religion and mythology through art, the attempt of a young culture to formulate its idea of God. He writes that the taste for grotesque figures once was thought to be an attribute of a young fantasy in religion as in art. This taste was indulged to a great degree. Serious and holy mythology, thought to be religion itself, was connected quite unconcernedly with these flighty games of childhood.[5] Indisputably, reference to the art, mythology, and religion of India is made here, especially as the language is couched in the frame of commonplaces identified with the mythical image: the childlike ingenuousness and inventiveness of mind.

One must conclude that Schleiermacher, like Fichte, made allusions to but did not share the uncritical ardor of the Early Romanticists for the mythical image of India.

> *Die christlichen Missionarien, die nach Indien kamen, glaubten den Bewohnern etwas Unerhörtes zu verkündigen, wenn sie lehrten, dass der Gott der Christen Mensch geworden sey. Jene . . . fanden bloss seltsam, dass bei den Christen nur einmal geschehen sey, was sich bei ihnen oftmals und in steter Wiederholung zutrage.* —SCHELLING

Susanne Sommerfeld, in her study of the involvement of Romantic philosophers with Indic thought, writes that the dissatisfaction with a rationalistic view of the world, which stemmed from the profound revolutions of European thought in the eighteenth and nineteenth centuries, drew the gaze of the Romanticists to the Orient, especially to the metaphorically rich profusion of India. To the Ro-

4. *Ibid.*, IV, 311.
5. *Ibid.*, IV, 298.

manticist, who had become painfully aware of himself in the icy
breath of the rationalistic, European-Christian atmosphere of a so-
bering disengagement from his own roots, India appeared like the
promised land, she says. There the link of life with the archaic, the
contact with the profoundly mysterious and ancient coherence of
existence had not been torn apart—the placenta was not yet cut
loose. In India prevailed the condition which Görres, in the introduction to the *Mythengeschichte*, describes as man still closely
joined to nature, as a child to its mother. Through their occupation
with Indic thought the Romanticists believed they had uncovered
an underground spring, a sealed well which preserved the water of
life. Here they saw the opportunity to join the bottomless profundi-
ty of an ancient *philosophia chtonica* to the European *philosophia
solaris*.[6]

Friedrich Wilhelm von Schelling (1775-1854) is *the* Romantic
philosopher. In his system nature is no longer an object, a means to
an end, as it is in Fichte, but rather a subject, the counterpart of
the mind. The conscious creative act of the mind synthesized with
the unconscious creative act of nature results in a work of art, an
aesthetic manifestation of the spirit immanent both in nature and
in mind. This conception of what might be called a co-operative
effort of nature and mind, while not cast in the mold of the mythical
image of India, nevertheless made the Romantic enthusiasm for the
aspect of nature in that image vital. Nature is quickened.

In *Über Mythen, historische Sagen und Philosopheme der ältest-
en Welt* (1793) Schelling points out the childlike character of
ancient myths, a combination of simplicity and the spirit of the
miraculous, the wonderful.[7] He calls attention, too, to the almost
inextricable mixture of historical tradition and philosophy (religion) in ancient myths (I, 1, 55). He speaks of the innocence of a
people in the paradise of a golden age. There the reader could see
man happy in his ignorance, unworried about the future, unaware
of higher things, not grasping for higher rank, for far-reaching
knowledge, for unlimited freedom which would bring evil to perfec-

6. Susanne Sommerfeld, "Indienschau und Indiendeutung romantischer Philosophen." Dissertation, Zurich, 1943, pp. 20-21.
7. Friedrich Wilhelm von Schelling, *Sämmtliche Werke*, ed. K. F. A. Schelling
(14 vols.; Stuttgart, 1856-1861), I, 1, 53. Further references to this work are parenthetical indications to volume, division, and page.

tion (I, 1, 70). Although he does not mention India either in the passages cited above or in the following reference, he doubtless was
thinking in terms of the mythical image of India. He speaks of a
people living in the closest harmony with nature, who, pressed by
the urgency of intellect, populate nature with the transcendental
figures of their gods, a people, living under the open sky on a bright
height of the world where nature reveals itself in its most sublime
and beautiful efficacy and is able to capture the attention of man in
a constant variation of phenomena and in the most manifold
changes in its loveliest and most placid forms. Such a people lingers
willingly in the company of this benevolent mother. Schelling writes
that they are pleased to follow her quiet procession and her secret
actions, easily forgetting the difficulties of the path because of delight in her beauty, and finally, when the requisites of understanding become too imperative to be held off, such a people stay yet as
close as possible to her and magically lure the supernatural poetry
out of the transcendental regions into the realm of nature (I, 1, 78).

In the *System des transcendentalen Idealismus* (1800) Schelling
divides history into three periods. The first he calls the tragic period,
in which destiny ruled paramount; this period undoubtedly included the ancient culture of India, the noblest people of antiquity, and
he expresses a longing for the return of this earliest era. There the
downfall of the glory and wonder of the ancient world belongs, the
collapse of that mighty realm of which hardly a memory remains
and whose greatness is surmised from its ruins. There can be
glimpsed the decline of the noblest of humankind ever to blossom,
whose return to earth is only an eternal desire (I, 3, 603-604).

In *Bruno* (1802) the influence of Hindu philosophy may be
traced, but no idealization of the mythical image of India is discovered (I, 4). In the *Vorlesungen über die Methode des akademi-
schen Studiums* (1803) he asserts that in Christianity the universe
is considered fundamentally as history, as a moral realm, and that
this is its principal and essential character in contrast to the religion
of the Greeks (I, 5, 287). Schelling further suggests that, contrary
to the religion of the Greeks, the religion of India does not stand
in contrast to Christianity; an affinity between the religion of
Christendom and that of India receives direct emphasis.[8] It might

8. Goethe also felt an affinity for Indic philosophy, as he indicated in a conversation with Eckermann in 1829 (Biedermann, IV, 71-72), not necessarily from a

be shown, he says, that as far back as historical knowledge extends there are even then two definitely disparate streams of religion and poetry distinguishable: one, discernible in the religion of India, transmitting the system of intellect and the oldest examples of idealism; the other, in the religion of the Greeks, containing a realistic appraisal of the world. That of India, after it had inundated all the Orient, found its permanent bed in Christendom and, mixed with the earth of the Occident, unfruitful in itself, it produced the progeny of the newer age. He continues to point to the similarities of Hinduism and Christianity, and places the deeper understanding of their religion with the Hindus. He writes that the missionaries who went to India thought they were proclaiming an unheard-of wonder to the inhabitants when they declared the God of the Christians had taken human form. But the Hindus were not amazed and in no way denied the incarnation of God in Christ—they only found it strange that such a thing had occurred only once among the Christians, for among them it had happened often and in constant repetition. Just as in Herder's essay ridiculing the clumsy attempts of the missionaries to make converts in India, the proselytizers must stand in second place to the people they intended to proselytize. Finally, even the Bible cannot compare with the religious books of the Hindus in genuine religious merit (I, 5, 298-300).

Lectures which Schelling delivered in Jena in the winter of 1802-1803, published after his death as *Philosophie der Kunst*, contain praise for the allegorical poetry of Hindu mythology and the lyric-epic character of the dramatic poems. He finds it undeniable that Indic mythology more closely approaches poetic significance than does Persian. The mythology of India is raised at least to the level of allegory, and the allegorical is its prevailing poetic principle. But since, through allegory, Indic mythology was poetic, further devel-

---

Christian standpoint but simply from a humanistic point of view. He said that the philosophy was not strange at all, rather it simply reiterated epochs through which every man goes. "We are sensualists when we are children; idealists when we are in love and place qualities in the beloved which are not really there. Love becomes unstable, we doubt fidelity and are skeptics before we know it. The rest does not matter, we let things go as they will, and end up with quietism, just as the Indic philosophers do" (author's translation). It is the Goethean sage speaking here, again adapting Indic wisdoms to his own uses, untouched by the mythical image. See Paul T. Hoffmann, p. 47.

opment of its allegorical feature produced true poetry by genuine poets (I, 5, 424).

Even where he does not discuss India specifically, Schelling at the outset of his career as a philosopher is often profoundly near to Indic thought, but it is in his *Einleitung in die Philosophie der Mythologie* (1826-1845), the work of his maturest years, that he expressly and thoroughly analyzes Indic thought and religion. The intensity and earnestness of his analysis adumbrates the mythical image, but it is still visible, as when he says that the Indian first became an Indian with the development of Indic mythology (II, 2, 470), that is, that the mythology of India contains the essence of the Hindu. In her monograph Miss Sommerfeld comments at length on Schelling's incisive probing of the Hindu triad, his concept of the sub-deities, his impressions of the essence of the Upanishads and the *Bhagavad-Gita*, and his conclusions about yoga and *maja*. Even though Schelling was not always successful in freeing himself of Western norms in his depiction of Indic thought in interpreting them within their own frame of reference, he nevertheless guards against magisterial interpretations. His ability to employ fantasy and empathy in the service of methodical investigation brought forth the following lines of praise in a poem by August Wilhelm Schlegel, dedicated to him:

> Bald werden, die in toter Weisheit schliefen,
> Die Götter, aufstehn und zu Priestern weihen
> Die Forscher, die vom Quell der Dichtung tranken.[9]

Indien ist überhaupt als gesuchtes Land ein wesentliches Moment der ganzen Geschichte.   —HEGEL

The deep awareness of Georg Wilhelm Friedrich Hegel (1770-1831) of the dynamic force of history, which distinguishes him from Fichte and Schleiermacher, made it inevitable that his gaze should encompass the Orient. But it was in his later works, published after 1808, that he becomes concerned with role of India in the historical development of mankind. Thus his philosophy does not contribute to the Romantic view of the mythical image of India, which received its formal contours before 1808. Although he reflects that view, he tempers it by a closer critical inspection.

9. Sommerfeld, pp. 41-56; the poem by August Wilhelm Schlegel is printed on p. 68.

Hegel mentions India in the role of the land of longing and fantasy, one aspect of the mythical image. He writes that India has always been the land of nostalgia, and that it still seems a wondrous realm, an enchanted world.[10] The longing for this bewitching land came into being not only because of its natural riches, but also because of the richness of its wisdom. From the oldest times, Hegel writes, all peoples have directed their wishes and desires toward India, hoping to find access to the most exquisite treasures of that wonderland (XI, 195). He makes India representative of the yearning for the golden age when he remarks that William Jones first sought out the poems of the golden age (XI, 217).

One admired trait of Hindu moderation is mentioned in language befitting the mythical image: "Das schwache Blumenvolk, die Indier, verzehren kein Tier."[11] The word *Blume* as descriptive of the people of India is a favorite term after Herder, and is an integral part of the projection of the mythical image. It is true that from Hegel's pen the word takes on connotations of *vegetative*.

The women of India in the Romantic mythical image are beautiful, tender, and graceful creatures. Hegel seems to reflect this quality when he says that there is a unique beauty of women whose faces are suffused with an unblemished skin, with a light, pleasing flush, not merely the flush of health and vivacity but a finer redness that is at the same time a spiritual tinge from within. Their features, the glance of their eyes, and the expression of their mouths seem gentle, tender, and unanxious. Such beauty, he concludes, is found most attractively formed in India (XI, 192-193).

Hegel mentions that the Hindu looks upon the animal and the natural world as being sublime and divine in themselves.[12] But he depreciates the magical and wondrous aspect of the Hindu world by remarking that in India everything is wonder and therefore nothing wondrous (XII, 498). He admits that the Hindu is known for his mildness, his tenderness, and the originality of his imagination —but he cautions that even decadent nations have their noble qualities (XI, 215). One critic comments that the Hindu achieved

10. Georg Wilhelm Friedrich Hegel, "Vorlesungen über die Philosophie der Geschichte," in *Sämtliche Werke*, ed. Glockner, XI, 191. This treatise is compiled from lectures held between 1822 and 1831.

11. *Ibid.*, "System der Philosophie, II. Die Naturphilosophie" (1804-1830), IX, 602.

12. *Ibid.*, "Vorlesungen über Aesthetik" (1818-1829), XII, 514.

knowledge of God by destroying his own vitality in the immersion
of his individuality in the substance of God. With this submergence
of the individual Hegel denies the Hindu a real moral concept. The
Hindu requires the suppression of desires and impulses not because
he envisions a goal of moral freedom, but in order to achieve the
destruction of the individual. Ethical behavior has no value for him
but rather exists only as a means to expedite his redemption. Thus
Hegel is correct in disputing the morality of the Hindu, for to the
Hindu good and evil are aspects of a single primal force.[13] Hegel
confesses that the tender feelings of the Hindu have a supreme
beauty, but he finds the devotion of the Hindu tramples down love
because it is without integrity. Under the relationships which pre-
vail in India, Hegel writes, the gentleness and charm of the tenderest feelings and the unending devotion of the personality necessarily
have great beauty, but only because this emotion, with such an
irrational basis, becomes beauty exclusively. However, because this
feeling of devotion is without honesty, it alternates with greatest
harshness, and the moment of self-assertion in the personality is
transformed into ferocity, into obliviousness to all bonds, even into
the destruction of love itself.[14]

Hegel's inspection of the religion of India is done mainly from
a historic-descriptive viewpoint and does not reveal a participation
in the longing for the mythical image. He does allude to the penetration of religion into every aspect of Hindu life: "Alles ist dem
Inder ein Gott" (XI, 194), and "die Phantasie macht hier Alles zu
Gott" (XV, 397), but he does not share the Romantic enthusiasm
for the ideal unity of religion and philosophy found in India. He
says deprecatingly that education is very developed, even splendid,
but the philosophy of the Indians is identical with their religion, so
that the interests of religion are there the same as of philosophy in
the West.[15]

Jean Paul, it will be remembered, finds the cultural omission of
a national history in India only right, but Hegel implies that he is
disappointed or at least quite surprised at this lack: "Indien hat
nicht allein alte Religionsbücher und glänzende Werke der Dicht-

13. Sommerfeld, p. 80.
14. Hegel, *Werke*, "Philosophie der Religion" (1821-1831), XV, 396.
15. *Ibid.*, "Vorlesungen über die Geschichte der Philosophie" (1805-1831), XVII,
161.

kunst, sondern auch alte Gesetzbücher...und doch keine Geschichte" (XI, 99). The Indians lack the prosaic circumspection
and sobriety to assimilate and understand the actual form, the em-
pirical interventions, bases, purposes, and causes of events (XII,
477). This brings about the impossibility of a factual, true depiction
of history. Everything which happens takes refuge in the confusion
of dream (XI, 200). From Hegel, in whom a sense of history was
fundamental, these sentiments are understandable, and are perhaps
significant for the basis of his general disapprobation of the culture
of India. But even though India reveals no written history, the land
nevertheless had a place in the scope of world history, and Hegel,
in the spirit of the Romantic mythical image, finds the origin of
world history there. In Asia, he says, first flared the light of the intellect and with it the history of the world (XI, 145). He says, in
fact, that it was the childhood of history (XI, 151). But since India
has no history of its own, he must look to later historians for reports
about India as a nation, and he cites as the oldest and most reliable
sources the commentaries of Greek writers after Alexander had
opened the way to India. The Mohammedan historians offer another source, he concludes (XI, 222).

Hegel considers the Vedas the most important literary heritage of
India and finds that the dramas, such as *Sakuntala*, were overrated
when they were first discovered by Europeans (XI, 217). At another time he does find *Sakuntala*—that wonderfully delightful work
(XIV, 503)—to reveal most beautifully the essential devotion to
feeling of the Hindu, the spiritual people with the character of
plants (XIV, 399). In the Hindu epics he sees genuine national
poems (XII, 368), and he says that the earliest religious conceptions
of the Hindus contained a fruitful germ for an epic presentation of
mythology which then, ramified with the heroic deeds of man, were
developed into real epics.[16] The literature of India contains the earliest examples of pantheistic poetry (XII, 489). He points out that
the first, and wildest, attempts of a people to evoke their fantasies
in symbolic images were made by the Hindus (XI, 447). This specific Indic principle has long been recognized as determinant in the
artistic productions of the Hindus. Here is shown the endeavor to
achieve the conquest of individuality by observing the work of art

16. *Ibid.*, "Vorlesungen über Aesthetik," XIV, 399.

as symbolic of the absolute and the general and thus increasing its content beyond the directly perceptive and unique.[17] In order to attain this aim the Hindu had to burst the bonds of things and phenomena in order to comprehend a mighty content, in order to achieve a palpable, concrete peculiarity of the universal. So, without finally reconciling the absolute with the finite, Hindu art became colossal, grotesque, immoderate, and imprecise (XII, 452). The ugly, insane, and fantastic representations of the multi-armed, many-headed figures of Indic sculpture (XV, 362) revulsed Hegel as well as Goethe (see note 3 to Part II above). But Hegel's attitude toward the literature is an ambivalent one, not the wholehearted surrender of the Romantic spirit. He writes that the most beautiful poetry could be found among the Indians, but always with the most insane foundation. One is attracted by the winsomeness and repulsed by the confusion and nonsense (XV, 396). The mixture of wondrous magic and everyday reality, so rife in the Romantic mind and a projection of the mythical image, does not find favor with Hegel.

Hegel takes eminent cognizance of India in his philosophy, but the mythical image is not bright here—the time of its great brightness had passed, and Hegel, with philosophical qualifications and logical reservations, does not project the image but reflects only a pale imprint.

> *Die älteste Sprache die wir kennen, die Sanskrit, ist . . . die vollkommenste, reichste, und doch einfältigste, die wohlklingendste und rhythmischste.* —G. H. SCHUBERT

The influence of the unity of the wisdoms celebrated in the Romantic mythical image of India is found most markedly in the natural philosopher Gotthilf Heinrich Schubert (1780-1860), a student of Schelling, in his *Ansichten von der Nachtseite der Naturwissenschaft* (1808), a work which profoundly influenced the writings of the later Romanticists, particularly E. T. A. Hoffmann.

At the very beginning of his book, in a statement of purpose, Schubert emphasizes one aspect of the mythical image: the close communion of man and nature, the harmony of the individual with the whole. The oldest relationship of man with nature, he says, the

17. Sommerfeld, p. 82.

cohesion of a present existence with a higher existence in the future, and the gradual unfolding of the bud of a future, new life in the midst of this life will be the main subject of his work.[18] He at once strikes a yearning note and adjures the soul to seek the stillness of a woods near Delphi and marshal itself for a new meditation (p. 6). He turns his glance toward the Orient, whence is to come the new happiness, the new redemption of mankind (p. 11).

First of all, he finds in the mythologies of all ancient peoples the report of a vanished age when mankind enjoyed a flourishing culture in intimate communion with nature (p. 3). The birthplace of mankind seems for various reasons to have been in India, at the source of the Ganges or the Indus, where one day the great grave of the fallen race may be found (p. 24). Support for the thesis that the heartland of India sheltered the first culture is found in the perhaps partly spurious *Chartah Bhade*, where, before the development of agriculture, mankind is commanded to live from nature's fruits and from the milk of cows (p. 52).

Schubert seeks the beginnings of religion in the idyllic harmony of a culture such as that of ancient India. If religion is a product of fear, risen from a raw origin, he inquires, then how is it that the older the religion, the purer and more sublime are its concepts? He cites as an example the religion of India, admissibly almost completely misjudged until recent, more versatile views had disclosed the core of its profound and wise meaning (pp. 25-26). The pure and sublime religious expression of the people of ancient India included an expression of another wisdom, science: science and religion were one. The oldest beginnings of natural science are distinguished from its present state, Schubert writes, in that the primitive discipline was not so much science as it was a cult of nature, a dogma of religion among the people. Many religious legends of the Indians, he continues, discuss the history of the planet earth and its formation (p. 54).

Hindu preoccupation with astronomy goes 7,600 years into the past, he says, and the Hindu still predicts eclipses (pp. 30-31). According to Bailly, the Copernican theory of the universe orig-

18. Gotthilf Heinrich Schubert, *Ansichten von der Nachtseite der Naturwissenschaft* (Dresden, 1808), p. 3. Further references to this work are made parenthetically in the text.

inated with the Hindus, although one group of Brahmans considered the earth to be immovable. The ancient Hindus may even have developed a telescope, to judge by their knowledge of the heavens, and particularly since their astronomical charts bear a number of stars seen only through a telescope (pp. 40, 43).

Hindu speculation was not restricted to the heavens. Schubert finds a more understandable and complete theory of the formation of the continents out of the deluge in the mythology of the Hindus than in that of the Scandinavians. Other aspects of natural science found a place in the studies of the Hindu. An ancient Indic poem contains a kind of botany, in which natural forces of plants and the significance of their shapes and colors is discussed. Schubert adds, in a note, that the *Bhagavad-Gita* contains several remarkable observations about light, the ether, and so on (pp. 47-48).

Schubert shares the Romantic amazement that the oldest literatures, including that from the banks of the Ganges, are written in verse; even the observations of the peoples of the Orient (the Hindus) in the realms of natural science are couched in verse form. Taking a contemporary theory of the origin of language to task, he asks: If language came into being through the communication of individuals who variously imitated the variously comprehended sounds from nature, such as the cries of animals, then how did it happen that, as could be illustrated, the metric form of language preceded prose? Mythology, the oldest historical record of the world, from the banks of the Ganges to the coasts of the Arctic Sea, was contained in verse. Even the most ancient astronomical observations and natural theories among the Asiatic peoples were preserved in poetry (p. 26). The high development of the civilization of ancient India is reflected in the complexity of its language, considered by Schubert to be the oldest known. Sanskrit, thought commonly to be the most imperfect, he says, is rather the most perfect language, the richest and yet most artless, the most harmonious and most rhythmic (p. 60).

Schubert was the philosopher who most vividly experienced the mythical image. Though his work appeared too late to be of influence upon the transmutation of that image by the Early Romanticists, it was due in part to him that features of the image endured.

Hat ... der Leser auch schon die Weihe uralter Indischer Weis-
heit empfangen und empfänglich aufgenommen; dann ist er auf
das allerbeste bereitet zu hören, was ich ihm vorzutragen habe.
                                                    —SCHOPENHAUER

Arthur Schopenhauer (1788-1860) very justifiably expressed his
indebtedness to Friedrich Majer for introducing him to the enchant-
ments of Indic thought for, among the philosophers of the age, it
was he who apprehended in himself the closest kinship to the basic
views of Indic philosophy. In *Die Welt als Wille und Vorstellung*
(1844) he acknowledges his conscious adaptation of the elemental
views of Indic philosophy from the holy writings of the Hindus,[19]
and later he confesses that his theories could never have come into
being had it not been for the philosophical luminosity of the
Upanishads, Plato, and Kant.[20] Although his first encounter with
the metaphysical literature of the Hindus occurred when the brilliance of the mythical image was at its apogee, he was not blinded
by an idealized impression of India itself, and he cannot be said to
have shared in the yearning glow generated by the image. He absorbed the teachings of the Hindu sages in their writings as a plant
drinks in the sunlight, and like a plant he made the warmth and
light into his own substance.

He writes rapturously of Anquetil's *Oupnek'hat,* perceiving in it
the breath of the holy spirit of the Vedas. Whoever reads the Per-
sian-to-Latin rendering of the Upanishads will be gripped to his
innermost being, he says. Every line is full of firm, positive, and
consistently coherent significance. On every page one meets profound, original, and lofty thoughts, while a noble and divine gravity
hovers over the whole work. It is full of the breath of Indic air and
a primitive presence with an affinity for nature. Schopenhauer finds
it the most rewarding and inspiring text in the world and says it has
been the consolation of his life and will be still at his death (V, 418).
He further calls the Vedas the fruit of the highest human knowledge and wisdom, and their kernel, the Upanishads, the gift of the
century (I, 457). Of the authors of the Upanishads, he says that
they can hardly be conceived of as having been mere men (II, 558).

19. Arthur Schopenhauer, *Sämtliche Werke,* ed. Eduard Grisebach (3rd ed.;
6 vols.; Leipzig, [1921-1924]), I, 533. Further references to this edition are given
parenthetically in the text by volume and page.
20. Arthur Schopenhauer, *Handschriftlicher Nachlass,* ed. Eduard Grisebach (4
vols.; Leipzig, [1926-1931]), IV, 343.

In the foreword to the first edition of his principal work Schopenhauer says that if the reader has already received initiation into ancient Indic wisdom then he is best prepared to hear what the philosopher is about to present. Although he would not like to be boastful, Schopenhauer asserts that any of the single, isolated maxims forming the Upanishads could be deduced from his own thoughts, even though, contrarily, his ideas were by no means to be found there (I, 13). It is not surprising then to find that Schopenhauer makes frequent references to the writings of the Hindu holy wisemen in his works.

Schopenhauer had little understanding and no tolerance for the poetic and artistic productions of India. However much he revered its religious and philosophical literature, he could find little in the poetic literature which pleased him. At times, he says, it even appeared to him that they were as tasteless and monstrous as Indic sculpture. He appreciated the dramatic works chiefly for the instructive illustrations and proofs of the religious beliefs and customs of the Indians woven into them. He surmises that the problem may be the impossibility of translating poetry, particularly the difficulty of transplanting a foreign poetry into the unfertile minds of most translators. Moreover, he says, since there is no lack of poetry in Europe, but a great impoverishment of metaphysical views, he is of the opinion that the translators of Sanskrit should apply their efforts less to poetry and more to the Vedas, Upanishads, and the philosophical works (V, 416).

As an example of a transcendental truth and precept which is incomprehensible to the common man except in a mythical representation, Schopenhauer mentions the doctrine of metempsychosis. No myth has conformed, nor ever will conform more closely to a philosophical truth comprehensible to but a few than this ancient doctrine of the noblest and oldest of people. Even though the people have degenerated into many sects, says Schopenhauer, the doctrine of metempsychosis prevails still as a general folk belief and exerts a determinative influence on their lives just as it did four thousand years ago. He mentions that Pythagoras and Plato were almost certainly devotees of the doctrine, but that Europeans send English clergymen and Moravian linen weavers to teach the Brahmans a better doctrine and to convince them they were formed out of nothing and should be gratefully happy. Religious sects from Europe will never gain a foothold in India, he says. On the other hand, he concludes with conviction, Indic wisdom streams back to Europe and will produce a basic change in the thought and knowledge of Europeans (I, 459). Schopenhauer himself was instrumental in making his prediction come true by his own absorption of Indic thought and its transmutation through his own speculations.

IV. The Projection of the Image: The Romantic Authors

1. Auch seine Seele schien, wie ein Bramin, von poetischen Blumen zu leben, und seine Sprache war oft, wie seine Sitten, indisch, d.h. poetisch. —JEAN PAUL

Some literary historians are reluctant to place Jean Paul Friedrich Richter (1763-1825) among the Romantic authors, but since he reveals Romantic tendencies, he is considered by all to be a precursor of Romanticism. Certainly, with regard to the Romantic mythical image of India, he may be considered the first to weave this image into artistic expression.

In his autobiography Jean Paul says that the word *Morgenland* had, in his youth, been to him like an open gate to Heaven.[1] The

---

1. Jean Paul [Friedrich Richter], *Sämtliche Werke*, ed. Eduard Berend (32 vols.; Weimar, 1927-1960), I, 2, 462, n. 206. Parenthetical references are to division, volume, and page of this edition.

use of the word *Morgen* in combination with *Land, Hauch, Luft, Sonne* to strike a note of longing or new hope or expectation occurs too frequently in the works of the Romanticists to be cited repeatedly. Such usage does not necessarily imply the Indic image, for Persia, Arabia, Palestine, even Greece lay eastward, and longing for or interest in these lands was often expressed by *Morgen* compounds. But since the Romantic tendency is to look beyond Greece and embrace the older East, and particularly India, one may assume that the mythical image is implied in almost every such utterance on the part of a Romantic author. This certainly was the case with Jean Paul.

In *Die unsichtbare Loge* (1793) Jean Paul reveals a distinct longing for the East: "Morgenland, Morgenland! auch nach deinen Auen neigte sich sonst meine Seele wie Bäume nach Osten:—'ach wie muss es da sein, wo die Sonne aufgeht,' dacht' ich" (I, 2, 206). That he has India in mind is undeniable. Of some influence upon this work was Wilhelm Friedrich von Meyern's (1762-1829) *Dya-Na-Sore*,[2] a work purported to be a translation from the Sanskrit. It is actually based on the Oriental legend of princely brothers separated and educated by a secret organization and reunited finally for the purpose of freeing their kingdom from forces of tyranny. Von Meyern wrote the novel apparently with only the faintest notion of India: he places the action in Tibet, but despite the precipitous mountain trails of India's northern wilderness, no cultural flavor of India adds spice to the book. It is an incoherent, absurdly idealistic work, but was influential in spurring Jean Paul on to integrate the mythical image of India into his writings.

A statement such as "Alles Schöne aber ist sanft; daher sind die schönsten Völker die ruhigsten" (I, 2, 61) is reminiscent of Herder's evaluation of the inhabitants of India as beautiful and gentle people. Jean Paul says further: "Alles Grosse oder Wichtige bewegt sich langsam: also gehen gar nicht die orientalischen Fürsten." He probably alludes here to the practice of transporting personages of importance either in litters or palanquins. He also mentions the secrecy surrounding the names of Oriental princes and the teachings of the Vedas (I, 2, 126).

The island of Teidor in *Die unsichtbare Loge*, although actually

2. Wilhelm Friedrich von Meyern, *Dya-Na-Sore oder die Wanderer. Eine Geschichte aus dem Sam-skritt übersetzt* (3 vols.; Leipzig, 1787-1791).

in a lake in southern Germany, is said to be washed by the waves of the Indian Ocean (I, 2, 378). The island is a paradise where the brightness of nature cannot be imitated by color in a human dwelling; hence to approximate at least the accustomed brilliancy, the walls of the mansion are painted white: "Im Landhause waren die Wände weiss, weil für einen Menschen ... welcher aus der in lauter Feuer und Lichtern stehenden Natur in eine enge Klause tritt, kein Kolorit dieser Klause hell genug sein könne, um einen traurigen beschränkten Eindruck abzuwenden" (I, 2, 389). This is perhaps a poetic interpretation of Mandelslo's observation that white is a color esteemed by the Indians.

The visitors on the island wander about and are feasted and entertained in the splendor of nature in a leisurely, Oriental mood:

Alsdann ruhten wir aus, indem wir von einer beschatteten Grasbank der Insel zur andern gingen, von Birkenblättern und indischen Wellen angefächelt—dann musizierten—dann dinierten wir, erstlich am Tische eines Wirthes, der auf eine lustige Art fein und delikat zu sein weiss, zweitens vor den in alle Weltgegenden aufgeschlossenen Fenstern, die uns noch mehr in alle Strudel der freudigen Natur hinein drehten, als wären wir draussen gewesen, und drittens jeder von uns mit einer Hand, welche die weiche Beere des Vergnügens abzunehmen weiss, ohne sie entzwei zu drücken. (I, 2, 389)

Nature becomes a participant in the festivities, or rather the festivities extend out into nature.

One aspect of the mythical image of India as it manifested itself in the Romanticists was the profound sense of kinship of man and nature, a feeling which developed into a mystic adoration. This aspect of the image found expression in Jean Paul's writings. With the Hindu caste system in mind, he divides strollers into four castes, beginning with a light, ironic mood and turning finally a sober and reverent glance upon an immanent Supreme Being in nature. The fourth and highest caste of strollers through nature (i.e., of mankind) is formed not only of observers who linger over the beauties of nature, but of those who observe also with the heart, who perceive the immanence of God and who feel an identity with nature, an intimate kinship:

Ein Mann von Verstand und Logik würde meines Bedünkens alle Spazierer, wie die Ostindier, in *vier* Kasten zerwerfen.
In der I. Kaste laufen die jämmerlichsten ...

In der II. Kaste rennen die Gelehrten und Fetten . . . weniger, um zu geniessen, als um zu verdauen . . .

Die III. Kaste nehmen diejenigen ein, in deren Köpfe die Augen des Landschaftmalers stehen, in deren Herz die grossen Umrisse des Weltall [*sic*] dringen . . .

Eine IV. bessere Kaste, dächte ich, könnt' es nach der dritten gar nicht geben: aber es gibt Menschen, die nicht blos ein artistisches, sondern ein heiliges Auge auf die Schöpfung fallen lassen—die in diese blühende Welt die zweite verpflanzen und unter die Geschöpfe den Schöpfer— die unter dem Rauschen und Brausen des tausendzweigigen dicht einge- laubten Lebensbaums niederknien und mit dem darin wehenden Genius reden wollen, da sie selber nur geregte Blätter daran sind—die den tiefen Tempel der Natur nicht als eine Villa voll Gemälde und Statuen, son- dern als eine heilige Stätte der Andacht brauchen—kurz, die nicht blos mit dem Auge, sondern auch mit dem Herzen spazieren gehen. (I, 2, 389-390)

The plot of Jean Paul's next novel *Hesperus* (1795) may be seen to owe something to *Dya-Na-Sore*, but otherwise the influence of Von Meyern's novel has abated. The sharp characterizations of *Hesperus* are certainly no reflection of the dimly limned persons described by Von Meyern. The eulogistic enthusiasm concerning India which permeates all of *Hesperus*, particularly in the character of the Brahman hermit Emanuel and in the Eden-like setting of Maienthal, owe much more to *Sakuntala*, which Jean Paul read and excerpted at the latest in 1792 (I, 3, xxxvi). Kanna, the preceptor and foster-father of Sakuntala, is undoubtedly the prototype for Emanuel-Dahore, the teacher of both Viktor (in the person of Dahore) and Klotilde (in the person of Emanuel), the two chief personages in the novel. There are numerous traces of the influence of *Sakuntala* in other aspects of the novel, but the traditions of East and West seem actually to merge and mix in the character of the astronomer-teacher, as well as symbolically in his dual name.

The island of Teidor from *Die unsichtbare Loge* has its double in *Hesperus* in the island of St. Johannis, where the author (Jean Paul) is visited by the mail-carrying dog. The extraordinary lake of *Die unsichtbare Loge* is also here: "In *die unsichtbare Loge* hab' ich den ausserordentlichen Teich gesetzt, welcher unter dem Namen ostindischer Ozean bekannter ist" (I, 3, 33). That ocean trans- planted in spirit from the bewitching shores of the East to the foot- hills of the Alps also rolls against the shores of St. Johannis with waves illuminated like the fan of a peacock's tail (I, 3, 38).

Dahore, whose name echoes the Indian city of Lahore and *Dya-Na-Sore*, was the childhood teacher of Viktor. He is described as a man with a gentle spirit, handsome, and possessed of a pure soul. "Dahore hatte das Herz aller Kinder in seiner weichen Hand, blos weil seines niemals brausete and zürnte, und weil auf seiner jungen Gestalt eine ideale Schönheit und in seiner reinen Brust eine ideale Liebe wohnte" (I, 3, 41). In conversation with Klotilde, Viktor speaks of the impression made upon him by Dahore, whose sublimity of spirit, like the upward glissando of a harp, wafted him to the stars with lessons in astronomy; he was a man who imparted to the heart an echo of Eden (I, 3, 71-72).

Klotilde tells Viktor about her own teacher of astronomy, who has a spirit just as noble and just as quiet, who is the gentlest and the greatest of men, and who came from the East Indies:

[Klotilde] zeichnete . . . ihren eignen astronomischen Lehrer . . . ab—dass er eben so edel und eben so still—dass seine Gestalt so gut besser mache wie seine Lehre—dass er sich Emanuel nenne und keinen Geschlechtnamen führe. . . . dass leider seine veredelte Seele in einem zerknickten Körper lebe, der schon tief ins Grab einhänge—dass er nach der Versicherung ihrer Aebtissin der sanfteste und grösste Mensch sei, der noch aus Ostindien (seinem Vaterland) gekommen, wiewol man über einige Sonderbarkeiten seiner Lebensart in Maienthal wegzusehen habe. (I, 3, 72)

His peculiarities consist of qualities that distinguish a Brahman: he is a Pythagorean, wears only white, has himself lulled to sleep and awakened by flutes, eats neither legumes nor the meat of animals, and is wont to spend half the night with the stars (I, 3, 74).

Viktor can hardly wait to meet this man, who resembles his beloved Dahore so much. Through the years he has lost contact with Dahore, but he remembers him still with nostalgia. In a letter to Emanuel, Viktor mentions the second life for which Dahore longed. This *second life,* also called the *second world* (as in *Die unsichtbare Loge*) repeatedly in the novel, is undoubtedly based upon the Brahmanical conception of death as really a birth into a genuine existence, mentioned by Paulinus, who cites reports of Strabo. In a parting letter Dahore had told Viktor to seek his double, his twin, and Viktor believes he has found the image of Dahore in Emanuel:

Da mein grosser Lehrer *Dahore*—dieser glänzende Schwan des Himmels, der, vom zerknickten Flügelgelenk ans Leben befestigt, sehnend zu andern Schwänen aufsah, wenn sie nach den wärmern Zonen des zweiten Lebens zogen—aufhörte an mich zu schreiben: so that ers mit den Worten: "suche mein Ebenbild!" . . .—Emanuel, bist du nicht ruhig und sanft und nachsichtig? . . . Glaubst du nicht an Gott und suchst seine Gedanken auf in den Lineamenten der Natur und seine ewige Liebe in deiner Brust? . . . O! schöne, gute Seele, liebe mich! (I, 3, 106-107)

When Emanuel's reply is delivered to him by Klotilde, Viktor trembles and hesitates, reflecting upon the teacher's beautiful soul, which is likened to a quiet-flowing, blue river of Paradise. It is almost as though he had become submerged in the blue, still waters of that soul. In Emanuel's letter a deep reverence for nature is at once revealed with a simile typical of the mythical image, the child, and with flowers characterized as eyes of the earth:

Auf einen Berg steigt der Mensch wie das Kind auf einen Stuhl, um näher am Angesicht der unendlichen Mutter zu stehen und sie zu erlangen mit seiner kleinen Umarmung. Um meine Höhe liegt die Erde unter dem weichen Nebel mit allen ihren Blumenaugen schlafend—aber . . . der Erdball wälzt sich gross und trunken voll Blüten und Thieren in den glühenden Schooss des Morgens.

Viktor discovers to his joy that Emanuel is really his own Dahore, who admits his Indic origin nostalgically: "Meine trübe Geschichte liegt neben der Asche meiner Eltern im Gangesstrom." Viktor himself perceives Emanuel's nostalgia, saying: "Seine Seele ist noch das Echo seiner indischen Palmen und des Gangesstromes" (I, 3, 126-127, 130).

Viktor goes to Maienthal for a reunion with his former teacher and finds him smiling, transfigured, in communion with the universe through the stars (I, 3, 198). When Viktor awakens the next morning he is struck anew by the appearance of his teacher, before whose childlike, calm, smiling face he dissolves in mute rapture. In the vocabulary of the Early Romanticists "childlike" is used with the connotations of primeval purity, unspoiled innocence, and childlike fantasy, qualities which distinguish the ancient Hindus in the mythical image of India. Emanuel's spotless morning-room cleanses the soul, and the hermit is depicted performing the morning ablutions ordained for Brahmans: "Er war der grösste körperliche Purist, er wusch seinen Körper eben so oft als seine Kleider. . . . Eben so blieb sein Herz sogar von den blossen Bildern grosser Sünden unbesudelt" (I, 3, 201).

Emanuel, in his Eden-like Maienthal, lives, as do the sojourners in Kanna's grove, in the closest harmony with nature, revealing a deep affection for his flowers and bushes. His very spirit seems to take nourishment from poetic blossoms: "Auch seine Seele schien, wie ein Bramin, von poetischen Blumen zu leben, und seine Sprache war oft, wie seine Sitten, indisch, d.h. poetisch. So war überall . . . eine auffallende vorherbestimmte Harmonie zwischen der äusseren Natur und seinem Herzen." A most striking attribute of the mythical image of India held by the Romanticists is the presence in it of blossoms, flowers, blooms, not only in nature, but applied to human beings, human emotions, even to abstract ideas. This conception of a universal flower, a bloom-like quality inherent in every creature, emotion, or idea endowed with calmness, purity, and gentleness stems probably in part from the descriptions by travelers of exotic Indic blossoms as well as from the frequent flower-symbolism encountered in the literature of India. India seemed to be a land of flowers, both natural and symbolic, real and poetic. Even more important for this image, however, must have been *Sakuntala*, where human beings show a heartfelt love for flowers, and where flowers are personified even to the extent that two plants are joined in matrimony by Kanna. At this point in *Hesperus*, as though anxious for the kind reception of his Brahman, Jean Paul exclaims: "Erdulde, Leser, diese blumige Seele" (I, 3, 202). It is interesting to note the poet's equation of *indisch* with *poetisch*: to him the words are synonymous. This is a significant attitude found also in most other Romanticists. Even the word unspoken, the thought of India or of the mythical image in sum or in its parts, evokes a poetic response.

In the company of Emanuel, Viktor finds the earth as though it were newly created, fresh as a paradise. In nature he sees God and love reflected everywhere in many forms (I, 3, 214). The Romanticist, reawakened to the wonders of nature, but with a sense of deep separation from it (which accounts for the nostalgia and longing for a more harmonious intimacy with nature), conceives of the return of a golden age when love and nature are indissoluble, when one implies the existence of the other. To Emanuel, Maienthal is a Paradise, an Eden, a Heaven on earth, where time takes on a universal aspect, measured by bloom-lit hours like the passing of constellations (I, 3, 124). Emanuel, like the inhabitants of the grove in *Sakuntala*, tends his flowers affectionately: "Er liebte als Indier physische Blumen wie poetische" (I, 3, 167). He hurries to his place of introspection to expose his flowers to the rain (I, 3, 158). Just as Sakuntala bade farewell to her beloved plants and flowers, Emanuel goes about to take his departure from the blossoms and the heights he loves, when he feels that his death is near:

Den Morgen verbrachten sie in Abschiedbesuchen bei alten Steigen, Lauben und Anhöhen; aber Emanuel . . . schlug . . . keinen unphilosophischen Lärmen darüber auf, dass er die Blumen und die Saaten nicht mähen und das grüne Obst nicht gelben werde sehen; sondern mit einem höhern Entzücken, das sich jenseits des Erden-Lenzes noch schönere versprach, machte er sich von jeder Blume los, ging er durch jedes Laub-Gewinde und Schatten-Nachtstück hindurch, zog er seine gleichsam in der Erde liegende verklärte Gestalt aus jedem Spiegelteiche, und eine liebevollere Aufmerksamkeit auf die Natur zeigte an, dass er heute Nachts dem näher zu kommen hoffte, der sie geschaffen. (I, 4, 226)

In his last hours he is overcome with longing for his homeland, a nostalgia which he expresses to Viktor (also known as Horion) and Klotilde:

Da kam eine unendliche Stille, eine auflösende Wonne, ein unaussprechliches Sehnen in Emanuels Herz. Seine Kindheitfreuden—die Züge seiner Mutter—die Bilder indischer Gefilde—alle geliebte verstäubte Gestalten —der ganze gleitende Wiederschein des Jugendmorgens floss vor ihm glimmend vorüber—eine wehmüthige Sehnsucht nach seinem Vaterland, nach seinen gestorbnen Menschen dehnte seinen Busen mit süssen Beklemmungen aus. Dieses immergrüne Palmenlaub der Jugenderinnerung legte er als kühlendes Kraut um seine und Horions Stirne, und den ganzen ersten Kreis seines Daseins trug er aus dem indischen Eden in dieses enge Gehäuse vor seine zwei letzten Geliebten herüber.

(I, 4, 228-229)

Alone on the *Trauerberg*, Emanuel awaits the moment of his death in ecstasy, his face turned toward the moon in the southeast:

Da beschien der Mond einen Regenbogen aus blassen Farbenkörnern, der in *Südosten* (der Pforte nach *Ostindien*) durch die dunklen Fluthsäulen drang und sich über die Alpen bog—da sah Emanuel die vorige Himmelleiter wieder über die Erdennacht gelehnt—da kam die Entzückung ohne Mass, und er rief mit ausgebreiteten Armen: "Ach dort in

Morgen, in Morgen, über die Strasse nach dem *Vaterland,* da schimmert der Triumphbogen, da öffnet sich die Ehrenpforte, da ziehen die Sterbenden hindurch."

In what he believes to be the moment of his death, he makes a quietly impassioned farewell, a prose reminiscence of Herder's version of the Brahman's farewell: "Bleibe du gesegnet, du gute Erde, du gutes Mutterland, blühet, ihr Gefilde Hindostans, lebe wohl, du schimmerndes Maienthal mit deinen Blumen und mit deinen Menschen—und ihr Brüder alle, kommt mir nach einem langen Lächeln seelig nach. Jetzt, o Ewiger, nimm mich hinauf" (I, 4, 234). It turns out that he does not die in that moment—he lingers a whole day in delirium, believing at first that he has died, dreaming of the second world but then awakening into reality. His final departure is quiet and gentle, to the rapturous tones of a flute played by Julius, his blind companion.

It is not only Emanuel who reveals an intense love and an almost mystic communion with nature: Klotilde and Viktor also are transported into wonder and a singular peace of mind and spirit when they become aware of nature. Klotilde is reminded of a Hindu flower rite when she sees two moons shimmering about a flower reflected in a flowing stream: "Ich kann oft noch bei Mondschein an die Bäche hinausgehen und eine Blume aufsuchen, die vor dem fliessenden Spiegel zittert und um welche ein Mond oben und einer unten schimmert, und ich stelle mir das Blumenfest in Morgenland vor, bei dem man (wie man sagt) Nachts um jede Gartenblume einen Spiegel und zwei Lichter setzt" (I, 4, 95). Even before he is exposed to the beauties of Maienthal, Viktor shows a receptive spirit for nature and the sublimity of soul that is freed from the frailty of earth:

Wann Nachmittags unter der brütenden Sonne Wiesen stärker duftend und mit gesenkten Blättern Wälder sanfter brausend und ruhend dastehen, und die Vögel darin als stumme Figuranten sitzen: dann umfasste im Eden, worüber schwül das Blütengewölke auflag, eine sehnsüchtige Beklommenheit sein Herz—dann wurd' er von seinen Phantasien unter die Weinpalmen Hindostans verweht—dann ruhte er in jenen stillen Ländern aus, wo er ohne stechende Bedürfnisse und ohne sengende Leidenschaften auseinanderfloss in die träumende Ruhe des Braminen, und wo die Seele sich in ihrer Erhebung festhält und nicht mehr zittert mit der zitternden Erde. (I, 3, 145)

In *Hesperus* particularly, Jean Paul has poeticized the idealized picture of Hindus prepared by Herder from his gleaning of travel books and translations. The work is in a sense a proving of his own hypothetical formula, *indisch=poetisch*, a formula by which he transmuted the mythical image from Herder's enthusiastic but lackluster accumulation of Indic lore into a scintillating symbol whose penetrating beams radiate from the works of other Romantic authors.

> 2. *Wäre deine Seele einige hundert Meilen weiter nach Osten [von Afrika], auf dem Boden von Indien aufgegangen, so würdest du in kleinen, seltsamgestalteten, vielarmigen Götzen den geheimen Geist fühlen, der, unsern Sinnen verborgen, darinnen weht.* —WACKENRODER

Wilhelm Wackenroder (1773-1798), the earliest of the *Frühvollendeten* among the Early Romanticists, hardly had an opportunity to explore the mythical image of India and give it expression in his own work. His contribution to the image is much narrower (though important in a large sense) and much more cryptic than was Jean Paul's. Ricarda Huch says that since more religion can be found in a worldly work of art (as exemplified in Novalis and Wackenroder) than in an intelligent, warm essay on religion (Schleiermacher), this is proof that the source of this religion lies very near the source of art, namely in the unconscious, in the Orient, from which all religions have come, at least all of those which have transcendental or Christian elements and which might be called the religions of the unconscious.[1]

The idea that religion is an unconscious outgrowth, emanant in a simple culture and not the result of subjective speculation, was voiced by Dohm. Wackenroder praises the painters of olden times to whom religion was the lovely commentary through which they first learned to understand life and its purpose. To him nature and art are the two languages through which God reveals Himself to

1. Huch, I, 194.

mankind.[2] His main contribution to the promulgation of the mythical image, given without direct reference to India in this connection, is his conception of the unity of art and religion (a unity found in Hindu culture) and his perception of God in nature and in art, and thus man's ability to approach God in the contemplation of nature and art.

In the essay entitled "Einige Worte über Allgemeinheit, Toleranz und Menschenliebe in der Kunst" from the *Herzensergiessungen eines kunstliebenden Klosterbruders* (1797), Wackenroder reveals an awareness of India and voices an exhortation for religious understanding with regard to tolerance for the fantastic forms of Hindu art: "Wäre deine Seele einige hundert Meilen weiter nach Osten [von Afrika], auf dem Boden von Indien aufgegangen, so würdest du in kleinen, seltsamgestalteten, vielarmigen Götzen den geheimen Geist fühlen, der, unsern Sinnen verborgen, darinnen weht."[3]

In the *Phantasien über die Kunst für Freunde der Kunst* (1799), published after Wackenroder's death, is found the "Wunderbares morgenländisches Märchen von einem nackten Heiligen." The figure of the hermit in this tale is Oriental, although not expressly Hindu, and since in India there was a tradition of naked philosophers, or gymnosophists as they were called by the Greeks, one may perhaps assume that a particular grade of Hindu holy man is meant. The frantic hermit, who wrestles mightily with the relentless wheel of time in his solitude (one is reminded of the *ciacram* of Vishnu), but who reveals none of the benignity believed characteristic of the Brahman, is at last released from his weary occupation by the magic of music and is borne aloft as a spirit on a melody.

At the beginning of the tale Wackenroder says:

Das Morgenland ist die Heimat alles Wunderbaren, in dem Altertume und der Kindheit der dortigen Meinungen findet man auch höchst seltsame Winke und Rätsel.... So wohnen dort in den Einöden oft seltsame Wesen...die...als übernatürliche Wesen verehrt werden. Der orientalische Geist betrachtet diese nackten Heiligen als die wunderlichen Behältnisse eines höhern Genius, der aus dem Reiche des Firmaments sich in eine menschliche Gestalt verirrt hat. (I, 156)

2. Rudolf Haym, *Die Romantische Schule* (3rd ed.; Berlin, 1914), p. 122.
3. Wilhelm Wackenroder, *Werke und Briefe*, ed. Friedrich von der Leyen (2 vols.; Jena, 1910), I, 49. Parenthetical references are to volume and page of this edition.

The allusion to the Orient as the home of wonders, and the reference to antiquity and the childhood of impressions there, are reflections of facets of the mythical image of India. One may add *Wunder* to *kindlich* as a catchword used by the Romanticists who draw their symbols from the mythical image. The spiritualization of the hermit into a melodic strain is reminiscent of the sub-deities of Hindu musical modes and suggests that Wackenroder may have known Jones's essay on Indic music.

This tale is among the first Romantic *Kunstmärchen*, a genre adopted after Goethe's lead (*Das Märchen*, 1795) and developed in part in response to Herder's plea and Friedrich Schlegel's reiteration for a new mythology (here anticipated by Wackenroder). The genre, perfected and exemplified by Novalis and, with an admixture of the fantastic enchantingly close to reality, by E. T. A. Hoffman, drew heavily on the mythical image of India. Wackenroder's *Märchen* may perhaps be considered the first to reveal a projection of the image in this form. Although Wackenroder developed his perceptive sense for the relationship of art and religion on Western examples, he found adequate justification for an adoring attitude before art in the exemplary though horrendous religious art of India.

3. *Ich möchte Indiens seltsame Gesträuche besehen, und aus den Flüssen Wasser schöpfen, deren Name mich schon in den Kindermärchen erquickte.*   —TIECK

Edwin H. Zeydel, in his biography of Ludwig Tieck (1773-1853), finds that in his relations with the circle of Early Romanticists in Jena, Tieck

was a dissenting member in essential points. He had much more in common with the later Romanticists, the Heidelberg group.... For while the Schlegels and their circle harked back to antiquity, he ... was more rooted in the soil of medieval Germany and Böhmean mysticism and had been strongly under the influence of Storm and Stress. And while the Romantic philosopher wanted to infuse the light of the soul into nature, Tieck ... tried to show the restraining influence of nature upon human existence.[1]

1. Edwin H. Zeydel, *Ludwig Tieck, The German Romanticist* (Princeton, 1935), p. 131.

Zeydel's remarks are borne out by a study of Tieck's attitude toward the mythical image of India, an image perused and transformed by the other Early Romanticists but only peripherally acknowledged by Tieck in the course of his long and uneven productivity. Only once does he mention India by name, with longing for its plants and rivers. One does not find in Tieck the depiction of a character such as Jean Paul's Emanuel-Dahore—in fact, he had no appreciation for such a character, as he states in the preface to the second edition of *William Lovell*: "Ich hatte ihm [Jean Paul] aber in unsern Gesprächen auch niemals verschwiegen, wie wenig ich mit der Schilderung seiner erhabenen Charaktere und seinen sentimentalen Frauen einverstanden sei."[2] In Tieck's works nature mainly reflects man's moods, but is often capable of evoking a certain mood in man. Seldom is there the close communion characteristic of the mythical image. Undoubtedly, with reference to Tieck's attitude toward nature and to his allusions to plants and flowers, Jakob Böhme was of some influence—but not exclusively, for the presence of the image of India may be detected now and then. There is an attempt to reconcile the Orient and the West, a characteristic result of the Romantic preoccupation with the mythical image— but it is happenstance and is not accomplished in lofty terms nor imbued with the importance ascribed to it by other Early Romanticists.

The Oriental texture of *Abdallah* (1792) is chiefly Persian and of a diaphanous quality which reveals the basic Storm and Stress outline, but such a metaphor as "in lieblicher Stille schmiegte sich der Himmel umarmend um die Erde" (VIII, 83) might be gleaned from Hindu cosmology. The writing upon palm leaves (VIII, 93 ff.) was characteristic of India (in *Sakuntala* such materials are used in writing). When Zulma, the sultan's daughter, is glimpsed for the first time by Abdallah, she is depicted as having the grace and gentleness of Sakuntala: "Schlank und mit majestätischer Anmuth trat sie herbei, um auf dem Altan die Blumen und jungen Citronenbäume zu begiessen" (VIII, 48). This is reminiscent of the maidens in Kanna's grove, who carefully water the plants. Aside from these instances, however, there is nothing of the mythical image in this youthful work.

2. Ludwig Tieck, *Schriften* (20 vols.; Berlin, 1828-1846), VI, liii. Parenthetical references, unless otherwise noted, are to volume and page of this edition.

In *William Lovell* (1795-1796) several evidences of the image may be discerned. There is at times a close harmony between man and nature, an active concern for man on the part of nature. Lovell hears the friendly speech of trees, the sympathetic weeping of springs, and finds consolation in nature, but these actions often are merely imitative of his own attitudes: "Der Wald sprach mir mit seinem ernsten Rauschen freundlichen Trost zu, die Quellen weinten mit mir. Man kann nirgend verlassen wandeln; dem leidenden Herzen tritt die Natur mütterlich nach, Liebe und Wohlwollen spricht uns in jedem Klange an, Freundschaft streckt uns aus jedem Zweige einen Arm entgegen" (VI, 24). On the evening before his departure from home, Lovell takes farewell from the familiar places of his gardens, a gesture typical of the mythical image (VI, 33). But here the farewells are restricted to the portions of the gardens which have a special place in his memory, not to the gardens as quickened beings with which he feels a bond. He writes to Amalie that human beings are the children of nature and thus are susceptible to the natural laws of order and harmony (VI, 42). But the lack of identity is not in the spirit of the mythical image.

Man may have drawn his philosophy from nature (in agreement with the tenet of the mythical image), but in *William Lovell* Tieck endows him not with the humility and the gentleness of the Hindu but rather with superhuman qualities—he becomes a giant: "Frei stehe der kühnere Mensch, ohne Stangen und Latten, die ihn umgeben, in der hohen Natur da, aus Baumwipfeln und Morgenroth ziehe er seine Philosophie, und schreite wie ein Riese über die Zwerge hinweg" (VI, 211). Lovell does express a nostalgia for a far-off land; he would like to regain a natural and simple existence by shrugging off the servitude in which he is held by his humanity (VII, 23). He even expresses a longing for India: "Ich möchte in manchen Stunden von hier reisen und eine seltsame Natur mit ihren Wundern aufsuchen. . . . Ich möchte Indiens seltsame Gesträuche besehen, und aus den Flüssen Wasser schöpfen, deren Name mich schon in den Kindermärchen erquickte" (VII, 27). But this longing is not the painful, magnetic nostalgia expressed by other Early Romanticists. India remains shrouded in fairy tale unreality to Tieck. To him man is gnawed with an expectancy in regard to nature as to what she might reveal: but he is fearful of allowing the revelation to take place. Man's admiration of nature is tempered by a somewhat frightened and suspicious respect:

Ich erinnre mich aus meiner Kindheit, dass uns die weite Natur mit ihren Bergen in der Ferne, mit dem hohen gewölbten blauen Himmel, mit den tausend belebten Gegenständen wie mit einem gewaltigen Entsetzen ergreifen kann; dann streift der Geist der Natur unserm Geiste vorüber, und rührt ihn mit seltsamen Gefühlen an, die wankenden Bäume sprechen in verständlichen Tönen zu uns, und es ist, als wollte sich das ganze Gemälde plötzlich hervortreten und sich zeigen, das unter der Masse liegt und sie belebt; wir wagen es nicht den grossen Moment abzuwarten, sondern entfliehen. (VI, 346)

This is not the mythical image, which endows nature with a spirit kindred to mankind, indeed with the same immanent spirit of the Supreme Being that is in all things.

Tieck is not, however, insensitive completely to nature in the stamp of the mythical image, although it does not attain a chief place in his works. Balder, in *William Lovell*, has a soul which is most naturally responsive to nature; he seems to feel a kinship with flowers and plants which is similar to that represented in the image. Through this character Tieck dwells most clearly on the mythical image as revealed in nature. From his mountain retreat Balder writes Lovell of his feelings of a consanguineous relation with nature and alludes to its enigmatic, secret power:

Es ist alles hier um mich lebendig und voll Freundschaft; die Bäume grüssen mich, wenn ich aufwache, der Himmel zieht purpurroth über meinen Kopf weg und seine bunten Lichter spielen um mich herum und necken mich. —Ach Freund, wenn man die Blumen und Pflanzen näher kennen lernt, was sie dann anders sind, als man gewöhnlich glaubt, sie sind klüger als die Leute denken, und haben auch mehr Gewalt, als man meint. Die Menschenwissenschaft kennt nur einen Theil ihrer geheimen Kraft.

> Blumen sind uns nah befreundet,
> Pflanzen unserm Blut verwandt.... (VII, 35)

In nature Balder finds a kinship of spirit and a mystic response to, or preutterance of, his every thought in a single harmonious tone: "In der freien Natur ist alles mit der Seele verwandt und auf einen Ton gestimmt, in jedes Lied stimmt sie freiwillig ein und ist das Echo und eben so oft der Vorsänger von allem, was ich denke: ein kleiner Vogel kann mir vielen Verstand in meinen Kopf herein-

locken" (VII, 37). A reciprocal affection develops between him and
the nature around him:

> Die Stauden winken mir, zu ihnen zu kommen, und ein Wort mit ihnen
> zu sprechen, denn sie halten alle viel von mir; meinen Rosen muss ich
> noch Wasser zu trinken geben, und dann muss ich die kranke Pappel
> besuchen, die der Wind eingeknickt hat. Es ist ganz mein freier Wille,
> aber ich habe es mir selbst zum Gesetze gemacht; ich helfe ihnen in
> vielen Sachen, und die Blumen und Bäume hier würden sich sehr
> grämen, wenn ich einmal fortzöge. (VII, 38)

In his solitude Balder seems to have developed a religion of his own,
in that there has come to be an ethical system which governs his
relationship with nature. But he is not to find the serenity he seeks,
and his end is almost as violent as Lovell's.

Several essays written by Tieck during the period of his intimate
friendship with Wackenroder found their way into the *Phantasien
über die Kunst* (1799). Here, in the essay "Über die Kinderfiguren
auf den Raphaelschen Bildern," there is a statement concerning
the figures of children which has in it an echo of the mythical
image, in that the faces of the children seem like tender plants
returned from a long vanished golden age:

> Wenn wir der Kinder holdseliges Angesicht betrachten, so vergessen wir
> gern und leicht die Verwickelungen der Welt, das Auge vertieft sich in
> den wunderbaren reinen Zügen, und wie Propheten einer schönen
> Zukunft, wie zarte Pflanzen, die unerklärlich aus der längst entflohenen
> goldenen Zeit zurückgekommen sind, stehen die Kinder um uns.[3]

In the essay "Die Farben," Tieck likens colors to the world spirit
which hides and discloses itself in a thousand ways; the incomprehensible language of color brings to man the memory of an ancient
friendship with spirits—one might say, a condition of harmony with
nature and the universe:

> Wir können nicht aussprechen, wie uns jede Farbe bewegt und rührt,
> denn die Farben selber sprachen in zarterer Mundart zu uns: Es ist der
> Weltgeist, der sich daran freut, sich auf tausend Wegen zu verstehen zu
> geben, und doch zugleich zu verbergen; die abgesonderten Farben sind
> seine einzelnen Laute, wir horchen aufmerksam darauf hin, wir merken
> wohl, dass wir etwas vernehmen, doch können wir keinem anderen, uns
> selber nicht Kunde davon bringen; aber eine geheime magische Kraft

3. Wackenroder, I, 253.

durchströmt uns, wir glauben uns selbst zu erkennen, und uns einer alten, unendlich seligen Geisterfreundschaft zu erinnern.[4]

In the musical realm, in "Unmusikalische Toleranz," Tieck strikes a similar chord which stirs perhaps even more obviously the sympathetic notes of the motifs of the mythical image: like magic seeds, tones send down roots in the poet; a thousand wonderful flowers whisper; childhood and an even earlier past play impishly on the leaves and in the crowns of the trees; and the flowers quicken and walk in a throng.[5] If these thoughts on color and music are, indeed, features of the projection of the mythical image of India, they are transfigured into an intense emotion where sensations are often synesthetic. But it is remarkable that Tieck fails to allude to India itself.

In *Der blonde Eckbert* (1797), while there is again no direct reference to India, there is present the mingling of the wonderful with the ordinary which results in an enchanted world.[6] It was noted by Herder that the magic of wonders was mixed in a natural and thrilling manner with the world of reality in *Sakuntala*. India, from ancient times, was known to the West as a land of wonders. This commingling of ordinary reality and wondrous magic is another lineament of the mythical image of India, one brought to distinction by E. T. A. Hoffmann.

In *Franz Sternbalds Wanderungen* (1798) man's relation to nature is whimsical, depending usually upon the mood of the person concerned (or sometimes upon the whim of the author). Franz feels a sense of communication with nature: "Welche Welten entwickeln sich im Gemüthe, wenn die freie Natur umher mit kühner Sprache in uns hinein redet, wenn jeder ihrer Töne unser Herz trifft und alle Empfindungen zugleich anrührt" (XVI, 21). He even appears to express a tender affection for flowers: "Er drückte sein heisses Gesicht an den Boden und küsste mit Zärtlichkeit die Blumen" (XVI, 39), but his fervor is from the impulse of an emotional moment and is not directed to the flowers for their own sake. He is aware of the strange language nature speaks; he senses signifi-

4. *Ibid.*, I, 269.
5. *Ibid.*, I, 284.
6. Ludwig Tieck, *Ausgewählte Werke*, ed. Georg Witkowski (4 vols.; Leipzig, [1903]), I, 89.

cant meaning, and harks gladly to her wondrous accents (XVI, 82), but coherent communication is not possible.

In a letter to his friend Sebastian, Franz counsels him to heed nature: "Heisse die süsse Frömmigkeit willkommen, die unter alten Eichen beim Schein der Abendsonne, wenn Heimchen zwitschern und Feldtauben girren, auf Dich niederkömmt. Nenne mich nicht zu weich und vielleicht phantastisch, wenn ich Dir dieses rathe" (XVI, 26). The apologetic tone of the concluding sentence dampens a response to the counsel.

Tieck tries to conjure too prematurely the image of India into the present; he seems to abandon the image without having understood it fully and without having succeeded in adapting it to his own nature. Franz, in conversation with the widely traveled Ludoviko, says: "O, wie gern möchte ich Euer Gefährte gewesen seyn! . . . die Gegenden wirklich und wahrhaftig zu sehn, die schon in der Imagination unsrer Kindheit vor uns stehn, die Oerter zu besuchen, die gleichsam die Wiege der Menschheit sind." The lines contain an implicit reference to India, but Ludoviko answers: "Darfst Du Dich in Deiner Heimath nicht verwundern?" (XVI, 327). Tieck's gaze could not dwell for long on foreign lands but was drawn magnetically back always to his own.

One may perhaps distinguish several murky reflections of the mythical image in *Leben und Tod der heiligen Genoveva* (1800). Grimoald, the charcoal-burner, loses his son in battle and plants a tree which is to be a mystic embodiment of the dead son:

Das Bäumchen hier bedeutet meinen Sohn,
Den Traugott; . . .

. . . .
Nun ist er hin, der Krieg hat ihn gefressen,

. . . .
So wachse und gedeihe, grüner Baum,
Du bist mir jetzt statt meines toten Sohns,
Und manchmal will ich Sonntags zu dir kommen
Und mich ins Gras zu deinen Füssen setzen
Und mit dir sprechen, als wenn er es wäre.[7] (II, 225)

The same Grimoald, when he feels compelled to leave his homeland because of his participation in the expulsion of Genoveva into the wilderness, bids a Brahmanical farewell to mountains and trees:

7. *Genoveva* references are to volume and page of *Ausgewählte Werke*.

> Leb' wohl, du Land, das du mich auferzogen,
> Ihr Berge, Bäume, denen ich gewogen,
> Ihr Linden, hohe Eichen, helle Buchen:
> Ich muss mir eine fremde Heimat suchen. (II, 225)

Cast into the wilds, Genoveva asks an immanent God for succor:

> Allgegenwärt'ger so in Gras wie Steinen,
> Du hörst mich jetzt, hast meiner nicht vergessen. (II, 227)

She finds her prayer answered as a doe comes forth to give milk to her son:

> Ich danke dir, Güt'ger!
> Der Steine erreget,
> Und Thiere beweget,
> Mir Retter zu sein.
> Komm, fromme Hirschin, du mir zugesendet,
> Du blickst mich an mit treuen, lieben Augen,
> Zu meinem armen, matten Kind komm,
> Es wartet dein und sehnet sich nach dir. (II, 227)

Later, when the icy winds of five winters have passed and little Schmerzenreich has not even a cloth to warm his body, a wolf comes carrying a sheepskin and lays it at the boy's feet:

> Da kam ein Wolf auf einmal hergegangen,
> Im Maule trug er eines Schafes Haut,
> Die warf er vor dem Kinde und der bangen
> Pfalzgräfin hin, die innerlich ergraut,
> Doch bald nimmt sie mit dankbarem Verlangen
> Und wickelt Schmerzenreich in diese Haut;
> So war er sicher vor dem schlimmen Frost,
> Und so fand Genoveva ihren Trost. (II, 240)

The wolf lingers near and becomes a member of the small company; he is even ridden by the boy, who becomes a friend to all the denizens of the wilderness:

> Es wurde auch das Wild zur selben Zeit
> Mit ihnen gar vertraulich und gemein,
> Das liebe Kind hat daran manche Freud',
> Dass sie um ihn so schön ergötzlich sein.
> Er ritt auf seinem Wolf gar oftmals weit
> Im Wald, die Hasen liefen hinterdrein,
> Die Vöglein sich auf Hand und Häuptlein schwungen,
> Erquickten ihn und sie, so wie sie sungen. (II, 240)

In this idyllic and simple existence the animals aid the boy in his search for herbs:

> Ging's Kindlein aus, um Kräuter aufzulesen,
> So liefen auch die frommen Tierlein mit,
> Und zeigten ihm die guten von den bösen
> Mit ihren Füssen, folgten jedem Schritt. (II, 240)

Death, when he comes to claim Genoveva, is intercepted by heavenly emissaries and says with some regret:

> So darf ich diese Blume noch nicht mähen. (II, 248)

Death as the reaper is not an Indic commonplace, but the expression *mähen* seems somewhat crass when applied to *Blume*. Because Tieck maintains so strict a silence with regard to direct mention of India, it is doubtful that these passages are clear reflections of the mythical image. After having read Tieck's verses, one is almost tempted to apply Jean Paul's equation of *indisch=poetisch* and conclude that the absence of any unequivocal manipulation of the mythical image here precludes poetic skill.

In *Kaiser Octavianus* (1804), which may be considered a companion piece to *Genoveva*, with more daring and a more sweeping panorama, there is much that is similar. Felizitas calls her twin sons "die zarten Blumen,"[8] and Romanze speaks of "Blumenvolle Wunderlande" (III, 104). Here also an animal, a lion, attaches itself affectionately and protectively to one of the boys, who is named Leo after his feline companion. The Oriental color in the play is provided by Persians, Palestinians, Babylonians, and the exotic religion (which is depicted absurdly as the most outlandish idolatry) is Mohammedanism. Nothing of India is here represented in this religion. A farewell to familiar objects in nature is alluded to when Arlanges, the king of Persia, speaking of Marzebille, the daughter of the sultan of Babylon, says:

> Von Ruh, Müssiggang, von Blumen
> Von dem Gartenduft, dem Chore
> Süsser Nachtigallen, klaren
> Quellen, aufsteigenden Bronnen
> Will sie gerne Abschied nehmen. (III, 152)

8. Ludwig Tieck, *Werke*, ed. Eduard Berend (6 vols.; Leipzig, [1908]), III, 49. *Kaiser Octavianus* references are to volume and page of this edition.

The reconciliation between the Orient and the West, supplied in the plot by the *Volksbuch* source in the marriages of the princes to their lovely Oriental maidens, has been treated by Tieck from a subjective Western viewpoint; the effect cannot be compared with the most sublimely poetic mingling of cultures envisioned by Hölderlin.

Der Runenberg (1803) merely echoes the incomprehensible language of nature perceived in brooks, plants, forests, and other objects of nature that Tieck has dwelt upon previously in *William Lovell* and *Franz Sternbalds Wanderungen*. The wondrous and the ordinary are mixed here, too, but with a suggestion of insanity to justify it. One must finally decide that, in contrast to the other main representatives of Early Romanticism, Tieck found little receptivity in his spirit for the mythical image of India; he certainly did not exalt the image, nor did he adapt its most prominent marks for poetic projection. The trace of the image perceptible here and there becomes finally so distorted as to lose its charm and attraction. Tieck's failure to transform the image fully in his own poetic utterances may be ascribed either to an incapability of doing so or to the fact that the image did not have the fascination for him that it had for other Early Romanticists. But Tieck's lack of ardor lessened by no whit their enthusiasm and longing for the image.

4. Reizender und farbiger steht die Poesie wie ein geschmücktes Indien dem kalten, toten Spitzbergen jenes Stubenverstandes gegenüber. Damit Indien in der Mitte des Erdballs so warm und herrlich sei, muss ein kaltes starres Meer, tote Klippen, Nebel statt des gestirnvollen Himmels und eine lange Nacht die beiden Enden unwirtbar machen. —NOVALIS

The mythical image of India failed to take root in Tieck's mind perhaps because of his lack of an essential mythological sense, and Hindu mythology, as a mystic expression of man's conception of nature and God, was one aspect of the image. The extremely sensitive spirit of Novalis (Friedrich von Hardenberg, 1772-1801) conceived of a mythology to express the unfolding of man's poetic nature and in doing so sublimated the mythical image. Tieck, in the foreword to the third edition of Novalis' works in 1815, mentions a trait of Novalis which made possible the effectiveness of the influence of the image upon him:

> Ihm war es zur natürlichen Ansicht geworden, das Gewöhnlichste, Nächste als ein Wunder und das Fremde, Übernatürliche als etwas Gewöhnliches zu betrachten; so umgab ihn das alltägliche Leben selbst wie ein wundervolles Märchen, und jene Region, die die meisten Menschen nur als ein Fernes, Unbegreifliches ahnden oder bezweifeln wollen, war ihm wie eine liebe Heimat.[1]

By fusing the mythical image with his own conceptions, Novalis was to give a new dimension to his ideas.

In his aphoristic "Blütenstaub," printed in the *Athenäum* in 1798, Novalis first reveals his receptivity to the image. Poet and priest are one to him, and he longs for the time in the future when poet and priest again will become one person as they were in the past: "Dichter und Priester waren im Anfang *eins*, und nur spätere Zeiten haben sie getrennt. Der echte Dichter ist aber immer Priester, so wie der echte Priester immer Dichter geblieben. Und sollte nicht die Zukunft den alten Zustand der Dinge wieder herbeiführen?"[2] Although he does not mention India here, he undoubtedly had in mind the Brahman, who served in the double role of poet and priest in ancient India. This supposition is enforced by the following remark, which in the manuscript immediately precedes the fragment just quoted: "In Indien ist an einigen Orten Feldherr und Priester getrennt gewesen, und der Feldherr hat die zweite Rolle gespielt" (II, 39).

The union of poet and priest in one person is the union of poetry and religion, an ideal cultivated by the Early Romanticists for which they found their model in India, where almost every expression of human wisdom found poetic form. The Romanticists desired to poetize all experience, all records of human activity and every emotion, even poetry itself (*Poesie der Poesie*). Novalis writes:

---

1. Novalis [pseud., Friedrich von Hardenberg], *Schriften*, ed. Jakob Minor (4 vols.; Jena, 1923), I, xxii-xxiii.
2. Novalis, *Schriften*, ed. Paul Kluckhohn (4 vols.; Leipzig, [1929]), II, 27. Parenthetical references are to volume and page of this edition.

"Der Geist ist jederzeit poetisch. Der poetische Staat ist der wahrhafte, vollkommne Staat" (II, 41). India had been described repeatedly as the cradle of mankind and as being inhabited by a childlike, innocent people; Novalis says: "Wo Kinder sind, da ist ein goldnes Zeitalter" (II, 33), combining two important ideas embodied in the mythical image, and setting down a programmatic note for his later evocations of the golden age. It has been noted that India lacked a written history as such, and that the history of India had been preserved instead in its mythology and epic poetry; Novalis declares: "Die Fabellehre enthält die Geschichte der urbildlichen Welt, sie begreift Vorzeit, Gegenwart und Zukunft" (II, 34). This statement contains the kernel of the new mythology as it is revealed by him later in Klingsohr's *Märchen*.

The notebooks from which Novalis gleaned the aphorisms for "Blütenstaub" were pored over after his death by Friedrich Schlegel and then again by Eduard von Bülow. The fragments selected by Schlegel were arranged by Tieck and printed first in the 1802 edition of Novalis' works. Among these "Fragmente vermischten Inhalts" there are several based on various aspects of the mythical image. The warm, melodious speech of the Hindu had been admired by the travelers to India; the inhabitants were known to have been a musical people from ancient times, for many of their epics were sung or chanted and they possessed verse plays to be accompanied by choruses and dances. Novalis writes: "Über die allgemeine *n* Sprache der Musik. Der Geist wird frei, *unbestimmt* angeregt— das tut ihm so wohl—das dünkt ihm so bekannt, so vaterländisch —er ist auf diese kurzen Augenblicke in seiner indischen Heimat" (III, 100). In what appears to be a mathematical reference, the unknown but infinite quality of music calls forth a longing for the land where music perhaps had its birth. The Orient was the home of mathematics: "Im Morgenlande ist die echte Mathematik zu Hause." And just above: "Reine Mathematik ist Religion" (III, 296). Here science and religion are united once again, just as they seem to have been when the ancients calculated the positions of stars and peopled the heavens with their gods.

The Romanticist who perceives the mythical image delves through Greek thought and art in search of the Oriental influence; Novalis reveals this tendency: "An einigen *Grenzen* [hat] ägyptischer und orientalischer Mystizismus [die griechische Kunst und Philosophie] angegriffen und modernisiert. In *Ionien* merkt man den erweichenden Einfluss des warmen asiatischen Himmels" (II, 409). One finds here, too, the influence of climate exerted on a people; the Hindus were thought to have developed their culture partly because of the beneficent gentleness of the Asiatic climate.

Novalis could combine Christian theology, Hinduism in what many considered its most abhorrent form, and sensuality in a startling but altogether natural fashion: "Es gibt nur *einen* Tempel in der Welt und das ist der menschliche Körper. Nichts ist heiliger als diese hohe Gestalt. Das Bücken vor Menschen ist eine Huldigung dieser Offenbarung im Fleisch. (Göttliche Verehrung des Lingam, des Busens—der Statuen.) Man berührt den Himmel, wenn man einen Menschenleib betastet" (III, 292). Thus religion is filtered into the display of every human act of physical love and into the veneration of erotic symbols.

The natural bent which Novalis had for a mingling of the natural with the supernatural, or the ordinary with the wondrous, was pointed out by Tieck. Novalis even sought to establish a logical connection between the two:

Alle Überzeugung ist unabhängig von der Naturwahrheit—Sie bezieht sich auf die magische oder die Wunderwahrheit. Von der Naturwahrheit kann man nur überzeugt werden—insofern sie Wunderwahrheit wird. Aller Beweis fusst auf Überzeugung, und ist mithin nur ein Notbehelf im Zustand des Mangels an durchgängiger Wunderwahrheit. Alle Naturwahrheiten beruhen demnach ebenfalls auf Wunderwahrheit. (II, 345)

Novalis also offers a clue to his inclination to dwell upon the magical and wondrous: "Hang zum Wunderbaren und Geheimnisvollen ist nichts als Streben—nach *unsinnlichem—geistigem* Reiz" (III, 85).

The greater simplicity of the Orient and the differences of its inhabitants in relation to the West is suggested by Novalis in a fragment taken from the notebooks: "Grössere Einfachheit—wenigere aber besser verteilte Massen der Natur, des Lebens und der Menschen im Orient. Die orientalischen Menschen, Lebensalter, etc. unterscheiden sich sehr von den unsrigen" (III, 335). In spite of these differences, Novalis adapted the mythical image of India for his own purposes: a lofty vision of the image revealed in a longing for poetry, and a cosmology of poetry in the shape of a new mythology.

The notebook *Fragmente* selected by Von Bülow also contain several examples which are evidence of Novalis' interest in the mythical image. In a cryptic fragment he mentions the mystic dogmatism of the Orient, a passivity which acts indirectly: "Mystischer Dogmatism des Orients—(entstanden aus *Trägheit* und *Ahndung*) höhere Mitteilung der Erkenntnis—intellektueller Quietismus— System des Wissens, wie System der Gnade—passives System—indirekt tätiges System" (III, 168). He refers to the Hindu conception of metempsychosis and wonders if earthly birth might not be the result of death in the beyond: "Wer hier nicht zur Vollendung gelangt, gelangt vielleicht drüben—oder muss eine abermalige irdische Laufbahn beginnen. Sollte es nicht auch drüben einen *Tod geben*, dessen Resultat *irdische Geburt* wäre" (III, 33). Thus Novalis offers a logical extension to the Hindu concept of death as birth into a perfect existence, an idea which Jean Paul championed in *Hesperus* in a mystical amalgamation of Hindu-Christian faith.

The cryptic, sometimes almost mystic, fragments which Novalis jotted down in his notebooks were meant to serve as a guide and a source for an encyclopedic work in which experiences and ideas from different realms of knowledge would mutually illuminate, support, and enliven one another.[3] Although this work did not come about, and might never have come about even had Novalis lived a long life, the notes are evidence of a wide-ranging curiosity and an actively probing intellect. Some of the ideas contained in them do appear in his creative endeavors.

In the fragmentary *Lehrlinge zu Sais* (1798) Novalis sees in all of nature a secret language, incomprehensible to man: "Man verstehe die Sprache nicht, weil sich die Sprache selber nicht verstehe, nicht verstehen wolle; die echte Sanskrit spräche, um zu sprechen, weil Sprechen ihre Lust und ihr Wesen sei" (I, 11). Here Sanskrit is placed among the mysterious languages found in nature, which, if understood, would reveal the secrets of the universe. It is paradoxical that one should attempt to understand languages which do not communicate—but the very fact that they are languages, signs, symbols, and sounds repeated in an orderly and yet

3. Novalis, *Schriften*, ed. Minor, I, v.

infinitely various fashion, signifies that the riddle can ultimately be comprehended.

Novalis mentions the humanization of nature by a childlike people in a past age, when mankind dwelled in close communion with nature. That time has vanished and now mankind thinks of it with nostalgia, longs for its return. Only the poets have felt, says one of a group of travelers, what nature can be to man: "Ihnen allein bleibt die Seele derselben nicht fremd, und sie suchen in ihrem Umgang alle Seligkeiten der goldnen Zeit nicht umsonst" (I, 31). He says further that the wise men of old were correct in seeking the origin of all things in water, but that they spoke of a more sublime water than that of oceans and springs: the fluid that is the source of all things. He continues:

Wie diese Wellen, lebten wir in der goldnen Zeit; in buntfarbigen Wolken, diesen schwimmenden Meeren und Urquellen des Lebendigen auf Erden, liebten und erzeugten sich die Geschlechter der Menschen in ewigen Spielen; wurden besucht von den Kindern des Himmels und erst in jener grossen Begebenheit, welche heilige Sagen die Sündflut nennen, ging diese blühende Welt unter. (I, 36)

Here Novalis combines biblical ideas with Hindu mythology to achieve a synthesis expressing a longing for the golden age. In nature he sees a multitude enclosed in a singleness, a unity of all in one. His young traveler says: "Glücklich preis ich diesen Sohn, diesen Liebling der Natur, dem sie verstattet sie in ihrer Zweiheit, als erzeugende und gebärende Macht, und in ihrer Einheit, als eine unendliche, ewigdauernde Ehe, zu betrachten. Sein Leben wird eine Fülle aller Genüsse, eine Kette der Wollust und seine Religion der eigentliche, echte Naturalismus sein" (I, 38). Here religion, nature, and eroticism are one.

The teacher and his apprentices approach, and the strange travelers then tell about their experiences:

Voll Sehnsucht und Wissbegierde hatten sie sich aufgemacht, um die Spuren jenes verloren gegangenen Urvolks zu suchen, dessen entartete und verwilderte Reste die heutige Menschheit zu sein schiene, dessen hoher Bildung sie noch die wichtigsten und unentbehrlichsten Kenntnisse und Werkzeuge zu danken hat. Vorzüglich hatte sie jene heilige Sprache gelockt, die das glänzende Band jener königlichen Menschen mit überirdischen Gegenden und Bewohnern gewesen war, und von der einige Worte, nach dem Verlaut mannichfaltiger Sagen, noch im Besitz

einiger glücklichen Weisen unter unsern Vorfahren gewesen sein mögen. Ihre Aussprache war ein wunderbarer Gesang, dessen unwiderstehliche Töne tief in das Innere jeder Natur eindrangen und sie zerlegten. Jeder ihrer Namen schien das Losungswort für die Seele jedes Naturkörpers.
(I, 38)

Novalis seems to have the mythical image of India in mind here. The ancient Hindus possessed a holy language, revealed to them by the gods, which contained their mythology, their religion, their science, and their entire culture. Novalis felt that the understanding of this language, the key to that culture, would reveal the secret of their intimate understanding of the universe. It is undoubtedly significant that in the paralipomena to this unfinished work Novalis should have noted: "Kosmogonie der Alten. Indische Gottheiten" (I, 41).

A relationship between Christianity and India is expressed very clearly in the *Hymnen an die Nacht* (1800). Novalis says that wise men from the East, who came bearing gifts for the Holy Infant, were the first to recognize the dawn of a new age: "Des Morgenlands ahndende, blütenreiche Weisheit erkannte zuerst der neuen Zeit Beginn" (I, 61). This is obviously a biblical reference, but the phrase *blütenreiche Weisheit* nevertheless gives it a mythical cast.

From a distant coast a Greek bard comes to Palestine to adore the Child, and then travels on to Hindustan, carrying tidings of the Lord: "Von ferner Küste, unter Hellas heiterm Himmel geboren, kam ein Sänger nach Palästina und ergab sein ganzes Herz dem Wunderkinde. . . . Der Sänger zog voll Freudigkeit nach Indostan— das Herz von süsser Liebe trunken; und schüttete in feurigen Gesängen es unter jenem milden Himmel aus, dass tausend Herzen sich zu ihm neigten, und die fröhliche Botschaft tausendzweigig emporwuchs" (I, 62). Who was this singer, this bard?

Friedrich Hiebel, in his study on Novalis, says that the minstrel is a puzzling figure, given no name, influenced by no literary ancestor. He enters in the middle of the fifth hymn and departs without further mention. Hiebel then essays to connect the figure with John the Evangelist (in regard to Novalis' allusion to Greece), with the story of Orpheus (in connection with the *Sänger*, and in an effort to effect here a reconciliation of Christianity and heathenism), and with the symbol of the poet transfigured. He concludes that the singer bears three different countenances and is for this reason anonymous: as a disciple of Christ he resembles John, as a Greek bard he is related to Orpheus, and he is lastly a transfigured objectification of the poet himself. With reference to the anonymity of the figure, Hiebel himself points out that not even Joseph, Mary, or Jesus are named in the fifth hymn,[4] so it would seem that the namelessness of the singer from Hellas is not necessarily explained by his being a threefold symbol. Without doubt, Novalis did intend a fusion of Christianity and heathendom to be represented: this reconciliation is accomplished by the allusion to Hellas and India. But there is also present here Novalis' equation of *Dichter*= *Priester*. The *Sänger* need not be taken literally to mean a bard. He is rather the highest conception of a poet: the poet-priest.

Heinz Ritter, in his essay on the *Hymnen*, notes that various historical personalities have been postulated as prototypes for the singer. For example, the apostle Thomas, who is said to have evangelized in India, or Apollonius of Tyana, or a certain Diodorus of Smyrna. But it can be none of these, he decides, partly because they were known in Germany only later, partly because the course of their lives does not agree with the legend in the hymn.[5] In a note Ritter says emphatically that it cannot be Thomas, not only because the source of the legend of St. Thomas was published in Germany only in 1822 and could not have been known to Novalis, but also because the content of the legend of the *Hymnen* does not agree with the story of the saint.[6] Ritter's first objection to an analogy with St. Thomas, that the legend of the saint was not known in Germany in Novalis' time, is certainly not admissible. The legend of the preaching of St. Thomas in India is told by St. John Chrysostom (*ca.* 347-407), St. Jerome (*ca.* 347-419?), St. Gregory of Tours (538-594), and by St. Isidore of Seville (*ca.* 560-636) in his *Life and Death of the Saints*. Jacobus de Voragine (*ca.* 1230-1298), in his *Legenda Sanctorum*, which was widely translated and appeared in many editions, relates the story.[7] Marco Polo returned to Europe

4. Friedrich Hiebel, *Novalis, der Dichter der blauen Blume* (Bern, 1951), p. 189.
5. Heinz Ritter, *Novalis' Hymnen an die Nacht* (Heidelberg, 1930), p. 137.
6. *Ibid.*, p. 167.
7. Jacobus de Voragine [better, Varagine], *The Golden Legend*, trans. Granger Ryan and Helmut Ripperger (2 vols.; London, 1941), I, vii, and 39-46. The first German translation was published in Ulm in 1470 and appeared in ninety editions before 1800.

from India with first-hand descriptions of the tomb of St. Thomas and tales of miracles worked by him among the Hindus.[8] Later travelers make reference to the legends of St. Thomas which they have encountered in India. Among the pseudoepigrapha are a gospel and an acts of Thomas. It seems that there is an abundance of sources, some of which may easily have come to the attention of Novalis to supply a prototype for the *Sänger* who traveled to India. Furthermore, in the Bible,[9] Thomas is called Didymus, or the *twin*, and the legend says that he was born in Antioch, a twin (variously with a sister or a brother), of Greek parents. The chief objection to assuming the *Sänger* to represent Thomas is that he did not go to India until after the Crucifixion, whereas in the *Hymnen* the *Sänger* departs for India before the death of Christ. One might assert that close attention to chronology is not important in this respect; neither would the skepticism of Thomas with regard to Christ's Resurrection be pertinent to the thought of the fifth hymn. However it may be, Novalis has used yet another aspect of the mythical image of India to suggest a harmony of Christianity and heathenism.

The Romantic mythical image of India found its most poetic expression in *Heinrich von Ofterdingen* (1800), in which it finally is transfigured and absorbed into the new mythology, the mythology of poesy, through the suprarational, magical qualities of the *blaue Blume*. This supreme Romantic symbol has been imperfectly comprehended because of the slighting by scholars of Novalis' allusions to India, the result of the poet's acquaintance with Indic lore in his time. Suggestions of an Indic aspect of the *blaue Blume* have in the past been relegated exclusively to skeptical footnotes. Indic influence on the symbol is undeniable, and recognition of this fact enlarges and gives a new dimension to the symbolism of the *blaue Blume*.

The mystery of the *blaue Blume* provoked speculation about its origin from the time the novel was published. Attempts were made at first to find a botanical prototype of the flower. On seeing the blue gentian, the Germanist Friedrich von der Hagen declared in 1816 that it was the real *blaue Blume*. Because of the cryptic cry of

8. Marco Polo, II, 341, 353, 355, and notes 355-359.
9. John 11:16, 20:24, 21:2.

the treasure flower of the Kyffhäuser legend, "Vergiss das Beste nicht," efforts have been made to connect the *blaue Blume* with the forget-me-not. Because the meadows about the Kyffhäuser are covered with bluebells, this flower also has been suggested as the model for Novalis' image. However, Jutta Hecker, in her monograph on the flower symbolism of the Romantic period, states categorically that such efforts to identify the *blaue Blume* with actual flowers are superficial and absolutely wrong since the representation of the *blaue Blume* has nothing in common with real flowers.[10] But if this is so, why could the *blaue Blume* not have been influenced by flowers used as symbols? Miss Hecker admits this possibility by herself suggesting three sources for Novalis' symbol. The first provided him with a flower endowed with enigmatic powers of prophecy and revelation: it is the old Thüringian legend of the treasure flower of the Kyffhäuser mountain. The second source offers not only a blue flower but also the vision of this flower in a dream: it is the dream of Gustav in Jean Paul's *Die unsichtbare Loge*. The third source presents a blue flower as a symbol of poetry in the role of a redeemer and a guide to the beyond: it is the mystic blue flower of Tieck's allegorical poem "Der Traum."[11] Very likely each of these sources influenced Novalis in his choice and use of the symbol of the *blaue Blume*. His flower reveals aspects suggested by each of them. But a unitive function of the flower seems still to be lacking.

An important function of a symbol is its unitive force, which links various worlds, combines experiences, and mediates between disparate realms.[12] If one may assume, as does Hiebel in his Novalis biography, that ideas are comprehended by symbols and that symbols are thus forms of expressing a process, a becoming,[13] then the symbol of the *blaue Blume* is representative of this definition; and when considered in all its aspects, the *blaue Blume* can perhaps reveal a progression of diverse ideas to an ultimate meaningful synthesis.

Of particular importance to the symbolism of flowers among the Romanticists is what may be considered the goal of Romantic effort:

10. Jutta Hecker, *Das Symbol der Blauen Blume im Zusammenhang mit der Blumensymbolik der Romantik* (Jena, 1931), p. 30.
11. *Ibid.*, pp. 29-34.
12. William York Tindall, *The Literary Symbol* (New York, 1955), p. 16.
13. Hiebel, *Novalis*, p. 122.

the creation of a new mythology. Friedrich Schlegel's reiteration of a call for a new mythology was really the articulation of a longing in the heart of every Romantic poet. The new mythology was to be achieved by the intermingling and combining of the most varied myths into a new union, a new and universal expression of metaphysical truths. Novalis indicates this program when he proudly notes (concerning his *Ofterdingen* novel): "Die entferntesten und verschiedenartigsten Sagen und Begebenheiten verknüpft. Dies ist eine Erfindung von mir" (I, 245). Although his idea was not original, he was the first to implement it on a grand scale. With this program stated, Novalis selected his symbol to impart a unifying force to an amalgamation of varied myths, the singularity of the whole being his own invention.

The *blaue Blume* is a many-faceted symbol. According to Miss Hecker, it is the symbol of recognition which is eventually to lead to the restoration of the golden age. She continues that it is the way to redemption, perhaps even redemption itself, for in it ideas and things become all-encompassing; it is the symbol of holy mysteries which are revealed in a cryptic secret or in a dream or in a visionary premonition.[14] Hiebel says that *Heinrich von Ofterdingen* is the novel of poetry and the *blaue Blume* is its basic motif for the unfolding of the sense for poetry. It is a mediator, a sensual medium of prophetic recognition. It awakens the sense for the inner progress of mankind by a mystic revelation of poetic maturation.[15]

But the primary concept of the *blaue Blume* as a symbol is in its use as the object suggesting the unfolding of poetic growth, the development of poetic vision, the germination of poetic accomplishment. A collateral and increasingly important symbolistic function in the course of the novel is its use as the mediator in the reconciliation of divergent religions, a motif of perfect, transcendental love, and a symbol of the merging into harmonious synthesis of the disparate qualities of man and nature.

It was in *Sakuntala* that the German poets saw the focused form of the diffused outlines of the mythical image of India: here was

14. Hecker, pp. 22-23.
15. For other interpretations of the symbolism of the *blaue Blume*, see Frederick Hiebel, "Zur Interpretation der 'blauen Blume' des Novalis," *Monatshefte*, XLIII (1951), 328-329; see also Edgar Ederheimer, *Jakob Boehme und die Romantiker* (2 vols.; Heidelberg, 1904), II, 6.

the magical and marvelous in the company of the realistic, here was the wonder of the Hindu pantheon couched in obscure references, here was the impressive exchange of sentiment between human beings and nature, particularly between human beings and flowers. Miss Hecker remarks upon the place of *Sakuntala* in the development of flower symbolism among the Romanticists. Although flowers in the play do not function as personifications, they are more than mere blossoms. Novalis was certainly intensely aware of the drama. Sophie von Kühn, his young fiancée, was known and addressed as "Sakontala," and he mentions the name cryptically twice in the paralipomena to the second part of his *Ofterdingen* (I, 240, 242).[16] His *Sakuntala* experience was decisive in the formation of the *blaue Blume*.

There was an intimate relationship between flowers and India in Novalis' mind. In the *Fragmente* he equates mankind with flowers slumbering in a mythic world. He says: "Die Siesta des Geisterreichs ist die Blumenwelt. In Indien schlummern die Menschen noch immer, und ihr heiliger Traum ist ein Garten, den Zucker- und Milchseen umfliessen." The following fragment continues: "Alle Märchen sind nur Träume von jener heimatlichen Welt, die überall und nirgends ist" (II, 352). In effect Novalis here identifies the people of India with flower-like spirits at home in the delightful world of mythology, a world that is nowhere and everywhere. Does Novalis allude here to India as that homeland, a homeland that now exists as a myth, ideally everywhere, physically nowhere?[17]

In "Die Christenheit oder Europa" (1799) one passage brings to mind Jean Paul's *indisch=poetisch* metaphor: "Reizender und farbiger steht die Poesie wie ein geschmücktes Indien dem kalten, toten Spitzbergen jenes Stubenverstandes [des Rationalismus] gegenüber. Damit Indien in der Mitte des Erdballs so warm und herrlich sei, muss ein kaltes starres Meer, tote Klippen, Nebel statt des gestirnvollen Himmels und eine lange Nacht die beiden Enden

16. Hecker, pp. 28-29.

17. Hiebel, "Zur Interpretation," says it is very significant that Novalis' first literary products were published under the title *Blütenstaub* and designated as "literarische Sämereien." He quotes the aphorism: "Wie kann ein Mensch Sinn für etwas haben, wenn er nicht den Keim davon in sich hat? Was ich verstehen soll, muss sich in mir organisch entwickeln" (II, 17). Then Hiebel gives the fragment just quoted, except that he omits the sentence beginning: "In Indien schlummern die Menschen noch immer . . ."; see p. 329 of the Hiebel article.

unwirtbar machen" (II, 80). Novalis uses the mythical image here to state that imaginative poetry could not exist were it not for the prosaic and the rational.

In the first of his "Geistliche Lieder" Novalis, in a eulogy to Christ, uses the verb *blühen* in reference to India:

> Hat Christus sich mir kundgegeben,
> Und bin ich seiner erst gewiss,
> Wie schnell verzehrt ein lichtes Leben
> Die bodenlose Finsternis.
> Mit ihm bin ich erst Mensch geworden;
> Das Schicksal wird verklärt durch ihn,
> Und Indien muss selbst im Norden
> Um den Geliebten fröhlich blühn. (I, 68)

Here is reflected the Böhmean idea of the immanence of God. Since he thought God was in every creature, there was for Böhme no essential difference between religions.[18] Plotinus spoke of the immanent God, and the Romanticists found the idea of a universal, omnipresent God also in Hindu religious thought. In the poem Novalis hints at a synthesis of Christianity and the religion of India —or, more fundamentally, at the essential unity of all religions. He also conceives of India here in the sense of Indic-poetic, making India a synonym for poetry and alluding, then, to the poetic transfiguration of the person of Christ.

To relate one referent of the *blaue Blume* with an Indic symbol, it is necessary to show a constant infusion of the mythical image of India throughout *Heinrich von Ofterdingen*. Aspects of the image here are numerous. At the very beginning Heinrich says: "Ich hörte einst von alten Zeiten reden; wie da die Tiere und Bäume und Felsen mit den Menschen gesprochen hätten. Mir ist gerade so, als wollten sie allaugenblicklich anfangen, und als könnte ich es ihnen ansehen, was sie mir sagen wollten" (I, 101). Then he dreams a fantastic dream in which he is transported into an exotic land and experiences metempsychosis:

Der Jüngling verlor sich allmählich in süssen Phantasien und entschlummerte. Da träumte ihm erst von unabsehlichen Fernen, und wilden, unbekannten Gegenden. Er wanderte über Meere mit unbegreiflicher Leichtigkeit; wunderliche Tiere sah er; er lebte mit mannichfaltigen

18. Ederheimer, p. 18.

Menschen ... in stillen Hütten. ... Alle Empfindungen stiegen bis zu einer niegekannten Höhe in ihm. Er durchlebte ein unendlich buntes Leben; starb und kam wieder, liebte bis zur höchsten Leidenschaft und war dann wieder auf ewig von seiner Geliebten getrennt. (I, 101-102)

Then he wanders into a grotto in a blue world and encounters the *blaue Blume*, which is to haunt and guide him ever after:

Dunkelblaue Felsen mit bunten Adern erhoben sich in einiger Entfernung ... der Himmel war schwarzblau und völlig rein. Was ihn aber mit voller Macht anzog, war eine hohe lichtblaue Blume, die zunächst an der Quelle stand, und ihn mit ihren breiten, glänzenden Blättern berührte. ... Er sah nichts als die blaue Blume. ... die Blütenblätter zeigten einen blauen ausgebreiteten Kragen, in welchem ein zartes Gesicht schwebte. (I, 103)

The human features framed tenderly by the petals of the *blaue Blume* lend it mystery in personification which heightens its symbolic power. The flower-enclosed face is reminiscent of a passage in Jean Paul's *Hesperus*.[19]

Heinrich's father reports a similar dream which he had in his youth. He says that he met an old man in a tavern, who knew well and longed for the old, heathen times (I, 106). After the meeting Heinrich's father had the dream, in which in a hot but not oppressive atmosphere he saw a strange landscape with gigantic trees and flowers everywhere, but one flower in particular which pleased him and seemed set above the others. Heinrich interrupts to ask if it was blue, but his father does not recall. However, the old man of the tavern meeting appears in the dream and says: "Gib nur acht, auf ein blaues Blümchen, was du hier oben finden wirst" (I, 108). In this dream, where there is a suggestion of a tropic wonderland, the *blaue Blume* holds promise of future bliss. When Heinrich leaves Eisenach for Augsburg, it is as though he approaches the blue flower: "Er sah sich an der Schwelle der Ferne. ... Er war im

19. Viktor, waiting outside a church, sees Klotilde through a windowpane: "Klotildens Angesicht schwebte, wie durch Magie vorgerufen aus der zweiten Welt, dicht am Glase, und er konnte unvertrieben seine Schmetterlingflügel um diese Blume schlagen; er konnte frei in ihre grossen Augen wie in zwei mit Thauglanz gefüllte Blumenkelche sinken. Er sah nie einen so reinen Schnee des Augapfels um die blaue Himmelsöffnung, die weit in die schönere Seele ging; und wenn sie das Auge in den Garten niederschlug, stand das grosse verhüllende Augenlied mit seinen zitternden Wimpern eben so schön darüber wie eine Lilie über einer Quelle" (Jean Paul, *Werke*, I, 4, 151).

Begriff, sich in ihre blaue Flut zu tauchen. Die Wunderblume stand vor ihm" (I, 111).

The merchants whom Heinrich meets along the way speak always with one voice, in the plural (a hint of the multitude revealed as a single entity).[20] They remark to Heinrich: "Auch neigt Ihr Euch zum Wunderbaren, als dem Elemente der Dichter" (I, 114). They tell a fairy tale in which a king, who declares his daughter may marry only a poet, reveals a deep prejudice for a caste system:

Er war aus einer uralten morgenländischen Königsfamilie entsprossen. ... Seine Dichter hatten ihm unaufhörlich von seiner Verwandtschaft mit den ehemaligen übermenschlichen Beherrschern der Welt vorgesungen, und in dem Zauberspiegel ihrer Kunst war ihm der Abstand seiner Herkunft von dem Ursprunge der andern Menschen, die Herrlichkeit seines Stammes noch heller erschienen, so dass es ihn dünkte, nur durch die edlere Klasse der Dichter mit dem übrigen Menschengeschlechte zusammenzuhängen. (I, 121)

It should be remembered that the ruling class, the princes, was the second highest in the hierarchy of the Hindu caste system. At the pinnacle stood the Brahman, the poet-priest.

In the tale there is also an old man from distant lands who lives in a cottage in the woods with his son (I, 121). When his son has met and fallen in love with the princess and finally become her lover, the dawn of their awakening into a new, blissful world is heralded by a blue morning (I, 127). It is possible that *Morgen* here contains the ambiguity of meaning which it often has in Jean Paul's *Hesperus*, that is, both *morning* and *Orient*. After the princess has been away from her father for a year, lost from his ken, living with the youthful poet, there appears one evening in the garden of the palace a minstrel, dressed in an exotic but simple costume, singing a song and playing a lute (the instrument of the Indian bard). It was a strange, wondrous song about the beginning of the world, the origin of stars, plants, animals, and mankind, of a mighty sympathy of nature, of an ancient golden age and its rulers, love, and poetry; hate and barbarism appear and conquer love and

20. Bruce Haywood, in *Novalis: The Veil of Imagery* (Cambridge, Mass., 1959), pp. 96-97, makes the interesting suggestion that "the merchants . . . personify the inquiring, mercantile spirit that throughout history has led man to leave his familiar surroundings to explore new realms." They could, then, in a manner of speaking, personify those travelers to India whose books Novalis must have perused.

poetry, but the song ends with a prediction of the triumph of these two and the return of an eternal golden age (I, 130). The song has the characteristics of Hindu cosmology outlined lightly, and although the scene in the fairy tale is placed in Atlantis, Novalis' Atlantis is not the pseudo-historical land mentioned by Plato and Solon, rather it is his term for the mythic but homelike world which is everywhere and nowhere. The mythical image of India is here transformed and illuminated.

Heinrich meets Zulima, who tells him of her homeland: "Vorzüglich hielt sie sich bei dem Lobe ihrer Landsleute und ihres Vaterlandes auf. Sie schilderte den Edelmut derselben, und ihre reine starke Empfänglichkeit für die Poesie des Lebens und die wunderbare, geheimnisvolle Anmut der Natur" (I, 141). Although Zulima is from Arabia, what she says applies equally to India as it is represented in the mythical image. It is a two-fold world, a physical world enhanced by the reflection in a world of poetry:

Das Leben auf einem längst bewohnten und ehemals schon durch Fleiss, Tätigkeit und Neigung verherrlichten Boden hat einen besondern Reiz. Die Natur scheint dort menschlicher und verständlicher geworden, eine dunkle Erinnerung unter der durchsichtigen Gegenwart wirft die Bilder der Welt mit scharfen Umrissen zurück, und so geniesst man eine doppelte Welt, die eben dadurch das Schwere und Gewaltsame verliert und die zauberische Dichtung und Fabel unserer Sinne wird. (I, 142)

Here again one senses the magical world of India and thinks of *maja*, illusion.

Farther along on his journey Heinrich meets an old miner who conducts the party on an exploration of a cave. In the cavern they are astonished to find a hermit who, on his part, seems to have been expecting them. The hermit speaks of the renowned treasure of the Orient and tells of his family: "Meine Maria hatte mir zwei Kinder im Orient geboren. Sie waren die Freude unsers Leben. Die Seefahrt und die rauhere abendländische Luft störte ihre Blüte. Ich begrub sie wenig Tage nach meiner Ankunft in Europa" (I, 167). Not only did his children perish, his wife also did not survive long in the strange and harsh climate of Europe, which Novalis had before contrasted with warm and splendorous India. While the hermit and the travelers go on an inspection of the cavern, Heinrich remains behind to leaf through an amazing book in which he finds profuse illustrations which seem to depict himself in former existences (I, 168-169).

When Heinrich falls in love with Mathilde, the daughter of the poet Klingsohr, he becomes suddenly aware that the face in the heart of the blue flower was her face: "Ist mir nicht zumute wie in jenem Traume, beim Anblick der blauen Blume? Welcher sonderbare Zusammenhang ist zwischen Mathilden und dieser Blume? Jenes Gesicht, das aus dem Kelche sich mir entgegenneigte, es war Mathildens himmlisches Gesicht. . . . Sie wird meine innerste Seele, die Hüterin meines heiligen Feuers sein" (I, 181). In a second dream, then, Heinrich is united with Mathilde in a land beneath the waters, where flowers and trees address him. Here again the color pervading the dream is blue; the land beneath the stream suggests the lost Atlantis, again Novalis' "heimatliche Welt, die überall und nirgends ist," but the mythical image of India has furnished the landscape with its hues (I, 182-183).

Klingsohr is cognizant of the awakening poet in Heinrich, for he says: "Das Land der Poesie, das romantische Morgenland, hat Euch mit seiner süssen Wehmut begrüsst" (I, 187). Although he does not name India, one thinks again of the formula: India=poetic. The same proposition is apparent in a remark in the paralipomena: "Die Morgenländerin ist auch die Poesie" (I, 241). The mystic relationship between love, poetry, and nature is suggested when Klingsohr says: "Die Liebe ist stumm, nur die Poesie kann für sie sprechen. Oder die Liebe ist selbst nichts, als die höchste Naturpoesie" (I, 191). Here there is an echo of the travelers' fairy tale and the song sung by the youthful poet, a transfiguration of the idyllic golden age reflected in the mythical image.

In Klingsohr's *Märchen*, when Ginnistan leads Eros into the *Schatzkammer*, which is a large garden filled with strange animals and colorful flowers, Eros is witness to a vision that seems to depict the Flood and could almost have been a description of a Hindu painting:

Eine wunderschöne Blume schwamm glänzend auf den sanften Wogen. . . . Ein Lilienblatt bog sich über den Kelch der schwimmenden Blume; die kleine Fabel sass auf demselben, und sang zur Harfe die süssesten Lieder. In dem Kelche lag Eros selbst, über ein schönes schlummerndes Mädchen hergebeugt, die ihn fest umschlungen hielt. Eine kleinere

Blüte schloss sich um beide her, so dass sie von den Hüften an in *eine* Blume verwandelt zu sein schienen. (I, 203)

Hindu gods are often represented floating on a lotus, and sometimes one finds a god and a goddess in the most intimate embrace on a lotus blossom. Although the flower in the vision is not described as blue, it nevertheless suggests the image of the lotus.

When Fabel and Eros are wed the world seems reborn, the golden age returns: "Die Blumen und Bäume wuchsen und grünten mit Macht. Alles schien beseelt. Alles sprach und sang. . . . Die Tiere nahten sich mit freundlichen Grüssen den erwachten Menschen. Die Pflanzen bewirteten sie mit Früchten und Düften, und schmückten sie auf das zierlichste" (I, 216). The triumph of love and poetry in the *Märchen* is a fabulous remolding of the mythical image into the shape of a new mythology.

In the second part of *Heinrich von Ofterdingen* the realization of the world of poesy is even nearer for Heinrich. Sylvester, the physician, the strange mentor of Heinrich's development, says that flowers are his friends (I, 231), and describes the unique power of the poet to apprehend nature. One is reminded of the secret language of nature imagined by Novalis in the *Lehrlinge zu Sais*, a language which he equates with "die echte Sanskrit" which speaks from sheer joy:

Die Gewächse sind so die unmittelbarste Sprache des Bodens; jedes neue Blatt, jede sonderbare Blume ist irgend ein Geheimnis, was sich hervordrängt und das, weil es sich vor Liebe und Lust nicht bewegen und nicht zu Worten kommen kann, eine stumme, ruhige Pflanze wird. Findet man in der Einsamkeit eine solche Blume, ist es da nicht, als wäre alles umher verklärt und hielten sich die kleinen befiederten Töne am liebsten in ihrer Nähe auf? Man möchte für Freuden weinen, und abgesondert von der Welt nur seine Hände und Füsse in die Erde stecken, um Wurzeln zu treiben und nie diese glückliche Nachbarschaft zu verlassen. Über die ganze trockne Welt ist dieser grüne, geheimnisvolle Teppich der Liebe gezogen. Mit jedem Frühjahr wird er erneuert, und seine seltsame Schrift ist nur dem Geliebten lesbar wie der Blumenstrauss des Orients. (I, 232-233)

In this passage, too, one is reminded of the yogi in *Sakuntala* seen by Dushmanta on the mountain meadow, the yogi who has almost become one with nature in his sublime contemplation, who is almost literally rooted in the earth, as Sylvester would like to be.

Heinrich, approaching the fulfilment of understanding, speaks of the poet's perception of a more sublime universe, the intricate intermingling of myth and history, and the essential unity of the Bible and mythology:

Auch in ihm [dem Dichter] redet die höhere Stimme des Weltalls und ruft mit bezaubernden Sprüchen in erfreulichere, bekanntere Welten. Wie sich die Religion zur Tugend verhält, so die Begeisterung zur Fabellehre, und wenn in heiligen Schriften die Geschichten der Offenbarung aufbehalten sind, so bildet in den Fabellehren das Leben einer höhern Welt sich in wunderbarentstandnen Dichtungen auf mannichfache Weise ab. Fabel und Geschichte begleiten sich in den innigsten Beziehungen auf den verschlungensten Pfaden und in den seltsamsten Verkleidungen, und die Bibel und die Fabellehre sind Sternbilder *eines* Umlaufs. (I, 236-237)

Here one senses again that Novalis intended to achieve a mystic fusion of the cultures of the Orient and the Occident through their religions and their mythologies.

Tieck, in his report about the planned continuation of the novel, says that after Heinrich had comprehended the heroic age and antiquity he was to go to the Orient, for which he had longed since childhood. The novel was to retain the same characteristic hue through the most varied events and was to be always charged with the glow of the blue flower; it was to mix the most varied myths with reminiscences of and allusions to Hindu mythology (I, 257). There were to be enigmatic references to America and the East Indies.

In the paralipomena to this fragmentary novel there are such entries as: "Ostindianische Pflanzen—etwas indische Mythologie. 'Sakontala.' Gespräche der Blumen und Tiere über Menschen, Religion, Natur und Wissenschaften" (I, 242). Novalis noted: "Die Poesie der verschiednen Nationen und Zeiten. Ossian. Edda. Morgenländische Poesie" (I, 244). And still another hint of the Oriental is given: "Kriegslieder. Orientalische Gedichte" (I, 246). Finally, reports Tieck, Heinrich the poet was to participate in a singing contest with Klingsohr; their songs were to symbolize the conflict of the forces of good and evil, religion and irreligion, the visible and the invisible worlds. Sciences were to be poetized and: "Indianische

Pflanzen werden besungen: indische Mythologie in neuer Ver-
klärung" (I, 258).

It was George Brandes who first suggested casually that in the
second part of the novel the lotus of India was intended to contribute to the nature of the *blaue Blume* symbol.[21] Later, E. Spenlé in
his Novalis study says, in a footnote to his retelling of Heinrich's
dream of the blue flower, that it is not possible from Novalis' description to identify the botanical species of the flower, but it nevertheless resembles the blue lotus of the theosophists. As a matter of
fact, he continues, Novalis proposed to extol the flowers of India in
the continuation of the novel.[22] These suggestions of a link between
the *blaue Blume* and the blue lotus, made as asides with no offer of
proof, have brought decided refutation which may have been over-
hasty. Hiebel, in his essay on the flower, sums up its symbolism with:
"Die blaue Blume ist also das Symbol eines Sinnes übersinnlicher
Erkenntnis." He then mentions in a footnote that in a yoga system
a heart-lotus is considered to be a super-perceptive sense organ. He
suggests further that Spenlé alludes to this aspect of the lotus, and
Hiebel implies that Novalis was cognizant of the symbolism of the
lotus in yoga. Although he admits that there are remarkable paral-
lels, Hiebel insists that the *blaue Blume* is in no way derived from
Indic religious philosophy.[23]

That the *blaue Blume* has any connection with the blue lotus of
India, Miss Hecker thinks questionable. In none of Novalis' works
is there mention of the lotus, she points out, and she sees no relationship between the religious connotations of the blue lotus and
the philosophical, aesthetical content of the *blaue Blume*. Further,
she discerns no immediate analogy between the *blaue Blume* and

21. George Brandes, *Main Currents in Nineteenth Century Literature*, trans.
Diana White and Mary Morison (6 vols.; London, 1901-1905), *The Romantic
School*, II, 217. Volumes I, II, and V were translated by the two individuals noted;
volumes III, IV, and VI were translated by Mary Morison alone. The original Danish
work, *Hovedstrømninger i det 19de aarhundredes litteratur*, was published between
1872 and 1890.

22. E. Spenlé, *Novalis* (Paris, 1904), p. 314, n. 2.

23. Hiebel, "Zur Interpretation," p. 334. In the article cited, Hiebel calls attention
to Arthur Avalon's [John George Woodroffe] *The Serpent Power*, a translation of
Shat-Chakra Nirūpana and *Pādūka-Panchaka*, two works on Laya Yoga containing
the descriptions of symbolic, supersensual lotuses. There was apparently no translation
of these works until the appearance of Avalon's book in 1924; certainly no translation
was extant during Novalis' lifetime.

the myths of animate flowers in India.[24] She considers that these observations refute Spenlé's identification of the *blaue Blume* with the lotus.

However, several objections may be made both to her remarks and to those of Hiebel. First, Novalis' awareness of the lotus was not gleaned from any knowledge of yoga but exclusively from remarks made by Herder, from travel books containing statements and illustrations concerning the mythological referents of the lotus, and from the slight number of translations of Sanskrit literature then available. Novalis knew almost nothing of yoga systems—no Sanskrit work on yoga had been translated in his time, and yogis were known simply as strange ascetics who sought to achieve perfect existence by self-punishing ritual and disembodied immersion in mystic thought. The idea of an inner sense-organ with intuitive powers came to Novalis probably from his readings of the Dutch philosopher Hemsterhuis.[25] Second, the *blaue Blume*, without yoga connotations, does merge in imagery with aspects of the Indic mythological lotus, and Novalis could have used the lotus as a corollary contribution to the symbol without ever having mentioned the flower by name in his works. The *blaue Blume* exists in association with images and events which clearly indicate an Indic connection. And last, although there is no personification of the flower, it can perhaps be shown that there is a direct relationship between the *blaue Blume* and the idea of metempsychosis.

A stream of Indic thought pervades the writings of Novalis, and the blue lotus pervades Indic thought. It is the symbol of the creative force in nature and is associated with every god or goddess endowed with creative powers in Hindu mythology. The blue lotus is present from the beginning of the cosmology of the Hindu, for Brahma, the creative principle of the *trimurti*, or Hindu trinity, is represented sitting on a lotus petal in contemplation when the world was still covered with primordial torrents. Parasakti-Bhavani, the mother of the *trimurti*, is depicted half-enclosed in a lotus blossom, sheltering three eggs. Lakshmi, the goddess of abundance, is shown floating in a lotus. One thinks of Eros' vision in the treasure chamber in Klingsohr's *Märchen*. The grotto in which Heinrich finds the

24. Hecker, p. 29.
25. Theodor Haering, *Novalis als Philosoph* (Stuttgart, 1954), pp. 630-632.

blaue Blume is reminiscent of the India of the mythical image in its exotic wildness. The female face which Heinrich sees peering from the heart of the *blaue Blume* links it even more closely to the lotus in its mythological images in India and also to the idea of metempsychosis.

Hans Peter Jaeger discerns an association in Novalis of India and the color blue. In his work on Novalis and Hölderlin, he says the time of fulfilment in Hölderlin stands under the aegis of the color green. But in Novalis, when the touch of the "Indic homeland" is felt, blue appears again and again.[26] Not only is blue in some respects native to Hindustan (the dye from India is called indigo), it also plays a significant role in Hindu mythology: Krishna means *blue*, and Vishnu in the avatar of Krishna has a blue body.

In the paralipomena to the novel, Novalis notes: "Farbencharacter. Alles blau in meinem Buche" (I, 245). It is easy to establish that Novalis follows his dictum. The hue of the whole novel is blue, reflecting the *blaue Blume* and infusing its spell at every turn. The attribute of blue is given to things which are blue by nature, such as the sky, waters, mist, the flower, the delicate veins of a fair skin; things which may appear to be blue, such as distances, shadowed columns, and walls; the manufactured blue of the veil of Sophie; and an appellative blue, Cyane (German: *Kornblume*, from the Greek Κύανος, meaning dark blue).

The main problem is to find, if possible, why Novalis chose the color blue to set the mood of his novel, why he endowed his wondrous flower with this color. Having read the novel, one might say with Goethe: "Wie wir einen Gegenstand, der vor uns flieht, gern verfolgen, so sehen wir das Blaue gern an, nicht weil es auf uns dringt, sondern weil es uns nach sich zieht."[27] There is in the color of blue a feeling of nostalgia, a sense of unfulfilled longing. Jutta Hecker notes that blue is the traditional color of the veil of the Madonna, and Hiebel interprets the figure of Sophie as that of the Madonna.[28] Such use of a blue veil in the novel occurs only once, revealing a Christian frame of reference emphatically. According to the paralipomena, Novalis intended a reconciliation of the Chris-

26. Hans Peter Jaeger, *Hölderlin-Novalis. Grenzen der Sprache* (Zürich, 1949), p. 40.
27. Goethe, *Werke*, II, 1, 315, No. 781.
28. Hecker, p. 23; Hiebel, *Novalis*, pp. 142-143.

tian religion with the heathen. By heathen he refers not only to the religion of ancient Greece but also to those of Arabia and India. Thus one important facet of the *blaue Blume* symbol, not hitherto noted, is the synthesis of Eastern and Western religions, a synthesis already effected in the symbol itself, which is in essence a macro-symbol, containing in itself a universe of referents. The blue in Heinrich's dream and the blue which appears throughout the work as a motif, a chord representing the longing for love, for poesy, for the land of fulfilment, is an aspect of the mythical image of India. It may be suggested that in his use of the color blue, and in particular in his choice of this color for the symbol which bears the heaviest meaning, Novalis had India also in mind and intended to create a new mythology by a mystic synthesis of traditional motifs from the East and the West.

But perhaps the most significant hint that the *blaue Blume* in one aspect may have been the blue lotus of India is given in a note, hitherto overlooked, which Georg Forster appended to his *Sakontala*: "Auch das musste die Lotosblume den Indiern wichtig machen, dass nirgends deutlicher die Bildung der Pflanze schon im Samenkorn sichtbar ist."[29] Novalis must have seen this note in his reading of the play. It gains special importance in relation to the *blaue Blume* in its primary function as the symbol of the unfolding of poetic vision.

In *Heinrich von Ofterdingen*, in which Novalis reveals the development and growth of a poet who contains the seed of poesy in his soul, he presents as the symbol of the most sublime poesy, as a symbol of the germination and flowering of the poet, a blue flower similar to the lotus of India, in the seed of which the unfolding of the blossom is foreseen. A further dimension is furnished the symbol in its unitive function, as the mediator between alien religions and the agent reuniting man and nature. Novalis has, in the prism of his imagination, taken this flower and other symbolic flowers and focused their innate characteristics into the shape of a supreme poetic symbol which is capable of an infinite number of interpretations within and even beyond the frame of the novel. Here the mythical image of India found its most skilled conjuror.

29. Forster, IX, 310.

> 5 . Des Ganges Ufer hörten des Freudengotts
> Triumph, als allerobernd vom Indus her
> Der junge Bacchus kam, mit heilgem
> Weine vom Schlafe die Völker weckend.
> —HÖLDERLIN

With fantastic, intricate symbols Novalis weaves the mythical image of India into the tapestry of a new mythology. Friedrich Hölderlin (1770-1843) presents a purer, more serene conception woven into a gossamer cloth with simpler and finer lines, but with a sense of the enigmatic sustained throughout. Both express a yearning for the golden age seen in the mythical image, but a golden age antedating Greek culture and located generally in the Indic landscape, an age when nature and man were joined in a bond of close understanding and sympathy, when philosophy and poetry and mythology were inextricably entwined. The essential aspect of the image which is present in Novalis but absent in Hölderlin is the sense for the magic, the wonder. In place of this pursuit of the fantastic, Hölderlin applies himself to the creation of an enchanted language of his own to proclaim a synthesis of East and West. Novalis' synthesis occurs on a mystic level, while Hölderlin's synthesis is concentered in great symbols. Wilhelm Böhm in his Hölderlin study says that Hölderlin's poetry always remains aesthetic, even when it treats myth. He refers undoubtedly to the lack of a sense of Wunder in Hölderlin. He says further that within the boundaries of aestheticism Hölderlin develops his myth of the synthesis of the Orient and the Occident with the greatest intrepidity.[1]

Two parallel attitudes toward the mythical image of India may be discerned in Hölderlin's works. Under the influence of Herder the attitude predominant in his early writings is one of longing for a more intimate intercourse with nature, praise for the simplicity of a young mankind, and a yearning for the return of the golden age of antiquity. His glance, and the glance of his creations, is turned toward the East. The second attitude is apparent after Hyperion, in the great hymns and elegies, when the mystic power of the East wings its way toward the West: he retains his nostalgia for the golden age, but he seeks to establish it anew in a fusion of the two cultures, by a synthesis of the East and the West.

---

1. Wilhelm Böhm, Hölderlin (2 vols.; Halle/Saale, 1928-1930), II, 372.

The motif of Dionysus, the god who legend says came to Greece from India, the god who was born in the shade of Meru, the Hindu Olympus, appears in "An unsre grossen Dichter" (1798) as the link between Asia and the West. L. S. Salzberger, in his monograph on Hölderlin, writes:

> For Hölderlin the link between the past and present is genius. In his eyes the genius is a god-like creature, and the historical panorama of his poetry consists in a chain of these beings rising like single luminous peaks in a mountain-range which stretches from prehistoric times down to the poet's own age. In the distance are the gods of Olympus, whose origins point far back into the mysterious Asiatic past.[2]

The Ganges and the Indus, holy rivers of India, are visited by Dionysus-Bacchus:

> Des Ganges Ufer hörten des Freudengotts
> Triumph, als allerobernd vom Indus her
> Der junge Bacchus kam, mit heilgem
> Weine vom Schlafe die Völker weckend.
>
> O weckt, ihr Dichter! weckt sie vom Schlummer auch,
> Die jetzt noch schlafen, gebt die Gesetze, gebt
> Uns Leben, siegt, Heroën! ihr nur
> Habt der Eroberung Recht, wie Bacchus.[3]

In the second verse cited, Hölderlin apostrophizes the poet, the modern Bacchus, urging him to awaken the people and quicken them. This theme is extended in a later version of the poem, in "Dichterberuf" (1801), in which the synthesis is more prominent (II, 1, 46-47).

The idyl of "Emilie vor ihrem Brauttag" (1799) contains a symbol which occurs frequently in Hölderlin: the spring which becomes a brook and a stream and a river, flowing into the sea and drawing with it the longing of a human soul for a different clime. Referring to the spring in the woods, Emilie says to Klara in her poetic letter:

> Wie oft, du Liebe! stand ich dort und sah
> Ihm nach aus seiner Bäume Dämmerung
> Hinunter in die Ferne, wo zum Bach'
> Es wird, zum Strome, sehnte mich mit ihm
> Hinaus—wer weiss, wohin? (I, 1, 277)

2. L. S. Salzberger, *Hölderlin* (New Haven, Conn., 1952), p. 43.
3. Friedrich Hölderlin, *Sämtliche Werke*, ed. Friedrich Beissner (6 vols.; Stuttgart, 1943-1961), I, 1, 261. References will be made to this edition parenthetically by volume, section, and page. The spelling has been modernized.

And then, in a letter from Corsica, her brother refers her to Horace and paraphrases him as follows:

> "Klagt nicht mehr! kommt in neues Land! so sagt' er.
> "Der Ozean, der die Gefild' umschweift,
> "Erwartet uns. Wir suchen seelige
> "Gefilde, reiche Inseln, wo der Boden
> "Noch ungepflügt die Früchte jährlich gibt,
> "Und unbeschnitten noch der Weinstock blüht,
> "Wo der Olivenzweig nach Wunsche wächst,
> "Und ihren Baum die Feige keimend schmückt,
> "Wo Honig rinnt aus hohler Eich' und leicht
> "Gewässer rauscht von Bergeshöhn. —Noch manches
> "Bewundern werden wir die Glücklichen.—
> "Es sparte für ein frommes Volk Saturnus Sohn
> "Dies Ufer auf, da er die goldne Zeit
> "Mit Erze mischte.—Lebe wohl, du Liebe! (I, 1, 280-281)[4]

The idyllic abundance offered by nature here, and the comparison of this beneficent land with that of the golden age, the nostalgia for an unspoiled and fruitful paradise is reminiscent of India as it is projected in the mythical image—it matters not that the land referred to here is Corsica, nor that the poet is Horace, for the landscape is illuminated by the eye of the poet who perceives the image.

The influence of Herder on *Hyperion* (1799) is suggested by Böhm, who says that the mythological religion and the love of antiquity taught by Adamas, and proclaimed by the seminarians, refer perhaps to Herder, who dominated Hölderlin's first ventures. It may also be due to Herder that Adamas sets out for the Far East to seek a people of a rare perfection, since in his *Ideen* Herder indicates that the course of civilization and history gives demonstrable proof that mankind originated in Asia. Böhm continues that in the poem which has been called "Hyperions Schicksalslied" the image of the bud is reminiscent of Herder's original idea that humanitarianism is only the preliminary formation of the bud of a future flower.[5] Böhm might have mentioned also the harmony of nature and man and the ideal, Sakuntala-like character of Diotima, both of which are aspects of the mythical image of India which Hölderlin could have gleaned from Herder.

4. Horace, *Epodes*, 16, 39 ff.
5. Böhm, I, 263-264.

A feeling of unity with all creation, a longing to return to the source of all being (exemplified in the Hindu idea of an emanant Supreme Deity) is found voiced by Hyperion:

Eines zu sein mit Allem, das ist Leben der Gottheit, das ist der Himmel des Menschen.

Eines zu sein mit Allem, was lebt, in seeliger Selbstvergessenheit wiederzukehren in's All der Natur, das ist der Gipfel der Gedanken und Freuden. (III, 9)

With his teacher Adamas, Hyperion goes out to study nature: "Bald stieg er auf die Berge mit mir; des Tags, um die Blumen der Heide und des Walds und die wilden Moose des Felsen, des Nachts, um über uns die heiligen Sterne zu schauen, und nach menschlicher Weise zu verstehen" (III, 14). Nature is friendly and endowed with an enchantment: "Wie Lüftchen über die Meeresfläche walteten über uns die freundlichen Zauber der Natur" (III, 30). The ancient harmony of man and nature no longer exists, however; nature has become an idea, emotionless: "Von Kinderharmonie sind einst die Völker ausgegangen, die Harmonie der Geister wird der Anfang einer neuen Weltgeschichte sein. Von Pflanzenglück begannen die Menschen und wuchsen auf. . . . Ideal wird, was Natur war . . . Ideal ist, was Natur war" (III, 63). In this passage two compounds reflect the mythical image: *Kinderharmonie* and *Pflanzenglück* are echoes of the idyllic existence of the ancient Hindus. Hyperion expresses a longing for the return of that time, when man was a god and untamed:

Der Mensch kanns nicht verleugnen, dass er einst glücklich war, wie die Hirsche des Forsts und nach unzähligen Jahren klimmt noch in uns ein Sehnen nach den Tagen der Urwelt, wo jeder die Erde durchstreifte, wie ein Gott, eh, ich weiss nicht was? den Menschen zahm gemacht, und noch, statt Mauern und totem Holz, die Seele der Welt, die heilige Luft allgegenwärtig ihn umfing. (III, 112)

The almost religious adoration of nature is signified by the use of *heilig* to modify natural phenomena: *heilige Sterne, heilige Luft.* Hölderlin does not go so far as to personify the lesser phenomena, as did the Hindus in their mythology; but he is aware of their religious function. He longs for the return of the golden age, which he sees reflected in children: "Dass man werden kann, wie die

Kinder, dass noch die goldne Zeit der Unschuld wiederkehrt, die Zeit des Friedens und der Freiheit, dass doch Eine Freude ist, Eine Ruhestätte auf Erden!" (III, 51). This is not a yearning for the innocence of childhood alone, but a yearning for the innocent state of man in nature. Another expression of the golden age, when beauty was eternal and man one with his gods, is the self-awareness man attains in art:

Das erste Kind der menschlichen, der göttlichen Schönheit ist die Kunst. In ihr verjüngt und wiederholt der göttliche Mensch sich selbst. Er will sich selber fühlen, darum stellt er seine Schönheit gegenüber sich. So gab der Mensch sich seine Götter. Denn im Anfang war der Mensch und seine Götter Eins, da, sich selber unbekannt, die ewige Schönheit war.
(III, 79)

He is aware of the intrinsic relation between philosophy, as a science, and poetry: "Die Dichtung . . . ist der Anfang und das Ende dieser Wissenschaft [der Philosophie]. Wie Minerva aus Jupiters Haupt, entspringt sie aus der Dichtung eines unendlichen göttlichen Seins. Und so läuft am End' auch wieder in ihr das Unvereinbare in der geheimnisvollen Quelle der Dichtung zusammen" (III, 81).

The direction of longing and fulfilment in *Hyperion* is the East: Asia and India. Adamas goes to India to seek an ideal people:

Es ist, als zürnt ich meinem Adamas, dass er mich verliess, aber ich zürn' ihm nicht. O er wollte ja wieder kommen!
In der Tiefe von Asien soll ein Volk von seltner Trefflichkeit verborgen sein; dahin trieb ihn seine Hoffnung weiter. (III, 16-17)

Hyperion and Diotima look longingly into the endless East: "Vorn am Rande des Berggipfels standen wir nun, und sahn hinaus, in den unendlichen Osten" (III, 54). And his friend Alabanda, at parting, goes eastward (III, 152).

Hyperion himself reveals a feeling of kinship with nature. When Alabanda deserts him the first time, he cries out: "Nun sprach ich nimmer zu der Blume, du bist meine Schwester! und zu den Quellen, wir sind Eines Geschlechts!" (III, 42). When he falls in love with Diotima, he compares their love to a flower image: "Wir waren Eine Blume nur, und unsre Seelen lebten in einander, wie die Blume, wenn sie liebt, und ihre zarte Freuden im verschlossnen Kelche verbirgt" (III, 61). One thinks of Eros and his nameless companion floating together on a lotus, the lower part of their bodies hidden in a blossom. An empathy and affection for plants is even more striking in Diotima. On one occasion she cries out a greeting to the trees: "O meine alten freundlichen Bäume! rief Diotima, als hätte sie sie in langer Zeit nicht gesehen" (III, 72). She reveals the traits remarked in Sakuntala, an inborn gentleness and a loving sympathy for flowers:

Unter den Blumen war ihr Herz zu Hause, als wär' es eine von ihnen.
Sie nannte sie alle mit Namen, schuf ihnen aus Liebe neue, schönere, und wusste genau die fröhlichste Lebenszeit von jeder.
Wie eine Schwester, wenn aus jeder Ecke ein Geliebtes ihr entgegenkömmt, und jedes gerne zuerst gegrüsst sein möchte, so war das stille Wesen mit Aug und Hand beschäftigt, seelig zerstreut, wenn auf der Wiese wir gingen, oder im Walde.
Und das war so ganz nicht angenommen, angebildet, das war so mit ihr aufgewachsen.
Es ist doch ewig gewiss und zeigt sich überall; je unschuldiger, schöner eine Seele, desto vertrauter mit den andern glücklichen Leben, die man seelenlos nennt. (III, 56)

Diotima is here a projection of Sakuntala, the serene and poised Hindu princess who has the most loving regard and closest affinity for plants and blossoms. At the end of the novel Hyperion himself, in an ecstatic reunion with the powers and forces of nature, with the creatures of nature, experiences a mystic reunion with his dead, beloved Diotima:

O Sonne, o ihr Lüfte, rief ich dann, bei euch allein noch lebt mein Herz, wie unter Brüdern!
So gab ich mehr und mehr der seeligen Natur mich hin und fast zu endlos. Wär' ich so gerne doch zum Kinde geworden, um ihr näher zu sein, hätt' ich so gern doch weniger gewusst und wäre geworden, wie der reine Lichtstrahl, um ihr näher zu sein! o einen Augenblick in ihrem Frieden, ihrer Schöne mich zu fühlen. . .
Einst sass ich fern im Feld', an einem Brunnen, im Schatten epheugrüner Felsen und überhängender Blütenbüsche. Es war der schönste Mittag, den ich kenne. Süsse Lüfte wehten und in morgendlicher Frische glänzte noch das Land und still in seinem heimatlichen Aether lächelte das Licht. . . . allein war meine Liebe mit dem Frühling, und ein unbegreiflich Sehnen war in mir. Diotima, rief ich, wo bist du, o wo bist du? Und mir war, als hört' ich Diotimas Stimme. . .
Bei den Meinen, rief sie, bin ich, bei den Deinen, die der irre Menschengeist misskennt!

. . .

"O du, so dacht' ich, mit deinen Göttern, Natur! ... nur du lebst, und was die Friedenslosen erzwungen, erdacht, es schmilzt, wie Perlen von Wachs, hinweg von deinen Flammen!

"Wie lang ists, dass sie dich entbehren? o wie lang ists, dass ihre Menge dich schilt, gemein nennt dich und deine Götter, die Lebendigen, die Seeligstillen!

. . .

"Ihr Quellen der Erd'! ihr Blumen! und ihr Wälder und ihr Adler und du brüderliches Licht! wie alt und neu ist unsere Liebe! ... wir lieben den Aether doch all' und inningst im Innersten gleichen wir uns.

"Auch wir, auch wir sind nicht geschieden, Diotima.... Lebendige Töne sind wir, stimmen zusammen in Deinem Wohllaut, Natur! (III, 158-159)

On such a rapturous note does the novel close.

Salzberger remarks that Hölderlin's figure of Empedokles "is possessed by a most un-Greek longing for nature,"[6] and Böhm says that nature myths, the ether, springs, and trees which dominate *Hyperion* dominate also the early versions of *Empedokles*.[7] The un-Greek longing for nature is a projection of the mythical image of India. In *Der Tod des Empedokles*, the first version, which was written at the same time as *Hyperion* in its final version (particularly the second part), that is, 1797-1798, the same feeling of sympathy for nature exists: a quickening of the plant world, almost a personification of flowers. Panthea, speaking of Empedokles, says:

> Man sagt, die Pflanzen merkten auf
> ihn, wo er wandre, und die Wasser unter der Erde
> strebten herauf da, wo sein Stab den Boden berühre!
>
> . . . .
>
> und wenn er bei Gewittern in den Himmel blicke,
> teile die Wolke sich und hervorschimmere der
> heitere Tag.— (IV, 1, 3)

One feels here the first stirrings of a synthesis of the Orient and Christianity; Empedokles has a Christ-like power over the elements. Panthea speaks further of the attraction of nature for Empedokles:

> ... ihn zieht in seine Schatten
> Die stille Pflanzenwelt, wo er sich schöner findet.
> (IV, 1, 6)

6. Salzberger, p. 33.
7. Böhm, I, 428.

Empedokles himself is a poet-priest, such as Novalis envisioned, who praises nature and brings it offerings of song:

> Mir wieder, seid, wie sonst, ihr Glücklichen,
> Ihr irrelosen Bäume meines Hains!
> Ihr wuchst indessen fort und täglich tränkte
> Des Himmels Quelle die Bescheidenen
> Mit Licht und Lebensfunken säte
> Befruchtend auf die Blühenden der Aether.—
> O innige Natur! ich habe dich
> Vor Augen, kennest du den Freund noch
> Den Hochgeliebten kennest du mich nimmer?
> Den Priester, der lebendigen Gesang,
> Wie frohvergossnes Opferblut, dir brachte? (IV, 1, 14)

He counsels his adherents:

> O gebt euch der Natur, eh sie euch nimmt!— (IV, 1, 65)

The receptiveness of the spirit of Empedokles for the manifestations of nature is also perceived in these verses:

> Es sammeln in der Tiefe sich, Natur,
> Die Quellen deiner Höhn und deine Freuden,
> Sie kamen all' in meiner Brust zu ruhn,
> Sie waren Eine Wonne.... (IV, 1, 70)

The drama remained unfinished, but it was to end with the union of Empedokles with the seething heart of nature, the fiery gulf of Aetna.[8]

In "Der Archipelagus" (1800) springtime turns the poet's gaze to the island chain of Greece which points toward Asia, where man is reminded of a golden age:

> ...denn immer im Frühling,
> Wenn der Lebenden sich das Herz erneut und die erste

---

8. Walther Kranz, in *Empedokles, antike Gestalt und romantische Neuschöpfung* (Zürich, 1949), is completely oblivious to Oriental features of Empedokles' philosophy. With no knowledge, apparently, of its source, he quotes Karoline von Günderode's farewell lines as evidence of renewed Romantic interest in pre-Socratic philosophy, particularly Empedokles' sympathy with the elements as part of the cosmos and belief in the mutual interpenetration and harmony of nature (pp. 104-105). In a note to the quotation he analyzes the meter of the lines briefly and comments that Karoline first names five elements, as though she were a student of Aristotle, but at the end she sums up with the traditional four (p. 358). Kranz obviously has no idea that the lines are Indic.

Liebe den Menschen erwacht und goldner Zeiten Erinnerung,
Komm' ich zu dir und grüss' in deiner Stille dich, Alter!

(II, 1, 103)

Hölderlin addresses the ocean; the Asian moonlight and the Oriental sun do not merely approach from the east but are symbols of cul-
ture-bearers from the East. *Morgen* can be given the same ambiguity
which it has in Jean Paul's *Hesperus*:

> . . . oft am dämmernden Abend,
> Wenn von Asiens Bergen herein das heilige Mondlicht
> Kömmt und die Sterne sich in deiner Woge begegnen,
> Leuchtest du von himmlischem Glanz, und so, wie sie wandeln,
> Wechseln die Wasser dir, es tönt die Weise der Brüder
> Droben, ihr Nachtgesang, im liebenden Busen dir wieder.
> Wenn die allverklärende dann, die Sonne des Tages,
> Sie, des Orients Kind, die Wundertätige, da ist,
> Dann die Lebenden all' im goldenen Traume beginnen
> Den die Dichtende stets des Morgens ihnen bereitet,
> Dir, dem trauernden Gott, dir sendet sie froheren Zauber.

(II, 1, 104)

Concerning the fragmentary "Am Quell der Donau" (1800)
Böhm says that here the homage for Mother Earth who taught
mankind to speak becomes a homage to Mother Asia who sent the
West an awakener, the voice imparting culture to man.[9]

> . . . so kam
> Das Wort aus Osten zu uns,
> Und an Parnassos Felsen und am Kithäron hör' ich
> O Asia, das Echo von dir und es bricht sich
> Am Kapitol und jählings herab von den Alpen
>
> Kommt eine Fremdlingin sie
> Zu uns, die Erweckerin,
> Die menschenbildende Stimme. (II, 1, 126)

Asia as the source of religions is praised:

> O Asia, deiner Starken, o Mutter!
> Die furchtlos vor den Zeichen der Welt,
> Und den Himmel auf Schultern und alles Schicksal,
> Taglang auf Bergen gewurzelt,
> Zuerst es verstanden,
> Allein zu reden
> Zu Gott. . . . (II, 1, 128)

9. Böhm, II, 423.

One is reminded here of the yogi standing before the palace of Kasyapa, almost rooted to the earth in the unmoving, unwavering introspection and contemplation of God.

In "Unter den Alpen gesungen" (1801) Hölderlin says that innocence is beloved by nature and is privy to the language of nature, whence come the religions. Only from such innocence can man discover the revelations of God:

> Siehe! das rauhe Tier des Feldes, gerne
> Dient und trauet es dir, der stumme Wald spricht
> Wie vor Alters, seine Sprüche zu dir, es
> > Lehren die Berge
>
> Heil'ge Gesetze dich, und was noch jetzt uns
> Vielerfahrenen offenbar der grosse
> Vater werden heisst, du darfst es allein uns
> > Helle verkünden. (II, 1, 44)

Salzberger remarks: "The landscape of Hölderlin's mature poetry is topographical and symbolical at the same time. Everything has its being concurrently in space, time, and eternity. His grandiose geographical symbolism embraces all those countries of Indo Germanic civilisation which meant so much to him: India . . . ."[10] With this in mind, one might consider the Alps in this poem to be Meru, the seat of the Hindu gods.

In "Brot und Wein" (1801) the coming of the gods is described. Their first arrival is perceptible only to the children (in the mythical image the origin of religion is placed in the cradle of mankind, in ancient India, and the Hindus are held to be the epitome of a blissful childlike race); but when the gods are revealed to man matured, the revelation is of one who was known for ages before as the One and All, an immanent God:

> Unempfunden kommen sie erst, es streben entgegen
> Ihnen die Kinder, zu hell kommend, zu blendend das Glück,
> Und es scheut sie der Mensch, kaum weiss zu sagen ein Halbgott,
> Wer mit Namen sie sind, die mit den Gaben ihm nahn.
>
> . . . .
> > . . . dann aber in Wahrheit
> Kommen sie selbst, und gewohnt werden die Menschen des Glücks
> Und des Tags und zu schaun die Offenbaren, das Antlitz
> Derer, welche, schon längst Eines und Alles genannt,

---

10. Salzberger, p. 44.

Tief die verschwiegene Brust mit freier Genüge gefüllet,
  Und zuerst und allein alles Verlangen beglückt. (II, 1, 92)

One senses here a fusion of the religion of the Orient and of Christianity. The poem is a combination of heathen and Christian symbols brought into reconciliation, so it is not surprising to find the mythical image of India present here, too.

Böhm finds that Hölderlin gives freer rein in his mature poems to an inclination to combine abstract ideas with concrete details, for example, in his depiction of the flight to Asia in "Andenken" (1801), where the river, already broad as a sea, is transformed into the ocean leading to India.[11] Hölderlin asks where his friends have gone. The answer reminds one of the departures of Alabanda and Adamas in *Hyperion*, although here Bellarmin is included also among the departed.

> Wo aber sind die Freunde? Bellarmin
> Mit dem Gefährten? Mancher
> Trägt Scheue, an die Quelle zu gehn;
> Es beginnet nämlich der Reichtum
> Im Meere. Sie,
> Wie Maler, bringen zusammen
> Das Schöne der Erd' und verschmähn
> Den geflügelten Krieg nicht, und
> Zu wohnen einsam, jahrlang, unter
> Dem entlaubten Mast...
>
> . . . .
> Nun aber sind zu Indiern
> Die Männer gegangen,
> Dort an der luftigen Spitz'
> An Traubenbergen, wo herab
> Die Dordogne kommt
> Und zusammen mit der prächt'gen
> Garonne meerbreit
> Ausgehet der Strom. Es nehmet aber
> Und gibt Gedächtnis die See,
> Und die Lieb' auch heftet fleissig die Augen,
> Was bleibet aber, stiften die Dichter. (II, 1, 189)

Emil Lehmann, in *Hölderlins Lyrik*, says that India is for Bellarmin and Hölderlin's other friends a kind of fount, the land of the origin of human culture, the land from which the eagle of humanitarian-

---

11. Böhm, II, 372.

ism flew. The friends have gone there in order to return home with rich treasures, in order to aid in the renewal of their homeland by grasping the knowledge of the development of humanity.[12]

Lehmann perceives a connection between "Andenken" and "Der Einzige" (1801). Even the title of "Der Einzige" points to the resplendent festival of universal love in "Andenken." In the former the expedition into distances, the compulsion to the All was discernible everywhere—in the latter, images of imprisonment are in the foreground. The shipmen sail in "Der Einzige" to India; in "Andenken" the worship of Dionysus comes from India, from the Orient comes Christianity.[13] The mythical image of India furnished the Hindu Dionysus legend, which Hölderlin transmutes into an expression of the origin of Christianity, a mystic spiritual intoxication.

> ... zu sehr
> O Christus! häng' ich an dir,
> Wiewohl Herakles Bruder
> Und kühn bekenn' ich, du
> Bist Bruder auch des Eviers, der
> An den Wagen spannte
> Die Tiger und hinab
> Bis an den Indus
> Gebietend freudigen Dienst
> Den Weinberg stiftet und
> Den Grimm bezähmte der Völker. (II, 1, 154)

Dionysus becomes here the mystic founder of a religion, but in India, where the Romanticist saw the beginning of religion in the mythical image.

"Die Wanderung," "Der Rhein," and "Germanien" (all 1801) are three poems which Hölderlin designated as a cycle. Concerning these, Böhm says "Die Wanderung" and "Germanien" are amplifications of myth from the Orient and the Occident, of antiquity and the poet's homeland, and between these philosophically factual contrasts is "Der Rhein," which embraces an evenly hovering contrast of two types of men.[14] "Die Wanderung" contains a description of the intermingling of the Orient and the West through the

---

12. Emil Lehmann, *Hölderlins Lyrik* (Stuttgart, 1922), p. 260.
13. *Ibid.*, p. 265.
14. Böhm, II, 436.

symbolic meeting of peoples of Germanic stock with the peoples of Asia:

> Ich aber will dem Kaukasos zu!
> Denn sagen hört ich
> Noch heut in den Lüften:
> Frei sei'n, wie Schwalben, die Dichter.
> Auch hat mir ohnedies
> In jüngeren Tagen Eines vertraut,
> Es seien vor alter Zeit
> Die Eltern einst, das deutsche Geschlecht,
> Still fortgezogen von Wellen der Donau
> Am Sommertage, da diese
> Sich Schatten suchten, zusammen
> Mit Kindern der Sonn'
> Am schwarzen Meere gekommen;
> Und nicht umsonst sei dies
> Das gastfreundliche genennet.
>
> Denn, als sie erst sich angesehen,
> Da nahten die Anderen erst; dann setzten auch
> Die Unseren sich neugierig unter den Ölbaum,
> Doch als sich ihre Gewande berührt,
> Und keiner vernehmen konnte
> Die eigene Rede des andern, wäre wohl
> Entstanden ein Zwist, wenn nicht aus Zweigen herunter
> Gekommen wäre die Kühlung,
> Die Lächeln über das Angesicht
> Der Streitenden öfters breitet, und eine Weile
> Sahn still sie auf, dann reichten sie sich
> Die Hände liebend einander. Und bald
>
> Vertauschten sie Waffen und all
> Die lieben Güter des Hauses,
> Vertauschten das Wort auch und es wünschten
> Die freundlichen Väter umsonst nichts
> Beim Hochzeitjubel den Kindern.
> Denn aus den heiligvermählten
> Wuchs schöner, denn Alles,
> Was vor und nach
> Von Menschen sich nannt', ein Geschlecht auf. Wo,
> Wo aber wohnt ihr, liebe Verwandten,
> Dass wir das Bündnis wiederbegehn,
> Und der teuern Ahmen gedenken? (II, 1, 138-140)

Aspects of the mythical image are visible here: the hospitable Hindu, the children of the sun (the two chief ruling houses in Indic legend are descended from the sun and the moon), which may be interpreted simply as dwellers of tropic climes. In "Der Rhein," the great river—symbol of genius, the poet—desires to flow toward Asia, but fate decrees a different course:

> Er schied und wandern wollt', und ungeduldig ihn
> Nach Asia trieb die königliche Seele.
> Doch unverständig ist
> Das Wünschen vor dem Schicksal. (II, 1, 143)

In "Germanien" Hölderlin's incessant urge to achieve a synthesis of the Orient and the West is given its most lofty symbol: the eagle. Böhm comments that in this ode the poet is exalted by the mythical belief that spring goes from land to land. Here we experience the mythical process, how the prophetic eagle—which in "Rousseau" precedes his gods in flight—soars now from the Indus over Italy and Greece, then jubilantly mounts over the Alps and finds Germania matured for priesthood.[15] He points out the linking symbol of the eagle, commenting that in the purely Germanic poems, those relating only to the poet's homeland, the falcon is symbol, in contrast to the eagle, which connects the Orient and the Occident.[16] In the flight of the eagle from the land of the Hindus to Germany, Lehmann sees a symbol of Herder's program of the development of human civilization. He remarks that now one can look into the Orient, into the most ancient of ages, to the starting point of human history. One after another the great civilized nations pass by. The eagle, spirit of civilized life, hovers over one and then another. From the Indus it went to Hellas and Rome, and now it flies over the Alps, with greater assuredness and certainty than usual, until it sees the multifarious peoples lying below. Lehmann finds this to be a magnificent symbol of the development of humankind in the sense in which Herder conceived it.[17]

> Schon grünet ja, im Vorspiel rauherer Zeit
> Für sie erzogen das Feld, bereitet ist die Gabe

15. *Ibid.*, II, 440.
16. *Ibid.*, II, 501.
17. Lehmann, p. 252.

Zum Opfermahl und Tal und Ströme sind
Weitoffen um prophetische Berge,
Dass schauen mag bis in den Orient
Der Mann und ihn von dort der Wandlungen viele bewegen.
Vom Aether aber fällt
Das treue Bild und Göttersprüche regnen
Unzählbare von ihm, und es tönt im innersten Haine.
Und der Adler, der vom Indus kömmt,
Und über des Parnassos
Beschneite Gipfel fliegt, hoch über den Opferhügeln
Italias, und frohe Beute sucht
Dem Vater, nicht wie sonst, geübter im Fluge
Der Alte, jauchzend überschwingt er
Zuletzt die Alpen und sieht die vielgearteten Länder.

(II, 1, 150)

In "Patmos" (1802) again Hölderlin is transported to the East, where Christianity had its beginnings in the earliest religion:

O Fittige gib uns, treuesten Sinns
Hinüberzugehn und wiederzukehren.

So sprach ich, da entführte
Mich schneller, denn ich vermutet
Und weit, wohin ich nimmer
Zu kommen gedacht, ein Genius mich
Vom eigenen Haus'. Es dämmerten
Im Zwielicht, da ich ging,
Der schattige Wald
Und die sehnsüchtigen Bäche
Der Heimat; nimmer kannt ich die Länder;
Doch bald, im frischem Glanze
Geheimnisvoll
Im goldenen Rauche, blühte
Schnellaufgewachsen,
Mit Schritten der Sonne,
Mit tausend Gipfeln duftend

Mir Asia auf ... (II, 1, 165-166)

It is true that most of the place-names and rivers which Hölderlin mentions in this poem are found in Asia Minor—but surely his encompassing eye included among the thousand peaks Meru, the home of the gods of India, the mountain from whose flanks flow the holy rivers of India. Lehmann sees the religions of all the earth's peoples in this poem.[18] In the poem, too, Hölderlin depicts the collapse of the bond between the ancient religion of the East and its offspring in the West:

> Denn jetzt erlosch der Sonne Tag,
> Der Königliche und zerbrach
> Den geradestrahlenden,
> Den Zepter, womit
> Er hatte geherrscht, von Asia her,
> Seit unerforschlichen Zeiten. (II, 1, 168; II, 2, 773)

During his translation of Greek tragedies Hölderlin remained aware of the influence of the Orient on Greece. In a letter of September 20, 1803, to the publisher of his Sophocles translations, Friedrich Wilmans, he writes: "Ich hoffe die griechische Kunst, die uns fremd ist durch Nationalkonvenienz und Fehler, mit denen sie sich immer herumbeholfen hat, dadurch lebendiger, als gewöhnlich dem Publikum darzustellen, dass ich das Orientalische, das sie verleugnet hat, mehr heraushebe, und ihren Kuntsfehler, wo er vorkommt, verbessere" (VI, 1, 434). Hölderlin's very expression of this intention is symptomatic of a projection of the mythical image. One must not expect, of course, to encounter Sakuntala or Brahmans or any exact reference to India (in the sense of the mythical image) in the translations. However, it may be remembered that Hölderlin shared the Romantic conception of the origin of the gods of Greece: Dionysus was a wanderer from the Ganges and the Indus. In reference to this idea, it is remarkable that, both in his translations and in his poems, he refers to Zeus, for example, as "der Vater der Erde" or "der Vater der Zeit"; Poseidon is called "der trauernde Gott"; Apollo is "die Sonne des Tages." This intentional generalization has the effect of expanding the idea of the god; Brahma could be called "der Vater der Erde." Hölderlin himself, in his notes to "Antigone," offers a partial interpretation of this technique:

> Sie zählete dem Vater der Zeit
> Die Stundenschläge, die goldnen.

statt: verwaltete dem Zeus das goldenströmende Werden. Um es unserer Vorstellungsart mehr zu nähern. Im Bestimmteren oder Unbestimmter-

---

18. *Ibid.*, p. 287.

en muss wohl Zeus gesagt werden. Im *Ernste* lieber: Vater der Zeit oder: Vater der Erde, weil sein Karakter ist, der ewigen Tendenz entgegen, *das Streben aus dieser Welt in die andre* zu kehren *zu einem Streben aus einer andern Welt in diese.* Wir müssen die Mythe nämlich überall *beweisbarer* darstellen. (V, 268)

This very concept of symbolization has been applied throughout his works by Hölderlin in regard to the mythical image of India. His generalization is an illusion, for it actually makes more immediate the concepts he wishes to transmit to his readers.

Hölderlin, like Novalis, represents an apotheosis of the mythical image of India among the Romanticists, but his transmutation of the image is accomplished in a more personal and, if possible, in a more enigmatic manner. His early works reveal a nearly direct projection of the image, but in his mature works the image is transfigured mystically and his panoramic glance is broadened in the attempt to reconcile the Orient and the West through the prophecy of poetry.

6. *Wir machten zusammen Wanderungen in die entferntesten Gegenden Indiens, und forschten nach Denkmälern der vergangenen Herrlichkeit dieses Landes. . . . und mit Erstaunen sah ich, dass Indiens Kultur in ein Alterthum hinauf reicht, wo die Zeitrechnungen anderer Völker noch ungeboren sind.*

—GÜNDERODE

On February 20, 1806, Friedrich Creuzer wrote to Karoline von Günderode (1780-1806):

Lass mich Dir hierbei ein Urtheil über Deine Poesie überhaupt sagen. Sie ist, meine ich, ihrem Hauptelemente nach . . . mystisch, *offenbarend.* Darum bist Du im Morgenlande so einheimisch und der grosse Naturgeist (der die stille Hoheit des alten Indiens am würdigsten fand sich in ihr zu verkörpern) zeigt auch Dir nicht selten sein Angesicht ohne Schleier.

Deine Poesie ist mystisch, sei's in grosser Naturanschauung oder im kindlichen Spiele—eben darum ist sie *nicht plastisch.*

Folglich ist Dir alles fremd, was seiner Natur nach hervortreibende systematische Gestalt fordert, folglich das eigentliche systematische

Drama. Verstehe mich wohl. Im Sinn der Sakontala kannst Du, ja *sollst* Du Dramen dichten und Deine Uhdola [*sic*] neiget sich sogar dahin, aber nur noch nicht entschieden genug.[1]

Creuzer's judgment of this minor poetess among the Romanticists is gentle and reveals an acute insight into the essential form of her writings. The mystic elements of her attitude toward nature are direct reflections of the mythical image of India, where the conception of the Supreme Being in His emanant nature is incapable of being represented in a systematic, plastic figure.

Elisabeth Salomon, in her foreword to the *Gesammelte Dichtungen*, says that Karoline's writings are not masterworks of creativity. The poetess takes her motifs from the wide range of subjects of Romanticism, playing with Nordic, Oriental, ancient, medieval, and Ossianic moods, often awkwardly and generally dominated by the thoughts, similes, and idioms of Classicists and Romanticists. Karoline found inspiration in Schelling and Creuzer as well. Schelling's philosophy of nature and Creuzer's mythology were not only fruits of her reading, but became for her the cipher of a nobly striving, profound but also completely feminine mind.[2] Because she wrote after the climax of the productive period of those Romanticists who projected in various degrees the mythical image of India, Karoline had as a stimulus not only Herder but also the Romantic authors who had transmuted the image into sublime poetry. Miss Salomon remarks that Karoline filled her leisure hours with the company of friends and wide-ranging reading: historical and philosophical works, French and English literature, Hemsterhuis and Ossian, and among German authors particularly Goethe, Schelling, Herder, Schleiermacher, Hölderlin, Jean Paul, Jacobi, and Novalis (p. xiv).

In *Gedichte und Phantasien* (1804) Karoline (who published this work under the pseudonym of Tian) reveals a partiality for Hindu mythology and philosophy. In "Immortalita" a great fiery serpent, reminiscent of the world serpent in Hindu and Norse mythology, holds Immortalita ensnared in its circle (p. 35). "Der Adept" relates how Valus, a man of learning, comes to India where he is initiated into the priestly class and finally attains the Brah-

1. Creuzer and Von Günderode, *Briefe und Dichtungen*, p. 86.
2. Karoline von Günderode, *Gesammelte Dichtungen*, ed. Dr. Elisabeth Salomon (Munich, 1923), pp. xi-xii. Further references to this edition will be given parenthetically by page.

manical third order. This Faust-like man, who now holds nature in his sway, finds himself outside the eternal cycle and endures the ages sadly (pp. 44-46). "Ein apokalyptisches Fragment" reveals Karoline's pantheistic tendencies. Erich Regen, in his work on the dramas by Karoline, notes that she herself did not confess to a monotheistic faith, but rather devoted herself in fervent love of nature to an infinite pantheism.[3] In the prose piece the author finds time unhinged: inside her, it runs its regular course, but outside it races by crazily; spellbound, she falls asleep and beholds the primeval sea in a cosmological vision (sections 5 and 6, p. 47). She sinks into a deeper trance and then awakens without knowing how long she has slept. But she has a feeling of having experienced a peculiar origin in that ocean, rising as a drop of moisture separated from the flood, delighting in her airy existence but yearning for something unknown; then she becomes aware that the creatures which came from the flood return to it, and she realizes that this is what she yearns for (sections 9-12, pp. 48-49). Reunited with the great watery source, she is jubilant at being included in an immanent, all-containing and all-pervading substance:

14. Erlöset war ich von den engen Schranken meines Wesens, und kein einzelner Tropfen mehr, ich war allem wiedergegeben, und Alles gehörte mir mit an, ich dachte, und fühlte, wogte im Meer, glänzte in der Sonne, kreiste mit den Sternen; ich fühlte mich in Allem und genoss Alles in mir. (p. 49)

The poetess herself, having experienced this pantheistic, palingenetic vision, cries out at the end:

15. Drum, wer Ohren hat zu hören, der höre! es ist nicht zwei, nicht drei, nicht tausende, es ist Eins und Alles; es ist nicht Körper und Geist geschieden, dass das eine der Zeit, das andere der Ewigkeit angehöre, es ist Eins, gehört sich selbst, und ist Zeit und Ewigkeit zugleich, und sichtbar und unsichtbar, bleibend im Wandel, ein unendliches Leben. (p. 49)

This is a transmutation of the cosmology and religion of the Hindus as it was perceived in the mythical image. Karoline adds the new dimension of the inseparability of body and spirit and achieves a pantheistic immortality among the elements of nature, which are one with God.

3. Erich Regen, *Die Dramen Karolinens von Günderode* (Berlin, 1910), p. 71.

The action of the drama *Udohla* (1805) takes place in Delhi, where a conquered Hindu ruler has been killed by a Mohammedan sultan for instigating an uprising. At the sultan's court is Nerissa, whom he believes to be his sister and whom he wishes to marry, in violation of Moslem, but not Hindu, law. Actually, Nerissa is the daughter of the slain rebel. Achmed, who comes to the sultan to plead for the life of the traitorous Hindu, is in reality Nerissa's brother, Udohla. Through the machinations of Sino, a Hindu at the court, Udohla, who has fallen in love with his sister, is reunited with her, and the sultan, rejected by Nerissa, allows them to depart peacefully.

Concerning the sources which influenced this play, Regen says that Karoline certainly studied the customs and manners of the inhabitants of Hindustan. She is able to report the difference of Hindu and Moslem marriage laws: the Koran forbids sibling marriage, while Hindu law does not. She is clearly aware that the Hindus are polytheistic while the followers of the Koran support a monotheistic religion. She speaks of the belief in metempsychosis and briefly, without giving details, she mentions the history of the Hindus, knowing that many had for ages been under the subjugation of Moslems. Regen believes that Herder's *Ideen* could have given Karoline no instruction in these matters; at most they could only have stirred her interest to probe deeper into an understanding of the Hindus. He concludes that it is impossible to establish a definite source.[4] The number of sources available to Karoline was not large, but Regen's suggestion that Herder in his *Ideen* was nothing but a stimulation to further studies is rather arbitrary. Herder emphasizes the antiquity both of the Hindu religion and of the people of India. In the play Sino says to a Moslem dervish:

> Hör Priester! Lang eh der Mongolen Name
> Die Welt genannt; als sie ein Hirtenvolk
> Durch Asiens Steppen ohne Heimat irrten
> War dieses Land ein ruhmbegränzter Staat;
> Und grosse Fürsten haben es beherrschet,
> Und viele edle Thaten sind geschehn,
> Eh man an euch und eure Weisheit dachte,
> Eh euer Muhamed den Koran schrieb. (pp. 269-270)

4. *Ibid.*, pp. 76-77.

The incongruity of Mongolian Moslems does not seem to have bothered Karoline or her contemporaries. On another occasion Sino mourns the collapse of past Hindu glory and says that the gods chose India as the cradle of humankind:

> So tief sind wir gesunken, dass vom Ruhme
> Von dieses Landes alter Herrlichkeit
> Nur eine Sage unser Ohr erreichte,
> Ach! eine Sage, die wir kaum verstehn—
>
> .   .   .   .
>
> Ja, alle Götter sind uns gewogen.
> Zur Wiege weihten sie sich dieses Land,
> Weil es zuerst sich aus dem Meer erhoben. (pp. 290-291)

"Die zarte Amrastaude" mentioned by Sino (p. 267) was probably known to Karoline from Forster's lexicon in his translation of *Sakuntala*, in which he calls it a beautiful, flowering tree whose sweet-smelling blossoms are considered more fragrant than the water lily.[5] The *Laws of Menu* undoubtedly provided her with the information that a Hindu was permitted to marry his sister. The flower which is closed and inert by day and blooms at night is the lotus.[6]

Sino, disputing with the dervish, describes the qualities and duties of the Brahmans:

> Sie leben in der Abgeschiedenheit.
> Entfernt vom irdischen Geräusch und Treiben
> Stört nichts die heilige Betrachtung da,
> Hartherz'gen Eifer kennt nicht ihre Seele,
> Sie mischen sich nicht in der Menschen Thun,
> Der Friede Gottes ist in ihrem Busen
> Und ihnen spricht die heilige Natur
> Durch ihre Kinder, die noch nicht entweihet
> Durch frecher Willkühr irres Streben sind.
> Der heiligen Thiere Sprache, und der Pflanzen
> Noch unentwickelt zart und still Gemüth
> Zu deuten und ihr Leben zu verstehen,
> Das ist für sie ein würdiger Beruf.

Whereupon Mangu, the chief vezier, says:

> Mein Sino! Du verlierest in müss'ge Fabeln
> Und deines Landes Kinderträume dich. (pp. 270-271)

5. Forster, IX, 317.
6. *Ibid.*, IX, 216, 232, 261, and 340-341.

This interjection does not destroy the illusion of the image, however; rather it heightens the effect of Sino's nostalgia.

Nerissa, masquerading as a Moslem, longs for the gods of India while praying to Allah:

> Die Götter Indiens verlassen mich,
> Weil ich zuerst abtrünnig sie verlassen,
> Und zürnend sieht der Gott von Muhamed
> Gebete die ich zweifelnd zu ihm sende,
> Den falschen Dienst, der ungern ihm geweiht,
> Der halb noch stets die alten Götter meinet. (p. 286)

When she is reunited with her brother and they are about to set off for Bengal where their uncle resides, she looks forward joyfully to a reconciliation with the Hindu gods:

> Ich suche jenes Felsen stille Kluft
> In der mit meinem Vater lang verborgen
> In einsamer Betrachtung ich gelebt;
> Dort soll Vergangenheit mir Zukunft werden,
> Die grosse Vorwelt will ich wieder schaun,
> Geschicke, die verflossen, wieder suchen,
> Die alten Götter neu versöhnen mir. (p. 293)

In *Udohla* Karoline does not achieve a poetic transfiguration of the mythical image of India—these are inept projections, in part a mere repetition of information concerning India. The stamp of the mythical image has impressed itself, however, upon her art.

The "Geschichte eines Braminen" is the story of Almor, the son of a French merchant who has become a Mohammedan. He finally goes to India for the fulfilment of his wish to discover something more important in life than riches and the pleasures of the senses. He had not been religious; his father had considered religions merely "necessary political contrivances" (p. 382). But he was led to seek in religion the clue to a longing he felt for nature:

Ich sahe hinauf in die Sterne, und fand es traurig, dass mein Auge so gerne hinsehe, und doch an die Erde gefesselt sey; ich liebte das Morgenroth, dass ich zu seinen Umarmungen hätte auffliegen, und die wogende See, dass ich mich in ihre Tiefen hätte stürzen mögen. In dieser Sehnsucht, in dieser Liebe sprach der Naturgeist zu mir, ich hörte seine Stimme wohl, aber ich wusste noch nicht, wo sie herkäme; je mehr ich aber darauf lauschte, desto deutlicher war es mir, dass es eine Grund-kraft gäbe, in welcher Alle, Sichtbare und Unsichtbare, verbunden seyen. Ich nannte diese Kraft das Urleben, und suchte mein Bewusstseyn in Verbindung mit ihr zu bringen, (denn eine mir geheimnissvolle und unbewusste Abstammung von ihr schien mir gewiss); ich suchte mir allerley Pfade, zu ihr aufzusteigen, von dem Irdischen zum Himmlischen; die Religion schien mir endlich dieser Pfad zu seyn. (p. 389)

He studies the Koran, Zoroaster, Confucius, Moses, Christ, the remnants of the wisdom of Egyptian priests, and the holy myths of the Hindus. In them all he finds one thought, the constancy of existence, which strengthens his own perception of the mystery of nature revealed by religion:

Es ist eine unendliche Kraft, ein ewiges Leben das da Alles ist, was ist, was war und werden wird, das sich selbst auf geheimnissvolle Weise erzeugt, ewig bleibt bey allem Wandel und Sterben. Es ist zugleich der Grund aller Dinge, und die Dinge selbst, die Bedingung und das Bedingte, der Schöpfer und das Geschöpf, und es theilt und sondert sich in mancherley Gestalten, wird Sonne, Mond, Gestirne, Pflanzen, Thier und Mensch zugleich, und durchfliesst sich selber in frischen Lebensströmen und betrachtet sich selber in Menschen in heiliger Demuth. (p. 391)

Regen sees the influence of Spinoza in these words,[7] but the pantheism of the Hindu is also present, along with the Hindu idea of an emanant God. Karoline seeks here to reconcile all the religions of mankind. Almor continues:

Diese Anschauung der Dinge, die Anschauung ihres Urgrundes, ist die innerste Seele der Religionen, verschieden individualisirt in jedem Individuum; aber durchgehe sie selbst die Religionssysteme alle, in allen wirst du finden ein Unendliches, Unsichtbares, aus dem das Endliche und Sichtbare hervorging, ein Göttliches, das Mensch wurde, ein Uebergehen aus dem zeitlichen Leben in das ewige. (p. 391)

The contemplation emphasized would seem to favor a large Hindu influence. A further statement by Almor in this respect reveals even more the Hindu idea of an emanant Being, Who gathers all of creation finally into Himself:

Ja, es muss eine Zeit der Vollendung kommen, wo jedes Wesen harmonisch mit sich selbst und mit den Andern wird, wo sie in einander fliessen, und Eins werden in einem grossen Einklang, wo jede Melodie sich hinstürzt in die ewige Harmonie. (p. 392)

7. Regen, p. 71.

Almor goes to India, where he wanders about with a Brahman. He is astonished at the antiquity of Hindu culture; the Brahman says metaphorically that all of human wisdom had its origin in India:

Wir machten zusammen Wanderungen in die entferntesten Gegenden Indiens, und forschten nach Denkmälern der vergangenen Herrlichkeit dieses Landes. Eine heisse Liebe zu seinem Volk beseelte den Brahminen, er trauerte über dessen Fall, als sey es sein eigener, und weidete sich an dessen voriger Grösse. . . . er lehrte mich die Geschichte seines Vaterlandes genauer kennen, und mit Erstaunen sah ich, dass Indiens Kultur in ein Alterthum hinauf reicht, wo die Zeitrechnungen anderer Völker noch ungeboren sind. . . . [Er sagte] einst zu mir . . . im Morgenlande ist doch jede Sonne aufgegangen, die die Erde erleuchtet und erwärmt hat; später und bleicher sendet sie ihre Strahlen dem Abendlande. (p. 394)

Almor praises the qualities of the Brahman and is taught the Brahmanical wisdoms by him:

Göttliches und Menschliches waren in seinem Gemüthe auf das Innigste und Schönste verknüpft. Die Erde war ihm heilig wie ein Vorhof des Himmels . . . und er blieb rein und unschuldig in den Strudeln des Verderbens. . . . Bald vergass er, dass ich ein Fremder sey, und weihte mich ein in die Weisheit der Braminen. Er lehrte mich, wie in jedem Theile des unendlichen Naturgeistes die Anlage zu ewiger Vervollkommnung läge, wie die Kräfte wanderten durch alle Formen hindurch, bis sich Bewusstseyn und Gedanke im Menschen entwickelten; wie von dem Menschen an, eine unendliche Reihe von Wanderungen, die immer zu höherer Vollkommenheit führten, die Seelen warteten; wie sie endlich auf geheimnissvolle Weise sich alle vereinigten mit der Urkraft, von der sie ausgegangen, und Eins mit ihr würden, und doch zugleich sie selbst blieben, und so die Göttlichkeit und Universalität des Schöpfers mit der Individualität des Geschöpfes vereinigten. (pp. 394-395)

In this passage the earth as the outer court, the prelude, to heaven is reminiscent of Emanuel's conception of the second world in *Hesperus*. Bhartrihari's Brahman farewell also points to death as the departure into the second world; Herder's paraphrase of the poem was well known to all Romanticists. Metempsychosis leads here to fulfilment. The universality of the creator united with the individuality of the creation echoes the mythical image in the passage cited above, which Regen attributes to Spinoza's influence.

Almor cannot part from his older Brahman friend. And finally, when the Brahman dies on the banks of the Ganges, Almor remains with Lasida, the Brahman's daughter. One aspect of the mythical image of India not stressed heretofore is the Hindu belief that the memory of a man must remain fresh in those he leaves behind when he dies and that he must be in their prayers if he is to enter heaven. Before he dies, the Brahman says to Almor: "Du Almor, lebe wohl! für dich werde ich nicht sterben, denn mein Geist wirkt fort in dir. . . . lass mich allein; ich möchte in ungestörter Betrachtung des Todes sterben, möchte stille meinen Geist in die stille Natur zurück hauchen" (p. 397). In the continued existence of the dead in the memories of the living, Regen sees the influence of Schleiermacher upon Karoline. He remarks that it seems to him Karoline did not believe in a life in the Hereafter but rather in immortality as a continued existence in the memory of coming generations, as a further life and a further conduct of ideas of the dead. He then quotes Schleiermacher's *Monologen* (Berlin, 1800), pp. 125 f., where he finds similar ideas expressed:

Du der in frischer Blüthe der Jugend, mitten im raschen, frohen Leben unsern Kreis verlassen musstest—ja, ich darf anreden das geliebte Bild, das mir im Herzen wohnt, das mit dem Leben und der Liebe fortlebt, und mit dem Gram—nimmer hat Dich mein Herz verlassen; es hat Dich mein Gedanke fortgebildet wie Du Dich selbst gebildet haben würdest, hättest Du erlebt die neuen Flammen, die die Welt entzünden, es hat Dein Denken mit dem meinen sich vereint, und das Gespräch der Liebe zwischen uns, der Gemüther Wechselanschauung hört nimmer auf, und wirket fort auf mich als lebtest Du neben mir wie sonst.[8]

The viewpoint is emphasized again when Almor says that he is remaining with Lasida, who will not leave her father's hut:

zehn Jahre sind seit dem Tode ihres Vaters verflossen, und er lebt noch unter uns; ja Lasida verlässt ungern das Haus, um ihrem Geliebten zu folgen, weil sie fürchtet, von der nähern Gemeinschaft mit ihrem Vater durch eine kleine Entfernung ausgeschlossen zu werden. Und ich werde nimmer diese Hütte, diese Palmen, diesen Strom verlassen; ich bin hierher gebannt wie in Zauberkreisen, und der Friede weicht nicht von mir.

(p. 397)

On the banks of the Ganges Almor finds the fulfilment of the peace

8. *Ibid.*, p. 72.

he has sought and the realization of a religion which embraces nature as he has perceived it.

Melete (1806), published under the pseudonym of Ion, contains three works, all stemming from 1796, which reflect aspects of the mythical image. "Zueignung" makes reference to the Oriental wreath of flowers which speaks to the lover who is initiated into the meaning of their symbols, a custom mentioned previously in a simile by Novalis. Karoline writes:

> Es flechten Mädchen so im Orient
> Den bunten Kranz; dass vielen er gefalle,
> Wetteifern unter sich die Blumen alle.
> Doch Einer ihren tiefern Sinn erkennt,
> Ihm sind Symbole sie nur, äussre Zeichen;
> Sie reden ihm, obgleich sie alle schweigen. (p. 209)

"Die malabarischen Witwen" is a glorification of the practice of burning widows on their husband's biers:

> Zum Flammentode gehn an Indusstranden
> Mit dem Gemahl, in Jugendherrlichkeit,
> Die Frauen, ohne Zagen, ohne Leid,
> Geschmücket festlich, wie in Brautgewanden.
>
> Die Sitte hat der Liebe Sinn verstanden,
> Sie von der Trennung harter Schmach befreit,
> Zu ihrem Priester selbst den Tod geweiht,
> Unsterblichkeit gegeben ihren Banden.
>
> Nicht Trennung ferner solchem Bunde droht,
> Denn die vorhin entzweiten Liebesflammen
> In einer schlagen brünstig sie zusammen.
>
> Zur süssen Liebesfeyer wird der Tod,
> Vereinet die getrennten Elemente,
> Zum Lebensgipfel wird des Daseins Ende. (p. 216)

Karoline makes the practice a ritual of religion and a rite of love with the reunion of the lovers in the eternal embrace of elemental nature.[9]

9. While Karoline von Günderode raises *suttee* to an erotic pinnacle in metaphysical terms, Goethe's treatment of the subject ends in a paean to the purification of the spirit through inner grace and a god's mercy. Goethe's source for the legend of "Der Gott und die Bajadere" (I, 1, 227-230) was Sonnerat (I, 211), who took it from Rogerius (*Offne Thür*, p. 163). Goethe's version differs from the source principally in the spiritual transformation of the Hindu prostitute: she remains

In the "Briefe zweier Freunde" Karoline expresses the ideas one finds also in "Geschichte eines Braminen," a description of the bliss attained by contemplation and by surrender to the Elemental Spirit:

Es giebt eine Ergebung, in der allein Seligkeit und Vollkommenheit und Friede ist, eine Art der Betrachtung, welche ich Auflösung im Göttlichen nennen möchte; dahin zu kommen lass uns trachten, und nicht klagen um die Schicksale des Universums. Damit du aber deutlicher siehst, was ich damit meine, so sende ich dir hiermit einige Bücher über die Religion der Hindu. Die Wunder uralter Weisheit, in geheimnissvollen Symbolen niedergelegt, werden dein Gemüth berühren, es wird Augenblicke geben, in welchen du dich entkleidet fühlst von dieser persönlichen Einzelheit und Armuth, und wieder hingegeben dem grossen Ganzen. . . . In solchen Augenblicken, wo wir uns nicht mehr besinnen können, weil das, was das einzle und irrdische Bewusstseyn weckt, dem äussern Sinn verschwunden ist unter der Herrschaft der Betrachtung des Innern; in solchen Augenblicken versteh' ich den Tod, der Religion Geheimniss, das Opfer des Sohnes und der Liebe unendliches Sehnen. (p. 251)

In another part of the letter written by Eusebio, the only one of the two friends named, Brahma is mentioned:

die unendliche Natur will sich stets neu offenbaren in der unendlichen Zeit. In der Fülle der Jahrhunderte ist Brahma oftmals erschienen, aber in immer neuen Verwandlungen; dieselbe Gestalt hat er nie wieder gewählt. So thue und dichte doch Jeder das, wozu er berufen ist, wozu der Geist ihn treibt, und versage sich keinen Gesang als den missklingenden. (p. 253)

What Regen has to say about the influence of Schleiermacher upon the "Geschichte eines Braminen" applies perhaps even more to these expressions from "Briefe zweier Freunde." He remarks that in the "Geschichte eines Braminen" Karoline deposited her own view of religion after Schleiermacher. She proceeds from the moral, fundamental process of self-examination, which in the ego discovers a mirror of the universe. The problem of existence is solved through the view of one's own innermost being, which is inseparable from

---

unchanged in the Indic legend, but is transfigured in Goethe's poem. The German poet retains the Indic scene, the winsomeness of the girl, and her absolute devotion, but omits the moral. He was indifferent to moral appendages, unlike Herder, and paid no heed to Indic works such as the *Hitopadesa*, as Paul T. Hoffmann points out, p. 26; see also pp. 24-25.

religion and from existence in the eternal and infinite.[10] The passage in Schleiermacher's *Reden über die Religion* which Regen has in mind is "Auf dem Wege der abgezogensten Selbstbeschauung das Universum zu finden, war das Geschäft des uralten morgenländischen Mysticismus,"[11] which has been considered above as a projection of the mythical image. The fact that Karoline expressly mentions Hinduism and Brahma is significant, not only to reinforce the view that Schleiermacher's ideas are a projection of the image, but also to support the assumption that Karoline went beyond Schleiermacher to the image itself.

When Friedrich Creuzer and Karoline fell in love early in 1804, Creuzer was married to a widow ten years his senior. Both the mythographer and the poetess confided in trusted friends who reacted with various expressions of dismay or encouragement and offered advice to the lovers. Creuzer, caught in the insoluble predicament of a joyless marriage, vacillated in his schemes to extricate himself. For a time his wife seemed to agree to a divorce, but when finally she made up her mind to refuse any other course than separation, Creuzer resigned himself to life without Karoline and asked his friend Karl Daub to be the intermediary in advising Karoline that the lively exchange of letters through the course of two years had to end and the relationship be terminated. Daub wrote to Karoline's friend Susanna von Heyden, who in turn wrote to Karoline, enclosing the letter in another to Charlotte Servière with whom Karoline was visiting near Winkel on the Rhine and who was to prepare Karoline for the shock of the news. Karoline, who had been hungering for mail, met the postman, evidently recognized the disguised handwriting of her friend Susanna, and opened the letter addressed to Charlotte. In it she found two letters from Daub and the letter from Susanna, and read her sentence of death.[12]

Although it was in vain, the care her friends took to advise her of the turn of events was probably well calculated. As early as March, 1805, she had evidently written Creuzer of suicidal thoughts, for in a letter of March 21, 1805, he scolds her soundly.[13]

10. Regen, pp. 73-74.
11. Schleiermacher, IV, 311.
12. Creuzer and Von Günderode, *Briefe und Dichtungen*, p. 115.
13. *Ibid.*, p. 33.

Again on March 28 he wrote in gentle protest against Karoline's philosophical justifications for suicide: "Der Gedanke, sich durch Vernichtung des Leibes früher zu nahen dem Ewigen, der Sie beherrscht, ist unrichtig selbst nach den Grundsätzen der Philosophie, die Ihnen so lieb ist."[14]

Creuzer's earnest pleas and flatteries swayed Karoline from her intention. But the blow of his renunciation of her sixteen months later affirmed her idea and steadied her resolve. Later in the day on which she intercepted the letters, July 26, 1806, in an apparently cheerful mood she took her accustomed stroll alone along the Rhine, tied a scarf filled with stones around her neck, and stabbed herself in the heart. Her body fell not into the water, as she had imagined it would, to sink from sight, but onto the shore where she was found the next morning by a peasant, after a night of anxious search by her friends. She was buried in the churchyard at Winkel. On the stone wall behind her grave friends later affixed a large iron plaque with her valedictory to the world, the verses of Bhartrihari's farewell of the Brahman. Karoline evidently had written Herder's paraphrase from memory, since it diverges slightly from the original, and left it lying with the fateful letters on her desk.

Erde, du meine Mutter, und du mein Ernährer, der Lufthauch,
Heiliges Feuer, mir Freund, und du, o Bruder, der Bergstrom,
Und mein Vater, der Äther, ich sage euch allen mit Ehrfurcht
Freundlichen Dank; mit euch hab ich hienieden gelebt;
Und ich gehe zur andern Welt, euch gerne verlassend;
Lebt wohl denn, Bruder und Freund, Vater und Mutter, lebt wohl![15]

Thus Karoline's death bore the seal of the mythical image of India.

Karoline von Günderode, in a strange mixture of the glorification of the image and what amounts almost to mere reporting, betokens the beginning of the darkening of the image. The time of its bright apotheosis was past; the two poets who succeeded in fashioning its most sublime transfigurations were no more: Novalis died in 1801, and Hölderlin sank into the gloom of insanity in 1806, the same

14. *Ibid.*, p. 34.
15. Mention already has been made of Kranz's pre-Socratic interpretation of these lines; he errs because of his unfamiliarity with the source, although it is true that there is evidence of Oriental influence in the philosophies of Pythagoras, Empedokles, and other early Greek thinkers; see Kranz, pp. 104-105; 358; see also Burnet, pp. 15-18, 24, 84-89, 92-95.

year in which Karoline committed suicide. It is ironic that the darkening of the mythical image of India was brought about largely by Friedrich Schlegel, who had urged that his contemporaries look to the Orient for the highest expression of the Romantic spirit. His efforts to illuminate the very source, in Sanskrit studies, heralded the beginnings of linguistic scholarship in Germany but doomed the mythical image as a touchstone for poetry.

7. *[Friedrich] schreibt die indischen Lettern so vortrefflich wie irgend ein Bramine, wit welchem Charakter er überhaupt immer mehr Aehnlichkeit gewinnt.* —AUGUST WILHELM SCHLEGEL

Wo hat sich aber der Geist zarter und süsser gebildet als in Indien? —FRIEDRICH SCHLEGEL

The Romantic mythical image of India contained the seeds of its own destruction. So long as the Romantic yearning for the idyllic land and its unified culture remained a fervent yearning, unattainable and always beckoning, the mythical image endured. The Romantic longing for the synthesis of the Orient and the West preserved the mythical image; but any attempt to realize the synthesis through philological studies or comparative linguistics or philosophical speculation doomed the mythical image by accenting the thesis (India) and the antithesis (Greece and the West) and failing to achieve a synthesis (the mythical image made reality). Only Hölderlin's poetic transfiguration of the synthesis, not realized, not capable of attainment, but earnestly desired and envisioned, preserved the mythical image in a sublime transmutation.

Both August Wilhelm (1767-1845) and Friedrich Schlegel (1772-1829) shared with the other representatives of Romanticism around 1800 an enthusiasm for the mythical image of India. By 1802, when he was in Paris, Friedrich Schlegel's interest in the poetic transfiguration of the image had begun to wane, and, in a change of focus, he devoted himself to the eager study of Sanskrit itself, still possessed with a longing to find the fulfilment of the image as the source of religion revealed in the language of ancient India. But by

1808, with the publication of his *Sprache und Weisheit der Indier*, he had discovered that the longing was incapable of fulfilment. Paul T. Hoffmann in his dissertation describes Friedrich Schlegel's reaction to the Sanskrit studies. He remarks that the small volume which cleared the path for the philological and linguistic study of Sanskrit is a work of disillusionment. Desire and imagination had made it possible for Friedrich Schlegel to give the form of a religious *fata morgana* to the Herderian dream-image of India. But then his ever-hungry, ever-eager intellect had asserted itself, and in the sober light of day the dreamy nighttime ideal of the land of the Ganges had vanished in the face of bald, naked reality. The genuine and the true remained; the good and the beautiful shone in reality still. But he also now saw the ugly and the evil. This recognition may have contributed to his conversion to Catholicism. Hoffmann believes that if Friedrich Schlegel had found in India the fulfilment of his Romantic ideal, he would have discovered there a placidity of spirit. But after 1808 he had as much as abandoned India entirely.[1] The ardent acceptance of the image changed finally to an almost bitter criticism of the aspects which were shown to be illusory.

In "Die Kunstlehre," the first division of his *Vorlesungen über schöne Litteratur und Kunst* (held in Berlin, 1801-1804), August Wilhelm Schlegel discusses primarily the mythology of Greece as a realistic mythology; but he mentions, as an example of a contrasting idealistic mythology, the religion of the Brahmans which, despite its colorful polytheism, may be the most perfect formulation of such a mythology because it came into being in a climate which invites even the most excitable natures to peaceful contemplation.[2] But in the third series of lectures, "Geschichte der romantischen Literatur," he sees in India a combination of the realistic and idealistic religions, suggesting perhaps a common source.[3] These are the sober observations of a critic and theorist, not the exalted expressions of a poet. However, in his composed manner, August Wilhelm

1. Paul T. Hoffmann, p. 78. The work of Gerhard Holpfner, "Die indischen Studien Friedrich Schlegels im Zusammenhange seines Denkens" (Unpublished dissertation, Breslau, 1921), was not available for consideration of any contribution it may make to this subject.

2. August Wilhelm Schlegel, *Vorlesungen über schöne Litteratur und Kunst*, ed. Jakob Minor (3 vols.; Heilbronn, 1884), I, 332.

3. *Ibid.*, III, 91.

Schlegel acknowledges an influence of the mythical image.

Josef Körner reports that in the private lectures on "Enzyklopädie" of the summer of 1803, August Wilhelm Schlegel hoped that India would reveal much about the essence of poetry, religion, and philosophy; the suggestions of such revelations are found in the mythical image. In the same lectures, he speaks of that distant land as "die Pflanzenschule des Menschengeschlechts." The idea, echoing Herder's designation of India as the cradle of humanity, is expressed in an essay of 1805 (unpublished during August Wilhelm Schlegel's lifetime), "Considérations sur la civilisation": "*L'Inde est de tous les pays du monde celui qui a le plus l'air d'avoir été le berceau de genre humain.*"[4]

Although Friedrich Schlegel's poetic talent was limited, it was nonetheless greater than his brother's, and one finds in Friedrich Schlegel's early works and letters a Romantic transmutation of the mythical image. In the essay on "Das Studium der Griechischen Poesie" (1797) he defends the Romantic imagination, emphasizing that the fanciful images of Romantic poetry are not based on deviant temperaments, as is Oriental bombast.[5] Here he undoubtedly refers not to available Sanskrit translations but to the more fantastic and more luxuriant tradition of Arabic and Persian tales. He says further that Greek poetry was very early distinguished by a "certain something" from all other national literatures at a similar stage of culture, equally removed from Oriental pomposity and Nordic melancholy (Minor, I, 125). Again, the reference must be to Persian or Arabic prototypes, for in a subsequent statement he refers directly to India in a context which seems to reflect positive aspects of the mythical image. Faithful truth, he writes, original power, simple grace, and charming naturalness are advantages which the Greek poet may perhaps have shared with one or another of his Indic or Celtic brothers (Minor, I, 127).

In the essay "Kunsturtheil des Dionysios über den Isokrates" (1797) he mentions the attack of Dionysius on the style of oratory which had come from Asian caves and displaced the old, native,

4. Josef Körner, ed., *Briefe von und an August Wilhelm Schlegel* (2 vols.; Zürich, 1930), II, 131.
5. Friedrich Schlegel, *Seine prosaischen Jugendschriften* (1794-1802), ed. Jakob Minor (2d ed.; 2 vols.; Wien, 1906), I, 98. Further references to this work will be given parenthetically in the text by Minor, volume, and page.

Attic oratory (Minor, I, 195). Friedrich Schlegel's sentiments here lie with Greece, as they do in the "Geschichte der Poesie der Griechen und Römer" (1798), where in the chapter on the pre-Homeric period of the epic age he refers condescendingly to the priestly castes of the Orient (Minor, I, 262). Although the passages show an awareness of the mythical image, they emphasize the Greek interest which occupied him. Perhaps one may see the budding of his interest in India in the request to August Wilhelm Schlegel of January 19, 1796, for information about a readable translation of Arrian's history of Alexander.[6]

Friedrich Schlegel's early attitude, however, is exemplified in the rather unfavorable mention he made of *Sakontala* in a letter to his brother of August 26, 1791. He writes that, of new publications displayed at the book fair in Leipzig, he found an Indic drama, *Sakontala*, particularly remarkable. It was, he said, especially interesting because of its oddness. There were many fine sentiments in it, although he found the characters somewhat flat and the dialogue, and especially the plot, slow and dull. The play had, however, caused a stir, he concluded (Walzel, p. 15). In a letter of July 4, 1792, to his brother he makes what one suspects to be a rather deprecatory reference to Herder. He notes that the fourth volume of *Zerstreute Blätter* contains the beautiful "Gedanken einiger Bramanen" and a fine essay on *Sakontala*. But he continues: "Herder wandelt diessmal oft oben im Aether; er nimmt allmählig die erhabene Ruhe eines Bramanen an" (Walzel, p. 50). Friedrich Schlegel himself was later to be compared by his brother to a Brahman, and then much later still to return the compliment. By 1797 he is more appreciative of *Sakontala,* as may be seen in the profile he wrote on Georg Forster: "Wie tief und lebendig das von jenem Kunstgefühl wesentlich verschiedne *Naturgefühl* in ihm war, davon geben viele unnachahmlich wahre Ergiessungen in seinen Schriften vollgültiges Zeugnis. Auch für schöne dichterische Naturgewächse hatte er viel Sinn. Das beweist schon die Art, wie er eins der köstlichsten, die Sakontala auf vaterländischen Boden verpflanzte" (Minor, II, 136). The metaphor of a poetic, wild growing thing transplanted into the earth of Germany is couched in terms revealing the mythical image.

6. Oskar Walzel, ed., *Friedrich Schlegels Briefe an seinen Bruder August Wilhelm,* p. 257. The reader is reminded that further references to this volume will be given parenthetically in the text by Walzel and page.

In the jottings of his notebooks of the same year he makes two favorable references to *Sakontala*: "Wie viel mehr ist nicht *Sakontala* werth als *Ossian* und wie haben beide ein ungleiches Glück gehabt," and "*Sakontala* ein herrliches *fantastisches* Gedicht.—Viel Oriental-[isch]es Fant[astisch]."[7] Thus Friedrich Schlegel showed a gradual development toward an excited enthusiasm for the mythical image.

August Wilhelm Schlegel's remarks concerning *Sakuntala*, in his review of the *Thalia* volume (1791) which contained the first published scenes from Forster's translation, are more in the spirit of the image than was Friedrich Schlegel's estimation:

In das Gebiet der dramatischen und der schönen Litteratur überhaupt gehören nur folgende Stücke: Scenen aus der 'Sacontala', oder dem unglücklichen Ring, einem indischen, 2000 Jahre alten Drama.... Es wäre zu wünschen, man wüsste, wie genau der erste Uebersetzer sich an das Original gehalten hat; indessen beweist der durchaus fremde, nicht europäische Ton des Ganzen, dass er nichts hineingelegt hat, wenn auch vielleicht Vieles unter seinen Händen verloren gegangen ist. Die Scenen sind voll süssen kindlichen Geschwätzes, voll unschuldiger, naiver Koketterie; es herrscht eine feine Sensibilität darin, welche die zartesten Blüten des Genusses mit schonender Hand zu Pflücken weiss.[8]

Later, in 1796, August Wilhelm Schlegel refers to Indic drama in defending Shakespeare's poetry and urging that his plays be translated in a poetic form (in "Etwas über William Shakespeare bei Gelegenheit Wilhelm Meisters," 1796):

'Die Naktaks oder indischen Schauspiele,' sagt der berühmte Sir William Jones in seiner Vorrede zur Sakontala, 'sind durchgehends in Versen, wo der Dialog einen höheren Schwung nimmt, und in Prosa, wo er sich zur gewöhnlichen Unterredung herablässt....' Diess ist schon an sich merkwürdig genug: es liesse sich eine Abhandlung von Schlussfolgen darüber schreiben, welchen Grad der Bildung es bei den Hindus in dem Zeitpunkte voraussetzt, da jene Schauspiele geschrieben wurden.[9]

In the fragmentary poem "Die Weltalter," done around 1800, Friedrich Schlegel illuminates several aspects of the mythical image; his exhortation to the Romanticists to seek the highest expression

---

7. Friedrich Schlegel, *Literary Notebooks 1797-1801*, ed. Hans Eichner (London, 1957), Nos. 112, 362, pp. 29, 52.
8. August Wilhelm Schlegel, *Sämmtliche Werke*, ed. Eduard Böcking (12 vols.; Leipzig, 1846-1847), X, 34.
9. *Ibid.*, VII, 40.

of Romanticism in the Orient, had been voiced in the *Athenäum*, and he had written *Lucinde*, which glimmers with reflections of the mythical image. Like his contemporaries, he was particularly sensitive to the mythical image at the turn of the century; this was the moment of the Romantic apotheosis of the mythical image of India. The fragment, "Die Weltalter," glows with the bright sun of the Orient. It describes the Eden-like existence of mankind in the golden age; the characteristic phrases of the Romantic projection of the mythical image bloom in the poem: the holy sun, the golden life in golden dreams, the childlike heart, the children of light, the flowery zone of earth. That the earliest age is placed in India is made clear by the reference to repeated incarnations of the gods, to metempsychosis, and to *suttee*.[10]

In *Lucinde* (1799) Friedrich Schlegel meant to exemplify the Romantic idea of unity in multiplicity, or as one critic says: "Einheit in der Allheit, sie ist in Gott, und sowohl das Ich wie die Welt sind Emanationen Gottes."[11] The Romantic preoccupation with the idea of an emanant God may in part be ascribed to the influence of the mythical image of India. Paul T. Hoffmann says that Friedrich Schlegel believed he had found the prototype of the idea of an emanant God in India.[12] It is true that the mythical image of India is notable in several instances in *Lucinde*. In the "Dithyrambische

10. Friedrich Schlegel, *Kritische Friedrich-Schlegel-Ausgabe*, ed. Ernst Behler, with Jean-Jacques Anstett and Hans Eichner (Paderborn, 1958 ff.), edition in progress. This immense and invaluable edition will include all known published and unpublished works and letters by Friedrich Schlegel as well as letters addressed to him and statements made about him by contemporaries. The enrichment of Schlegel scholarship which will result is impossible to measure. Volumes which have thus far been published are:
    IV. *Ansichten und Ideen von der christlichen Kunst*, ed. Hans Eichner (1959);
    V. *Dichtungen*, ed. Hans Eichner (1962);
    VI. *Geschichte der alten und neuen Literatur*, ed. Hans Eichner (1961);
    XI. *Wissenschaft der europäischen Literatur, Vorlesungen, Aufsätze und Fragmente aus der Zeit von 1795-1804*, ed. and with an introduction by Ernst Behler (1958);
    XIV. *Vorlesungen über Universalgeschichte* (1805-1806), ed. Jean-Jacques Anstett (1960).
    XVIII. *Philosophische Lehrjahre 1796-1806*, I, ed. Ernst Behler (1963).
The text reference is to V, 285-286; further *Lucinde* references (and others made to the critical edition) are given parenthetically in the text as KFSA with volume and page.
11. Carl Enders, *Friedrich Schlegel, die Quellen seines Wesens und Werdens* (Leipzig, 1913), p. 351.
12. Paul T. Hoffmann, p. 72.

Fantasie über die schönste Situation," Julius says to his beloved: "Ich weiss, auch du würdest mich nicht überleben wollen, du würdest dem voreiligen Gemahle auch im Sarge folgen, und aus Lust und Liebe in den flammenden Abgrund steigen, in den ein rasendes Gesetz die indischen Frauen zwingt und die zartesten Heiligtümer der Willkür durch grobe Absicht und Befehl entweiht und zerstört" (KFSA, V, 11). Friedrich Schlegel condemns *suttee* as a universal law in India, but praises it highly as a voluntary demonstration of ultimate love. Karoline von Günderode, as has been shown, also sentimentalized the practice, seeing in it a declaration of fervent love. The passage in *Lucinde* reminds one of a similar statement made by Friedrich Schlegel in a letter to Novalis, December 17, 1798. Speaking of Dorothea Mendelssohn Veit, who in 1804 became his wife and who generously inspired his *Lucinde* fantasies, he writes: "Ihr ganzes Wesen ist Religion obgleich sie nichts davon weiss. Wenn sie mich verlöhre, sie würde mir nach Indischem Gebrauch folgen aus eigentlicher Religion, und ohne zu ahnden dass das ausserordentlich oder auch nur dass es recht wäre" (Körner, p. 20).

Reminiscent of passages by Novalis and Hölderlin is Julius' declaration: "Wir beide werden noch einst in Einem Geiste anschauen, dass wir Blüten Einer Pflanze oder Blätter Einer Blume sind, und mit Lächeln werden wir dann wissen, dass was wir jetzt nur Hoffnung nennen, eigentlich Erinnerung war" (KFSA, V, 12). In this passage Friedrich Schlegel gives a perceptible nod to metempsychosis, as well as to the metaphorical image of lovers united in a flower, which may be considered an expression of the mythical image. Other plant metaphors occur in *Lucinde*: "Je göttlicher ein Mensch oder ein Werk des Menschen ist, je ähnlicher werden sie der Pflanze; diese ist unter allen Formen der Natur die sittlichste, und die schönste" (KFSA, V, 27), and "Die Formen [der Menschen in Julius' Gemälden] selbst entsprachen vielleicht nicht immer den angenommenen Gesetzen einer künstlichen Schönheit. Was sie dem Auge empfahl, war eine gewisse stille Anmut, ein tiefer Ausdruck von ruhigem heitern Dasein und von Genuss dieses Daseins. Es schienen beseelte Pflanzen in der gottähnlichen Gestalt des Menschen" (KFSA, V, 56). Hans Eichner links the latter passage with an entry Friedrich Schlegel made in 1799 in his literary notebook: "Der Mensch ist allerdings der höchste Gegenstand der Mahlerei, auch der höchsten, aber der *Mensch als Pflanze.*—Die Madonna mit dem Kinde—Staude mit Frucht.—"[13] The equation of mankind=plant either as a simile, metaphor, or in an intimate relationship was very early made a part of the mythical image. Also in the notebook, from 1798, Friedrich Schlegel connects the plant-human symbol explicitly with India: "Schreiben die Frauen nicht leicht Orientalisch, Indisch?—Frauen als Pflanzen zu betrachten, doch eigentlich sehr Sultanisch."[14]

In a playfully erotic passage in *Lucinde* there is a description of the delight experienced by lovers who change the role of the sexes in an act of love:

Wir müssen ihre verzehrende Glut in Scherzen lindern und kühlen und so ist uns die witzigste unter den Gestalten und Situationen der Freude auch die schönste. Eine unter allen ist die witzigste und die schönste: wenn wir die Rollen vertauschen und mit kindischer Lust wetteifern, wer den andern täuschender nachäffen kann, ob dir die schonende Heftigkeit des Mannes besser gelingt, oder mir die anziehende Hingebung des Weibes. Aber weisst du wohl, dass dieses süsse Spiel für mich noch ganz andre Reize hat als seine eignen? Es ist auch nicht bloss die Wollust der Ermattung oder das Vorgefühl der Rache. Ich sehe hier eine wunderbare sinnreich bedeutende Allegorie auf die Vollendung des Männlichen und Weiblichen zur vollen ganzen Menschheit. Es liegt viel darin, und was darin liegt, steht gewiss nicht so schnell auf wie ich, wenn ich dir unterliege. (KFSA, V, 12-13)

One thinks of Plato's myth of the origin of love, but even more one thinks of Rogerius' Brahman informant, who declared: "Die alten Heyden haben vermeint / ihre Götter wären *utriusq: naturae,* das ist, so wol Mann als Weib; und zwar dergestalt / dass / so sie *in actu* begriffen / alsdann Männer; hingegen Frauen seyen / *cum pariendi haberent naturam.*"[15] From the literary notebooks of 1798 Eichner quotes a paragraph which brings the playful scene of *Lucinde* to mind in a direct reference to lovers in India: "Sollen sich denn nicht auch die *Geister* küssen, umarmen, befruchten, Eins werden?—‹Das Einswerden ist wohl bloss Ideal der Umarmung. Die Vermischung der Indier ist weder der Freundschaft noch der Liebe

13. F. Schlegel, *Literary Notebooks,* No. 1584, p. 160.
14. *Ibid.,* No. 1260, p. 133.
15. Rogers, *Offne Thür,* p. 237.

Ziel, nur innigste und vielseitigste Berührung.—› "[16] Böhme comes
upon a similar idea in a passage in *Morgenröthe im Aufgang* quoted
by Eichner: "Siehe, was die Gottheit thut, das thun sie [die Engel]
auch, wenn die Geister Gottes in sich fein lieblich einander gebären,
und ineinander aufsteigen, als ein liebliches Halsen, Küssen und
von einander Essen."[17]

In the chapter "Idylle über den Müssiggang" Friedrich Schlegel
seems to have the Brahman in mind when he speaks of the contemplation of eternal substances: "Gleich einem Weisen des Orients
war ich ganz versunken in ein heiliges Hinbrüten und ruhiges Anschauen der ewigen Substanzen, vorzüglich der deinigen und der
meinigen" (KFSA, V, 26). The wit of the ironic twist at the end
does not detract from the allusion to India. P. T. Hoffmann considers the following statement related in sense to the teaching of
yoga:[18] "Nur mit Gelassenheit und Sanftmut, in der heiligen Stille
der echten Passivität kann man sich an sein ganzes Ich erinnern,
und die Welt und das Leben anschauen" (KFSA, V, 27). And
Friedrich Schlegel refers to India directly in a later statement: "Je
schöner das Klima ist, je passiver ist man. Nur Italiener wissen zu
gehen, und nur die im Orient verstehen zu liegen; wo hat sich aber
der Geist zarter und süsser gebildet als in Indien?" (KFSA, V, 27).
Here the influence of climate, and its effect on human intelligence
through the repose of the body, is reminiscent of Jean Paul's comment: "Alles Grosse oder Wichtige bewegt sich langsam: also
gehen gar nicht die orientalischen Fürsten" (I, 2, 126). The softness of the Indic dialect, praised by travelers and Sir William Jones,
is mentioned in "Charakteristik der kleinen Wilhelmine": "Zur
Poesie glaube ich hat sie weit mehr Neigung als zur Philosophie; so
lässt sie sich auch lieber fahren und reiset nur im Notfall zu Fuss.
Die harten Übelklänge unsrer nordischen Muttersprache ver-
schmelzen auf ihrer Zunge in den weichen und süssen Wohllaut der
italienischen und indischen Mundart" (KFSA, V, 14).

In "Metamorphosen" there is reference to the golden age of human innocence in the divine peace of nature: "In goldner Jugend
und Unschuld wandelt die Zeit und der Mensch im göttlichen

16. F. Schlegel, *Literary Notebooks*, No. 1489, p. 152.
17. *Ibid.*, n. to 1489, p. 274.
18. Paul T. Hoffmann, p. 72.

Frieden der Natur, und ewig kehrt Aurora schöner wieder" (KFSA, V, 60). The idyllic landscape of ancient India is reflected in "Zwei Briefe": "Auf dem Lande können die Menschen doch noch beisammen sein, ohne sich hässlich zu drängen. Da könnten, wenn alles wäre wie es sollte, schöne Wohnungen und liebliche Hütten wie frische Gewächse und Blumen den grünen Boden schmücken und einen würdigen Garten der Gottheit bilden" (KFSA, V, 62-63). The omnipresent, emanant Supreme Deity of the Hindu finds allusion here: "Alles ist beseelt für mich, spricht zu mir, und alles ist heilig. Wenn man sich so liebt wie wir, kehrt auch die Natur im Menschen zu ihrer ursprünglichen Göttlichkeit zurück" (KFSA, V, 67). Friedrich Schlegel wrestled fruitlessly with plans and sketches for a continuation of *Lucinde*, in which he planned to insert an (unwritten) Indic *Märchen*, "Malitta" (KFSA, V, lxii). Soon after the poetic transmutation in *Lucinde* of his longing for the realization of the ideal unity, Friedrich Schlegel turned with the same yearning to the study of Sanskrit, which was to be the undoing of the Romantic contemplation and transfiguration of the mythical image.

August Wilhelm Schlegel showed an awareness of India even before Friedrich Schlegel, because of his communication with their older brother, Karl August Schlegel. Paul T. Hoffmann, discussing this relationship and its effect upon August Wilhelm Schlegel, suggests that Karl August Schlegel, who had lived for several years between the Himalayas and the coast of Coromandel and had begun a thorough study of the land, its system of government, and of the Indic mind, might have become the first German Indic scholar had he not succumbed to an early death in Madras in 1789. August Wilhelm Schlegel dedicated a sadly prophetic poem to his brother, "Die Bestattung des Braminen. Eine Phantasie an meinen Bruder in Ostindien,"[19] which appeared in 1787 in the *Göttinger Musenalmanach*. Hoffmann suggests it is possible he got the idea for the poem from Karl August Schlegel's written reports, but more probably perhaps that he culled the idea from current travel literature. The poem is quite immature and treats its subject matter in a thoroughly sentimental way and from a strictly German viewpoint.[20]

19. A. W. Schlegel, *Werke*, I, 82-86.
20. Paul T. Hoffmann, pp. 85-86.

August Wilhelm Schlegel was earlier than Friedrich Schlegel, also, in demonstrating an interest in the language of India. In "Die Sprachen," published in the *Athenäum* in 1798, he mentions Sanskrit, along with Persian and Arabic, as a harmonious language (I, 23). In 1799 in the *Athenäum* he addresses Tieck in a postscript to "Der Rasende Roland. Eilfter Gesang," expressing a wish to learn Sanskrit in order to translate Indic poetry.[21]

Friedrich Schlegel had not forgotten India, although he did not yet express a desire to learn Sanskrit. In a letter to August Wilhelm Schlegel of February 20, 1801, he says he is considering a canto to Apollo, and then as many Indic romances as good fortune will allow (Walzel, p. 463). Later, in a letter of April 17, 1801, he promises to send his brother an Indic *Märchen*, the "Pandaram oder den Sänger des Schiwa" (Walzel, p. 476). However, nothing came of these plans. The turning point came with his move to Paris in 1802. On September 16, 1802, he writes his brother of plans to study Sanskrit, and, if necessary, Persian (Walzel, p. 497). This announcement resulted in the following lines, written by August Wilhelm Schlegel, in "An Friedrich Schlegel" in the autumn of 1802:

> Und schon dich dein Gemüthe
> Hinlockt mit kühnerm Triebe,
> Gleich weltumfahrnen Schiffern,
> Zu lauschen, wie am Ganges
> Getönt voll sel'gen Klanges
> Manch indisch Blumenlied,
> Und Weisheit zu entziffern
> Aus heiliger Sanskrit.[22]

Then on January 15, 1803, Friedrich Schlegel writes his brother that he has already acquired knowledge of the common Indic dialect but will postpone the study of Sanskrit until spring because the library has no heat (Walzel, p. 507). Even the zealous scholar could not persuade himself to endure the wintry cold of an unheated library to study the Sanskrit manuscripts. In the same letter the aspiring student of Sanskrit gives the first hint that he is thinking in the direction of a comparative grammatical investigation of Persian, Sanskrit, and German (Walzel, p. 507).

21. A. W. Schlegel, *Werke*, IV, 127; *Athenäum*, II, 281.
22. A. W. Schlegel, *Werke*, I, 245.

Friedrich Schlegel's progress with Sanskrit may be followed in the letters he wrote to August Wilhelm Schlegel. In a letter of May 15, 1803, he reports that he is receiving aid from Alexander Hamilton, a member of the Asiatick Society of Calcutta, who had spent several years in India and was, on his way home to England, caught in Paris by the tides of the Napoleonic wars. He is jubilant that he has at last reached the "great goal," and says that he will be able to read *Sakuntala* in the original Sanskrit within four months, although he would undoubtedly still have to refer to the translation (Walzel, p. 511). By November 26, 1803, he is able to write that through thorough application he has become such an expert copyist of Sanskrit characters that he could earn his living in India as a scribe.[23] Also, in this letter, he first mentions his intention to make a metrical translation of *Sakuntala* (Walzel, pp. 522-523). In the same letter he offers to send his brother metrical translations from a Sanskrit didactic work and an essay on the language; he also expresses his wish to contribute to a journal, should his brother publish one, and he reiterates his plan to do a poetic translation of *Sakuntala* or a similar Indic play (Walzel, p. 525).

It was at this stage, in the winter of 1803-1804, that Friedrich Schlegel still believed he could find the fulfilment of his yearning in the revelations Sanskrit might bring. He wrote to Tieck on September 15, 1803, that his original preoccupation with art and Persian in Paris had now been supplanted by the study of Sanskrit. He exclaims: "Hier ist eigentlich die Quelle aller Sprachen, aller Gedanken und Gedichte des menschlichen Geistes; *alles, alles stammt aus Indien* ohne Ausnahme. Ich habe über vieles eine ganz andere Ansicht und Einsicht bekommen, seit ich aus dieser Quelle schöp-

---

23. Goethe himself, in his interest for things Indic, covered sheets with copies of Sanskrit characters, evidently not as the result of serious study but simply from the pure pleasure of imitating, perhaps to get a feeling for the form of the Indic script (I, 7, 297, 300; see also III, 6, 147). Kosegarten was often requested to translate Indic texts for him literally, so that he could make comparisons with the translations of Sir William Jones, Horace Wilson, and August Wilhelm Schlegel (I, 7, 239; I, 42, ii, 52). He discussed Indic poetry with Christian Lassen (Biedermann, III, 383). He promoted Indology however he could, acquired Indic works for the libraries of Weimar (IV, 33, 164, 317-318), and encouraged Duke Karl August to purchase Indological studies on his travels (IV, 28, 108). After August Wilhelm Schlegel began to print Sanskrit texts in Bonn in 1818, Goethe wrote to Carl Dietrich von Münchow on September 2, 1820: "A Sanskrit press on the Rhine seems to me an immense and almost unfeasible undertaking. Thus it is all the more respectable. May the Indus and the Ganges bestow their blessings on it" (IV, 33, 196; author's translation). See Paul T. Hoffmann, pp. 36-37.

fen kann."[24] The same eager enthusiasm for the language, the religion, and the culture of India, reflecting the idea contained in the mythical image, that India was the great source of all human wisdom, is reflected in the essays he wrote for the journal *Europa*, discussed previously.

In Paris, from November 25, 1803, to April 11, 1804, Friedrich Schlegel held initial lectures on the history of European literature for a small circle of listeners, lectures which he repeated in Cologne between June 28 and September 18, 1804, and gave again with a revised and enlarged text in Vienna in 1812.[25] He praises the "restless activity" of European scholars who are broadening their researches into Asiatic literature. In a passage significantly omitted from the Vienna lectures, he declares that the hypothesis that the source of Greek mythology is to be sought in India is very substantial (KFSA, XI, 15). He also dwells on the concept of God in Indic mythology, emphasizing the infinite spirit of God, the idea of the singularity and uniqueness of God, as well as other attributes of the Christian God that find echoes in Indic religion, such as that of the Trinity and that of Incarnation (KFSA, XI, 25). At this point he still seems to be seeking the lodestone of religion, and perhaps his own salvation, through India.

By 1804 Friedrich Schlegel had achieved a thorough knowledge of Sanskrit and could now devote himself wholeheartedly to studies in the language and philosophy of India. F. Imle, in his study of Friedrich Schlegel, says that with the continuing studies of the Indic language and culture he was laying the groundwork for a lifetime occupation which would have been sufficient to make him immortal to the civilized world. One scholar is even of the opinion that in Paris the eager student of Sanskrit became Indic himself, echoing August Wilhelm Schlegel's own estimate of his brother. Just as he had shown new paths to classical antiquity through his singularly profound knowledge of sources, Friedrich Schlegel was able to gain the Orient for Europe and become himself the founder of Oriental

24. H. Von Lüdeke, ed., *Ludwig Tieck und die Brüder Schlegel* (Frankfurt a.M., 1930), p. 140.
25. The small circle of listeners was composed of the brothers from Cologne who so excited Friedrich Schlegel's interest for the art and architecture of the Rhine area, Sulpiz and Melchior Boisserée, their friend Johann Baptist Bertram, and Helmina von Hastfer, later the wife of the Paris Orientalist Antoine-Léon de Chézy. The repetition of the lectures in Cologne was to a larger group, and in Vienna to a still larger audience—but in each case it was a private enterprise (KFSA, XI, xxx, xxxvi).

studies in Germany.[26] However, in his deeper probings into the original Sanskrit works, he looked beyond the mythical image of India. He came to realize that the ideal he sought was not to be found in the intellectual treasure house of India after all. His studies probably contributed to his conversion to Roman Catholicism in the search for the realization of his religious yearnings. Imle does not doubt that Friedrich Schlegel, in the state of mind which governed him at that time, ransacked the philosophy of India for its religious merits. But the Orient did not drive him away from Christianity, rather it impelled him toward it, for he believed that the primordial verity, the revelation of the essence of God, was to be found in Christianity, while such a revelation was only palely visible in the religion of India.[27] By the time of his philosophical lectures of 1804-1806, the critical reaction that was to cause him to abandon his studies had begun to manifest itself. Imle comments that the moral injuries already were present, for in the lectures Friedrich Schlegel relates the ascetic excesses and moral deterioration of Hindu sects.[28] Information regarding the less attractive side of the culture and religion of India had been available at second-hand through the reports of travelers, but it had been eclipsed by the brightness of the mythical image; now Friedrich Schlegel had documented sources, immediate and undeniable, and fatal to the mythical image.

While Friedrich Schlegel was involved in coming to terms with the poetic and philosophical aspects of the mythical image in the studies which culminated in *Über die Sprache und Weisheit der Indier*, his more scientific and objective attitude is glimpsed in the text of the lectures on universal history which he delivered privately in Cologne from October, 1805, until June, 1806. Although the northern valleys of India, particularly Kashmir, are still felt to be paradisiacal, no mention is made of the role they were felt to have played as the cradle of humankind (KFSA, XIV, 16). He still insists that the languages and cultures of Persia, Greece, and ancient Rome can be derived from Indic sources—but he does not state categorically that this is the case, and he adds a significant name to the list: Germany (KFSA, XIV, 19). The alteration of Friedrich Schle-

26. F. Imle, *Friedrich von Schlegels Entwicklung von Kant zum Katholizismus* (Paderborn, 1927), pp. 18-19.
27. *Ibid.*, p. 19.
28. *Ibid.*, p. 113.

gel's cultural focus from that of a pan-European to that of a specifically German one—evident after his move to Vienna and his patriotic endeavors in the realm of politics—causes him to list strange antecedents: he finds that the superiority of the class of nobility at one stage in the history of Persia and Germany can be traced to a like division in India (KFSA, XIV, 28). Although he still insists that everything was poeticized in India, since Indic religion was equivalent to poetry, he now distinguishes "real poetry," that is, "heroic poetry," and places its Indic origins at a time when the ruling class was composed of burghers (KFSA, XIV, 29). His growing preference for the Catholic church can be seen in his statement that the religious constitution of the Middle Ages was comparable to that of India (KFSA, XIV, 167). The idealized image of India has begun to disintegrate, a process which was completed in his book on India.

Now that the mythical image had begun to fade for Friedrich Schlegel, he became aware more and more of the less pleasant aspects of Hinduism. However, this did not detract from the enthusiasm for the studies he was making in Sanskrit. He first thought of publishing a journal of essays and translations, as he writes to the Berlin publisher Georg Reimer from Cologne on September 14, 1804 (Körner, p. 464). By the spring of 1805 he had conceived of a treatise and devised an outline of its contents. In a letter of March 16, 1805, written to Reimer, he tells of his progress in Sanskrit and describes the work that was to be the forerunner of comparative linguistics in Germany and in particular the harbinger of a lively German Oriental scholarship. He writes that he has copied seven Sanskrit manuscripts and translated them into Latin with a commentary. He remarks that not everything is suitable for translation, a realization which must have been disappointing to him. He then sketches the contents of his proposed treatise. After a general introduction he indicates that he would present a discussion of the language of India, to be followed by metrical translations of Hindu poetry. As an introduction to the *Ramayana* he planned to translate the epic Sakuntala episode (which Charles Wilkins had done in English in 1795), which could be compared to the drama, he says, "as an Egyptian pyramid to a small, elegant miniature." As for the drama *Sakuntala*, his enthusiasm has decreased. It is too lengthy to be included in his book, and besides, his aim is to present a variety of examples of Hindu literature. Moreover, the work contains so much Prakrit and prose that he will be content to offer only a sample to his readers. The third section of his work on India is to consist of a philosophical poem, for whose subtlety and sublimity he believes the German language to be particularly suited. His whole purpose is to make the language and style of Indic poetry as vivid as possible for German readers (Körner, p. 59).

In the autumn of 1805 Friedrich Schlegel visited August Wilhelm Schlegel, reawakening in him the interest in Sanskrit he had shown earlier. August Wilhelm Schlegel wrote the poet Fouqué on March 12, 1806, that his brother had made him excited about Oriental literatures, particularly Persian and Indic, and that he would pursue the matter as soon as he had an opportunity. He notes that after the visit Friedrich Schlegel had gone on to Paris to continue the studies begun earlier. He continues: "[Friedrich] schreibt die indischen Lettern so vortrefflich wie irgend ein Bramine, mit welchem Charakter er überhaupt immer mehr Aehnlichkeit gewinnt."[29] The concentration with which Friedrich Schlegel applied himself to the study of Sanskrit might indeed be compared with the contemplative singleness of mind of a Brahman. The oft-discussed poetic version of *Sakuntala* was destined never to become reality; in the letter to Reimer in the spring of 1805 Friedrich Schlegel had indicated a disenchantment with the dramatic version. August Wilhelm Schlegel, whose interest in Sanskrit had been aroused earlier than his brother's, but who had turned to other occupations in the intervening years, was to be Friedrich Schlegel's successor, when the younger brother abruptly abandoned his studies after the publication of the *Sprache und Weisheit der Indier*—but August Wilhelm Schlegel's pursuit of Indic research and his translations of Sanskrit works was beyond the pale of the mythical image and was done in a scientific spirit which won him the name of Germany's first great Indic scholar.[30]

29. A. W. Schlegel, *Werke*, VIII, 150. Thirteen years later, long after he had ceased his pursuit of Indic studies, Friedrich Schlegel employs a like term in regard to August Wilhelm Schlegel, whom he calls "the leading German Brahman" (letter of November 13, 1819, to August Wilhelm Schlegel, Walzel, p. 631).

30. Goethe's involvement with Indic culture consisted of attraction to the literature (with the exception of the moral fables) and abhorrence for the art and mythology. He even resisted in light or drastic ironic guise the exaggerations and exuberance of literary products because he felt his own formal equilibrium to be thus endangered. When August Wilhelm Schlegel began the serious dedication to Sanskrit studies with

In 1808 the fate of the mythical image of India among the Romanticists was decided with the publication of Friedrich Schlegel's work, the culmination of half a decade of intense study and rumination. The mythical image was depreciated in the book by the author's critical, often somewhat prejudiced, look at certain features. The form of the work did not quite turn out to be what the author had hoped for. On March 30, 1808, he wrote to Friedrich Wilken, who read proof for the volume, that instead of presenting an Indic chrestomathy, which he could not have done without outside financial support, he had no choice but to delineate his Indic studies in a "universal-grammatical and universal-historical relationship to its total importance." In this endeavor he had encountered such limitations and omissions that he had had to content himself with small, though sure, steps forward with particulars instead of taking regard of the larger aspects (Körner, p. 104). He was aware of the shortcomings and deficiencies in the work; he realized that it was fraught with the errors inherent in a pioneering venture. But he was proud of his effort, as he reveals in a letter of May 2, 1808, to Christian Gottlob Heyne, the Göttingen philologist and his former teacher. He begs to be remembered and commends his book to Heyne's attention. He remarks that the work represents initial steps on a largely untrodden path, deserving of consideration and accomplished with great personal sacrifice, for which he asks and expects no reward except the interest of the curious and the approval of leading scholars (Körner, pp. 105-106).

In the foreword to the work, *Über die Sprache und Weisheit der Indier* (1808), Friedrich Schlegel speaks of the expectancy that gripped those who were interested in the literature and the culture of India when Wilkins and Sir William Jones published the first translations of Sanskrit: revelations about the dark history of the ancient world for scholars of antiquity, and for those devoted to poetry beautiful creations of the Asiatic spirit like Sakuntala, filled

---

his professorial chair at the University of Bonn, and with the publication of original texts in the journal *Indische Bibliothek* (3 vols.; [Bonn, 1823-1830]), Goethe wrote: "The announcement of the *Ramayana* can be frightening. It is a poem of 24,000 distichs. May Brahma have mercy on the editor" (IV, 39, 283). Goethe never saw Indic culture in the aura of the mythical image. Those examples of Indic legend or literature which he adapted for his own use bear the stamp of his own artistic and philosophical essence.

with charm and love.[31] He expresses his thanks to Hamilton for making possible his acquisition of knowledge about India through the perusal of original Sanskrit manuscripts (VIII, 273). He speaks of his original plan for the publication of a more scholarly work and of the difficulties which made this plan unfeasible:

Mein Wunsch ging eigentlich dahin, eine *indische Chrestomathie* in lateinischer Sprache und in den Original-Charakteren herauszugeben, welche ausser den Anfangsgründen der Grammatik eine Auswahl zweckmässiger indischer Stücke mit lateinischer Paraphrase, Noten und Glossar enthalten sollte. . . . aber freilich würde die Verfertigung indischer Typen eine Unterstützung erfordern, an welcher es mir bis jetzt fehlte. . . . Und so musste ich mich denn für's erste darauf beschränken, durch den gegenwärtigen Versuch nur einen Beweis mehr zu liefern, wie fruchtbar das indische Studium dereinst noch werden könne, die Ueberzeugung allgemeiner zu verbreiten, welche reiche Schätze hier verborgen seien, die Liebe für dieses Studium, wenigstens vorläufig, auch in Deutschland anzufachen, und für die Ansicht des Ganzen einen festen Grund zu legen, auf welchem sich nachher mit Sicherheit weiter fortbauen liesse.
(VIII, 274-276)

He mentions the names of other Germans who studied Sanskrit before him:

Noch führe ich die mir bekannt gewordnen Deutschen an, welche sich mit dem Studium der altindischen Sprache beschäftigt haben. Der erste, den ich erwähnt finde, ist der Missionarius Henrich Roth, der im Jahr 1664 "die samskretanische Sprache erlernt, um mit den Brahminen disputieren zu können." —Grossen Ruhm erwarb sich in diesem Fache der im Jahre 1699 nach Indien abgegangene Jesuit Hanxleden, der über 30 Jahre (1732 wird sein Tod gemeldet) in der malabarischen Mission arbeitete, selbst vieles in der altindischen . . . und in der gemeinen Landessprache . . . in Prosa und in Versen geschrieben, Sprachlehren und Wörterbücher darüber verfasst, und dessen wahrscheinlich sehr reicher und gehaltvoller Nachlass zu Rom sich befindet. Der durch mehre gelehrte Schriften über das indische Alterthum bekannte Paulinus a St. Bartholomäo beruft sich mehrmals auf Hanxledens Arbeiten und handschriftlichen Nachlass. (VIII, 276-277)

He mentions also a Hauptmann Wilford and his own older brother, Karl August Schlegel. Joseph von Hammer-Purgstall, in a letter of

---

31. Friedrich Schlegel, *Sämmtliche Werke* (2d ed.; 15 vols.; Wien, 1846), VIII, 273. Further references to this edition will be given parenthetically in the text by volume and page.

May 21, 1808, lauds Friedrich Schlegel for his attainments, point-
ing out that he will find no one equipped to judge the work. He
notes, too, that Paulinus is of Germanic stock (Körner, p. 107).

The first section of the volume, "Von der Sprache," lays the
foundation for subsequent scholarship in comparative linguistics.
Friedrich Schlegel writes that Sanskrit presents evidence of relationship with Latin, Greek, Persian, and Germanic tongues, not only
in the great numbers of common roots but even in structure and
grammar. It is no coincidental agreement, he declares, but a basic
one which points to a common descent. Furthermore, he continues,
comparison shows that the Indic language is the more ancient, and
the others more recent and derived from it (VIII, 278). Linguists
no longer hold the opinion that Sanskrit is the mother of languages;
perhaps Friedrich Schlegel was led astray by the mythical image,
which made India the primeval source of all human attainments.
He sees in comparative linguistics an opportunity to discover much
about the origin of peoples and their earliest wanderings (VIII,
279). He hopes to have shown how a true history of the development of language could be devised on the basis of comparative
grammar (VIII, 318).[32] However false his premises may sometimes
have been, Friedrich Schlegel's contributions in this book were invaluable for the linguistic studies that were to be continued by
other scholars.

It is in the section entitled "Von der Philosophie" that Friedrich Schlegel's critical attitude, which effectively did damage to the
mythical image, comes to the fore. Imle, in his monograph, discusses
Schlegel's reaction. Above all, he says, it was both the old, Orientally
colored pantheism or the Indic system of emanation with its ethical
consequences of fatalism and determinism and the philosophical
dualism with its sovereign declaration of the coexistence of the
principle of evil with that of good which brought Friedrich Schlegel's own personal struggle to an end. They wrestled inside of
him until a higher truth, namely, the manifested, absolute truth was
victorious. Pantheism, of course, did create unity, but it dulled the
concept of the Absolute and through its consequence of fatalism

---

32. In regard to this passage Paul T. Hoffmann says that Friedrich Schlegel "prägte
zuerst den Ausdruck 'vergleichende Grammatik' " (p. 81). He errs, for August Wilhelm Schlegel used the term as early as 1803 in the review for Friedrich Schlegel's
Europa of A. F. Bernhardi's *Sprachlehre;* see *Europa,* II, 203.

lamed the human ethos. Moral stupefaction and intellectual in-
dolence were the natural results, particularly of the pantheistic
systems of the Orient and their popular religious mystifications.[33]

The mythical image had reflected brightly the idea of unity in
multiplicity, singularity in universality, the microcosm in the macro-
cosm, and the idea was transmuted in poetic terms by the Romantic poets; now Friedrich Schlegel sees in it nothing but a void: "Hier
bemerken wir nur, dass das lebendige tiefe Gefühl des Unendlichen
und seiner Fülle der Allmacht schon sehr geschwächt und ver-
dunkelt sein muss, ehe es sich in diesen vom Nichts schwer zu un-
terscheidenden Schatten- und Scheinbegriff des Einen und Allen
auflösen kann" (VIII, 344). He would not deny that the ancient
Hindus had a knowledge of the true God, "da alle ihre alten Schriften voll sind von Sprüchen und Ausdrücken, die so würdig, klar und
erhaben, so tiefsinnig und sorgfältig unterscheidend und bedeutend
sind, als menschliche Sprache nur überhaupt von Gott zu reden
vermag," but he wonders how they could have fallen into such abundant error (VIII, 326-327). He says the system of emanation is
agreeable as a doctrine of the return to the source, but finds it has
been spoiled and degraded by superstition:

Von dem göttlichen Ursprunge des Menschen nimmt es überall Anlass,
ihn an die Rückkehr zu erinnern, und sich die Wiedervereinigung mit
der Gottheit als einzigen Zweck aller seiner Handlungen und Bestre-
bungen zu setzen. Daher die heilige Bedeutung so mancher indischen
Gesetze, Sitten und Gebräuche, und der erhabene Ernst ihrer ganzen
Lebenseinrichtung. Doch mag der Geist schon frühe entflohen sein, so
dass es nur todte Gebräuche und Bussübungen blieben. (VIII, 330)

However, Friedrich Schlegel defines Hindu metempsychosis pre-
cisely and concurs in the belief that the transmigration of souls in
the teachings of Pythagoras had its origin in India:

Nach der in diesem Systeme herrschenden Ansicht von der Abstufung
und den Geschlechten der in so mannichfacher Gestalt eingehüllten
lebendigen Wesen, ihrer allmähligen Annäherung und Entfernung von
dem gemeinschaftlichen Urquell, entstand der Begriff von der *Seelenwanderung*. Noch verwandt damit und ebenfalls ein wesentlicher Be-
standtheil desselben Systems ist die Lehre von einem vorigen Leben, von
der Präexistenz der Seelen, und von den Ideen oder höheren Gedanken

33. Imle, p. 113.

aus dunkler Erinnerung der im vorigen Zustande angeschauten göttlichen Vollkommenheit, die besonders beim Anblicke des Schönen wieder rege wird; eine Lehre, auf die sich Kalidas in der Sokuntola ... als auf eine allgemein bekannte, und ganz populäre Vorstellungsart bezieht und anspielt. Wo diese Seelenwanderung nicht bloss physisch gemeint, sondern mit der Meinung von der moralischen Verderbniss und Unseligkeit aller Wesen, und nothwendigen Reinigung und Rückkehr zu Gott verbunden ist, da ist sie sicher aus diesem System entlehnt, und also indischen Ursprungs. Auf diese Weise finden wir in der Lehre des Pythagoras den Begriff der Metempsychose mit allen seinen orientalischen Nebenbestimmungen zum sichern Beweise, dass es keine hellenische Erfindung war. (VIII, 330-331)

The Hindu idea of an incarnation is, to him, proof of the profoundness of Hindu thought and the level of their wisdom, "so sehr die Idee auch durch willkührliche Dichtung und Märchen entstellt ist" (VIII, 340).

The third section of the work is "Historische Ideen." Here Schlegel notes that the theory of emanation contained the germ of polytheism, which contributed to Hindu mythology; this mythology was "verschönert, auch bereichert ... durch die Lehre von den zwei Principien, die Religion des Lichts, und der frommen gottbegeisterten Helden; sobald aber, wo es auch sein mag, pantheistische Denkart herrschend ward, konnte die Mythologie nur noch als Allegorie, als esoterische Hülle oder Spiel der Dichtung stehen bleiben" (VIII, 352). As an appendix to his volume, he offers translations excerpted from four Hindu works: the *Ramayana*, the *Laws of Menu*, the *Bhagavad-Gita*, and the *Mahabharata* (X, 195 ff.). P. T. Hoffmann says that in spite of the disappointed hopes of its author, Friedrich Schlegel's work was still an enthusiastic call for Indic studies. The purpose was no longer to find in India the cornucopia of the religion fervently hoped for, but to illuminate the oldest history of the human intellect.[34]

Friedrich Schlegel's abandonment of Sanskrit studies after the publication of *Sprache und Weisheit der Indier* was of influence in the continuation of the studies by August Wilhelm Schlegel, who found it hard to forgive his brother for the abrupt desertion. Many years later, on March 28, 1828, August Wilhelm Schlegel wrote to his brother and asked a bitter, reproachful question: "Jene Arbeiten

34. Paul T. Hoffmann, p. 81.

haben auf Dich nicht gewirkt, was sie hätten wirken sollen. Ich habe bereitwillig Deine frühzeitigen Bemühungen anerkannt: aber kennst Du den heitigen Stand der Wissenschaft?" (Walzel, p. 657).

Friedrich Schlegel's study was a scientific work, and the mythical image of India, which held his attention at first and spurred him on to investigate further into the culture of the Hindus through their language, could not survive the scrutiny of scientific inquiry. His disenchantment meant that the mythical image could not endure. Yet it found sympathetic spirits among later German poets and enjoyed a brief respite from oblivion in the works of three in particular: E. T. A. Hoffmann, Heinrich Heine, and Adalbert Stifter.

V. *The Reflection of the Image*

The dissolution of the Romantic mythical image of India, as a result in part of Friedrich Schlegel's disillusionment after his unhampered inspection of the culture of India revealed in Sanskrit writings, was to produce a fragmentary reflection of its features as fantastic imagery, as an ironic device, and as a symbol of the impossibility of the fulfilment of a longing for perfect contentment. These three aspects of the reflection of the image are best represented in E. T. A. Hoffmann, Heine, and Stifter. Even though the idyllic existence as delineated in the mythical image was acknowledged to be unattainable, each of these authors persists in his yearning for it. To Hoffmann India is the never-never land of magic language and paradisiac, poetic being. Heine sees India as a place of metaphorical blossoms and incredible temporal and artistic contradictions. And, finally, Stifter laments the failure of an attempted synthesis of Indic and Germanic cultures.

1 . Heute kommen Sie nur herein, werter Anselmus, denn wir müssen in das Zimmer, wo Bhogovotgitas Meister unsrer warten.
    —E. T. A. HOFFMANN

E. T. A. Hoffmann (1776-1822) was the poet after Novalis who came closest to devising a new mythology, based in part on the mythical image. He was the poet who, because of the inborn harmonies of his musical talent, created the most nearly musical texture of prose in the skilled use of assonance and recurrent motifs, a union of two arts in an era when unity of the arts was a watchword. Ricarda Huch says that Hoffmann calls music the most Romantic of all the arts, even the only true Romantic art because as its theme it has infinity, Sanskrit spoken in melody—thus the primeval language.[1] The best example of Hoffmann's new mythology, among his works the one most fully imbued with abundant examples of fantastic metaphor after the mythical image and a work which offers an intricate mixture of the wondrous and the ordinary, is *Der goldene Topf* (1813).

A contemporary critical review of the *Märchen* reveals some characteristics of the mythical image of India that are here contained. The critic says that this work is reminiscent of the mystery of mysteries, the mystery of all finite creation, of decay, and of the return of the transitory in primordial Being. It could also be called a beautiful hymn to poetry itself, for it is a poetic temper in which that transfiguration of the unpretentious bud of earth is celebrated as the splendor of primeval bliss. The magnificent myth of Phosphorus, the tale of the love and lament of the salamander, and the story of Anselmus the student are basically one and the same sublime allegory of decay and eternal return. All three images designate the graduated distance and the emanation of the finite from the infinite.[2] Here is the great rhythm, the return to the source, the emanation of a Supreme Essence. The three tales told, that of Phosphorus, that of the salamander, and that of the youth Anselmus are three variations on the same theme: in them are glimpsed the cos-

1. Huch, II, 256.
2. In the "Heidelbergische Jahrbücher der Litteratur," VII (1815), No. 66, pp. 1050 ff.; see E. T. A. Hoffmann, *Werke*, ed. Dr. Viktor Schweizer (3 vols.; Leipzig, [1896]), I, 4-5.

mology of the ideal world and the attainment of that world through poetry. There is much here that is reminiscent of Novalis' *Ofterdingen*. In *Der goldene Topf* the mythical image is transformed into fantastic imagery symbolic of poetic bliss.

When Anselmus first learns that he may find work with Archivarius Lindhorst, he is told about the strange and exotic languages represented in the Archivarius' library: "Er besitzt ausser vielen seltenen Büchern eine Anzahl zum Teil arabischer, koptischer, und gar in sonderbaren Zeichen, die keiner bekannten Sprache angehören, geschriebener Manuskripte."[3] One suspects that one of these strange languages must be the mysterious Sanskrit. After he has begun his job as copyist for Lindhorst, Anselmus is greeted one day with Lindhorst's invitation: "Heute kommen Sie nur herein, werter Anselmus, denn wir müssen in das Zimmer, wo Bhogovotgitas Meister unsrer warten" (III, 72). So it *is* Sanskrit, a metamorphosing script, which the astonished Anselmus sees before him: "Anselmus wunderte sich nicht wenig über die seltsam verschlungenen Zeichen, und bei dem Anblick der vielen Pünktchen, Striche und Züge und Schnörkel, die bald Pflanzen, bald Moose, bald Tiergerstalten darzustellen schienen, wollte ihm beinahe der Mut sinken, alles so genau nachmalen zu können" (III, 73). Thus, as a poetic copyist, does Hoffmann describe the script of Sanskrit.

The room in which Anselmus is to do his copywork is just off a marvelous greenhouse filled with exotic flowers and trees. The first time that he enters this garden of wonders with the Archivarius, Anselmus is left for a moment by himself; when the Archivarius returns, he says: "Verzeihen Sie, werter Herr Anselmus ... dass ich Sie stehen liess, aber vorübergehend sah ich nur nach meinem schönen Cactus, der diese Nacht seine Blüten aufschliessen wird" (III, 55). Such concern for a creature of nature is worthy of Kanna's grove. Upon Anselmus' first visit to the garden, he finds a truly Indic wonder:

Sie kamen aus dem Korridor in einen Saal oder vielmehr in ein herrliches Gewächshaus, denn von beiden Seiten bis an die Decke hinauf standen allerlei seltene, wunderbare Blumen, ja grosse Bäume mit sonderbar gestalteten Blättern und Blüten.... Im tiefen Dunkeln dicker Cypressenstauden schimmerten Marmorbecken, aus denen sich wunderliche Fi-

3. E. T. A. Hoffmann, *Dichtungen und Schriften*, ed. Walther Harich (15 vols.; Weimar, 1924), III, 18-19. Parenthetical references are to volume and page of this edition.

guren erhoben, Kristallenstrahlen hervorspritzend, die plätschernd nie-
derfielen in leuchtende Lilienkelche; seltsame Stimmen rauschten und
säuselten durch den Wald der wunderbaren Gewächse, und herrliche
Düfte strömten auf und nieder. (III, 54)

The first time Anselmus glimpses his future workroom, he is awed;
it seems almost to be an extension of the greenhouse: "Aus den
azurblauen Wänden traten die goldbronzenen Stämme hoher Palm-
bäume hervor, welche ihre kolossalen, wie funkelnde Smaragden
glänzenden Blätter oben zur Decke wölbten" (III, 55-56). The
second time that he enters the greenhouse Anselmus is even more
amazed: blossoms have become colorful insects, birds are now flowers, and the sweet fragrances are melodies; there is an aura of yearning about (III, 72). This is a rich and colorful paradise transplanted
from another age and clime, endowed with the magic of metamor-
phosis and full of yearning for a lost homeland.

In the story of Phosphorus, told by Lindhorst, cosmology is unfolded in poetic enchantment:

Der Geist schaute auf das Wasser, da bewegte es sich und brauste in
schäumenden Wogen und stürzte sich donnernd in die Abgründe, die
ihren schwarzen Rachen aufsperrten, es gierig zu verschlingen. Wie tri-
umphierende Sieger hoben die Granitfelsen ihre zackicht gekrönten
Häupter empor, das Tal schützend, bis es die Sonne in ihren mütter-
lichen Schoss nahm und es umfassend mit ihren Strahlen wie mit glühenden Armen pflegte und wärmte. Da erwachten tausend Keime, die
unter dem öden Sande geschlummert, aus dem tiefen Schlafe und streck-
ten ihre grüne [sic] Blättlein und Halme zum Angesicht der Mutter
hinauf, und wie lächelnde Kinder in grüner Wiege ruhten in den Blüten
und Knospen Blümlein, bis auch sie, von der Mutter geweckt, erwachten
und sich schmückten mit den Lichtern, die die Mutter ihnen zur Freude
auf tausendfache Weise bunt gefärbt. (III, 22)

When Phosphorus dons armor to battle the dragon who guards the
fire lily, the wings of the dragon strike his coat of mail so that it
resounds: "Und von dem mächtigen Klange lebten die Blümlein
wieder auf und umflatterten wie bunte Vögel den Drachen, dessen
Kräfte schwanden, und der besiegt sich in der Tiefe der Erde ver-
barg. . . . Im hochjubelnden Hymnus huligten ihr [der Lilie] die
Blumen, die Vögel, ja selbst die hohen Granitfelsen als Königin des
Thals." At this point, Registrator Heerbrand, one of the philistine
listeners to the story, interrupts to say: "Erlauben Sie, das ist ori-

entalischer Schwulst, werter Herr Archivarius!" (III, 24). But the Archivarius assures Heerbrand that the story is true, for the fire lily was his ancestor.

From Serpentina, who assumes the form of a little green snake and is the daughter of Lindhorst, Anselmus hears the story of the salamander, who is Lindhorst himself. When the salamander lays waste the garden of Phosphorus, because of his despair over the loss of his beloved, he is banished from Atlantis, synonymous here, just as in Novalis, with Paradise or the mythic land of poetry:

Sein Feuer ist für jetzt erloschen . . . in der unglücklichen Zeit, wenn die Sprache der Natur dem entarteten Geschlecht der Menschen nicht mehr verständlich sein, wenn die Elementargeister, in ihre Regionen gebannt, nur aus weiter Ferne in dumpfen Anklängen zu den Menschen sprechen werden, wenn, dem harmonischen Kreise entrückt, nur ein unendliches Sehnen ihm dunkle Kunde von dem wundervollen Reiche geben wird, das er sonst bewohnen durfte, als noch Glaube und Liebe in seinem Gemüte wohnten,—in dieser unglücklichen Zeit entzündet sich der Feuerstoff des Salamanders aufs neue, doch nur zum Menschen keimt er empor und muss, ganz eingehend in das dürftige Leben, dessen Bedräng-nisse ertragen. Aber nicht allein die Erinnerung an seinen Urzustand soll ihm bleiben, sondern er lebt auch wieder auf in der heiligen Har-monie mit der ganzen Natur, er versteht ihre Wunder, und die Macht der verbrüderten Geister steht ihm zu Gebote. (III, 78-79)

The salamander will be released from his exile when his three daughters have married men who are kindred spirits. Phosphorus describes the sort of youth such a man must be, and tells what trials he must pass:

Findet sich dann in der dürftigen armseligen Zeit der innern Verstockt-heit ein Jüngling, der ihren Gesang vernimmt, ja, blickt ihn eine der Schlänglein mit ihren holdseligen Augen an, entzündet der Blick in ihm die Ahnung des fernen wundervollen Landes, zu dem er sich mutig emporschwingen kann, wenn er die Bürde des Gemeinen abgeworfen, keimt mit der Liebe zur Schlange in ihm der Glaube an die Wunder der Natur, ja an seine eigne Existenz in diesen Wundern glutvoll und lebendig auf, so wird die Schlange sein. (III, 79)

Here, in the most sublime poetic language, and clothed in the trans-figured imagery of the mythical image of India, the land of longing and universal poetry and harmony with nature, Hoffmann expresses his yearning for poetic innocence. Serpentina reports to Anselmus the quality of mind necessary for the attainment of this ideal: "Er hat mir oft gesagt, dass für die innere Geistesbeschaffenheit, wie sie der Geisterfürst Phosphorus damals als Bedingnis der Vermählung mit mir und meinen Schwestern aufgestellt, man jetzt einen Ausdruck habe, der aber nur zu oft unschicklicherweise gemissbraucht werde; man nenne das nämlich ein kindliches poetisches Gemüt" (III, 80). The catchwords of the apotheosis of the mythical image sparkle here in brilliant abundance.

When Anselmus has proved his worthiness, he goes to Atlantis to live with his bride. Hoffmann, the author, longs to know how Anselmus fares in the garden of poetry, and Lindhorst reveals it to him in a vision:

Das Azur löst sich von den Wänden und wallt wie duftiger Nebel auf und nieder, aber blendende Strahlen schiessen durch den Duft, der sich wie in jauchzender kindischer Luft wirbelt und dreht und aufsteigt bis zur unermesslichen Höhe, die sich über den Palmbäumen wölbt. —Aber immer blendender häuft sich Strahl auf Strahl, bis in hellem Sonnenglanze sich der unabsehbare Hain aufschliesst, in dem ich den Anselmus erblicke. —Glühende Hyacinthen und Tulipanen und Rosen erheben ihre schönen Häupter, und ihre Düfte rufen in gar lieblichen Lauten dem Glücklichen zu.... sehnsuchtsvoll schaut Anselmus nach dem herrlichen Tempel, der sich in weiter Ferne erhebt.... Da tritt in hoher Schönheit und Anmut Serpentine aus dem Innern des Tempels, sie trägt den goldnen Topf, aus dem eine herrliche Lilie entsprossen.

(III, 115-116)

The glorious lily is "die Erkenntnis des heiligen Einklangs aller Wesen" (III, 117), and thus transformed does the lotus revered in India symbolize the sacred union of all things in splendid harmony —the synthesis sought for is achieved. The author mourns his return to the pedestrian world, but is reprimanded by Lindhorst: "Still, still, Verehrter! Klagen Sie nicht so! —Waren Sie nicht soeben selbst in Atlantis, und haben Sie denn nicht auch dort wenigstens einen artigen Meierhof als poetisches Besitztum Ihres innern Sinns? —Ist denn überhaupt des Anselmus Seligkeit etwas anderes als das Leben in der Poesie, der sich der heilige Einklang aller Wesen als tiefstes Geheimnis der Natur offenbaret?" (III, 118). So Hoffmann finds surcease for his longing and attains his yearned-for Atlantis in poetic fantasy.

Throughout the *Märchen* there are glimmerings of the mythical image, echoes of the language of the myth transfigured. The use of the term *Atlantis* for a poetically transubstantiated existence into a state of innocence in harmony with all creation reminds one of Novalis' conception of the land of harmony and simplicity and contentment. It is the poet there who is welcomed to the court of the king of Atlantis, just as it is the enchantment of poetic fancy, abetted by the mythical image, which transports Hoffmann to the land of fulfilment.

2. *Komm mit nach Indien, nach dem Sonnenlande,*
   Wo Ambrablüten ihren Duft verbreiten,
   Die Pilgerscharen nach dem Ganges schreiten,
   Andächtig und im weissen Festgewande. —HEINE

Heinrich Heine (1799-1856), who called himself the last Romanticist, revives the mythical image of India almost to the level it reached among the Early Romanticists. He cherishes and expresses a deep yearning for the land of love, for the simplicity of existence on the banks of the Ganges, where the wondrous beauties of nature dwell intimately with a naïve people. A new element is added to the transmutation of the image, however: irony. Heine consciously conjures the image to echo his own sentiments, his moods, and his yearning. At times he breaks a lyric thought with a brash injection of irony, an immediate disclaimer of the mood, an admission that this is make-believe. At times a whole poem is playfully ironic, resulting in a bemused dissection of the image (see "Der weisse Elefant").[1] The irony serves notice of the author's awareness of the idealism of the image, but one discerns nevertheless a real longing for the qualities symbolized by the mythical image.

In the tenth poem of "Lyrisches Intermezzo" (1823), from the *Buch der Lieder*, Heine would fly on the wings of poetry to the

1. Heinrich Heine, *Sämtliche Werke*, ed. Oskar Walzel (10 vols.; Leipzig, 1911-1915), III, 8-14. Further references are given parenthetically by volume and page of this edition.

Ganges with his love. The poem is resplendent with the vocabulary typical of an expression of the mythical image:

> Auf Flügeln des Gesanges,
> Herzliebchen, trag ich dich fort,
> Fort nach den Fluren des Ganges,
> Dort weiss ich den schönsten Ort.
>
> Dort liegt ein rotblühender Garten
> Im stillen Mondenschein;
> Die Lotosblumen erwarten
> Ihr trautes Schwesterlein.
>
> Die Veilchen kichern und kosen,
> Und schaun nach den Sternen empor;
> Heimlich erzählen die Rosen
> Sich duftende Märchen ins Ohr.
>
> Es hüpfen herbei und lauschen
> Die frommen, klugen Gazelln;
> Und in der Ferne rauschen
> Des heiligen Stromes Welln.
>
> Dort wollen wir niedersinken
> Unter dem Palmenbaum,
> Und Liebe und Ruhe trinken
> Und träumen seligen Traum. (I, 74)

In the seventh poem of "Die Heimkehr" (1824) a wistful glance of longing is cast toward the Ganges:

> Wir sprachen von fernen Küsten,
> Vom Süden und vom Nord,
> Und von den seltsamen Völkern
> Und seltsamen Sitten dort.
>
> Am Ganges duftet's und leuchtet's,
> Und Riesenbäume blühn,
> Und schöne, stille Menschen
> Vor Lotosblumen knien. (I, 110)

In the series entitled "Friedrike," from *Neue Gedichte* (1844), but published earlier in *Salon* (1834), Heine once again desires to leave philistine Berlin and declare his love to his beloved in India:

> Verlass Berlin, mit seinem dicken Sande,
> Und dünnen Thee, und überwitz'gen Leuten,
> Die Gott und Welt, und was sie selbst bedeuten,
> Begriffen längst mit Hegelschem Verstande.

Komm mit nach Indien, nach dem Sonnenlande,
Wo Ambrablüten ihren Duft verbreiten
Die Pilgerscharen nach dem Ganges schreiten,
Andächtig und im weissen Festgewande.

Dort wo die Palmen wehn, die Wellen blinken,
Am heil'gen Ufer Lotosblumen ragen
Empor zu Indras Burg, der ewig blauen;

Dort will ich gläubig vor dir niedersinken,
Und deine Füsse drücken, und dir sagen:
Madame! Sie sind die Schönste aller Frauen. (II, 72)

After the saucy introductory stanza, Heine sinks into the mythical image with yearning for India. The caressing of feet was a commonplace expression of love in Hindu poetry (for example, in the *Gita-Govinda*). In other verses to Friedrike, Heine alludes to the Ganges, Kama, the Hindu cupid, and to Gandarvas, the musicians in Indra's heaven (II, 73).

In the appendix to the "Harzreise" (1826) Heine deplores the wanton killing of animals by hunters and in humanistic fervor implies that the most gentle people live in India: " 'Am Ganges, am Ganges wohnen Menschen' " (IV, 422). In the short essay "Über Polen" (1822) he compares the women of Poland to the legendary beauties in Hindu India: "—ich spreche von Polens Weibern. Mein Geist schweift an den Ufern des Ganges, und sucht die zartesten und lieblichsten Blumen, um sie damit zu vergleichen" (V, 296). The equation of *Blumen* for the women of India is quite typical of the mythical image. In the "Englische Fragmente" (1828) Heine visits a merchant ship docked in England and, at the sight of the Hindu crewmen, is transported in enchantment to the land of his dreams:

Im Hafen von London, wo die indischen Docks sind, stieg ich an Bord eines Ostindienfahrers ... der eben aus Bengalen angelangt war. Es war ein riesenhaftes Schiff und zahlreich bemannt mit Hindostanern. Die grotesken Gestalten und Gruppen, die seltsam bunten Trachten, die rätselhaften Mienen, die wunderlichen Leibesbewegungen, der wildfremde Klang der Sprache, des Jubels und des Lachens, dabei wieder der Ernst auf einigen sanftgelben Gesichtern, deren Augen, wie schwarze Blumen, mich mit abenteuerlicher Wehmut ansahen—alles das erregte in mir ein Gefühl wie Verzauberung ... und ich meinte schon, nun mussten ... fabelhafte Bäume und Tiere zum Vorschein kommen.

(V, 154-155)

In "Das Buch Le Grand" (1826) Heine mixes the conjuration of the magic land with abrupt interludes of Romantic irony. The narrator says:

Ich . . . liess mir . . . ein Glas Rheinwein vorstellen—
Essen konnt ich nicht und trinken noch viel weniger. Die heissen Tropfen fielen ins Glas, und im Glas sah ich die liebe Heimat, den blauen, heiligen Ganges, den ewigstrahlenden Himalaya, die riesigen Banianenwälder, in deren weiten Laubgängen die klugen Elefanten und die weissen Pilger ruhig wandelten, seltsam träumerische Blumen sahen mich an, heimlich mahnend, goldne Wundervögel jubelten wild, flimmernde Sonnenstrahlen und süssnärrische Laute von lachenden Affen neckten mich lieblich, aus fernen Pagoden ertönten die frommen Priesterergebete, und dazwischen klang die schmelzend klagende Stimme der Sultanin von Delhi. (IV, 140-141)

At this point in the narrative the idyllic picture in the imagination of the poet takes a sudden wild turn and then is shattered by Romantic irony: "—in ihrem Teppichgemache rannte sie stürmisch auf und nieder, sie zerriss ihren silbernen Schleier, sie stiess zu Boden die schwarze Sklavin mit dem Pfauenwedel, sie weinte, sie tobte, sie schrie—Ich konnte sie aber nicht verstehen, der Keller des Signor Unbescheiden ist 3000 Meilen entfernt vom Harem zu Delhi, und dazu war die schöne Sultanin schon tot seit 3000 Jahren" (IV, 141). Later irony breaks the mood again when the narrator, who has identified himself as the count from the Ganges, confesses to his feminine friend that he has deceived her:

Madame! ich habe Sie belogen. Ich bin nicht der Graf vom Ganges. Niemals im Leben sah ich den heiligen Strom, niemals die Lotosblumen, die sich in seinen frommen Wellen bespiegeln. Niemals lag ich träumend unter indischen Palmen, niemals lag ich betend vor dem Diamantengott zu Jagernaut, durch den mir doch leicht geholfen wäre. Ich war ebensowenig jemals in Kalkutta wie der Kalkutenbraten, den ich gestern Mittag gegessen. Aber ich stamme aus Hindostan, und daher fühl' ich mich so wohl in den breiten Sangeswäldern Valmikis, die Heldenleiden des göttlichen Ramo bewegen mein Herz wie ein bekanntes Weh, aus den Blumenliedern Kalidasas blühn mir hervor die süssesten Erinnerungen, und als vor einigen Jahren eine gütige Dame in Berlin mir die hübschen Bilder zeigte, die ihr Vater, der lange Zeit Gouverneur in Indien war, von dort mitgebracht, schienen mir die zartgemalten, heiligstillen Gesichter so wohlbekannt, und es war mir, als beschaute ich meine eigne Familiengalerie.

Franz Bopp—Madame, Sie haben gewiss seinen "Nalus" und sein "Konjugationssystem des Sanskrit" gelesen—gab mir manche Auskunft über meine Ahnherren, und ich weiss jetzt genau, dass ich aus dem Haupte Brahmas entsprossen bin und nicht aus seinen Hühneraugen; ich vermute sogar, dass der ganze Mahabharata mit seinen 200,000 Versen bloss ein allegorischer Liebesbrief ist, den mein Urahnherr an meine Urältermutter geschrieben— O! sie liebten sich sehr, ihre Seelen küssten sich, sie küssten sich mit den Augen, sie waren beide nur ein einziger Kuss — (IV, 147-148)

In this passage Heine makes numerous allusions to the mythical image, often with an ironic smile. He puns on the word Calcutta with *Kalkut* (=turkeycock, in accordance with the tradition which has the American bird—also called *Kalekutschhahn,* a corruption of *kalekutscher Hahn*—being brought to Europe by way of the Indian city); Valmiki is the poet of the *Ramayana,* and Ramo (=Rama) its hero; he mentions the Sanskrit scholar Franz Bopp (1791-1867) and two of his works: that of the conjugation system of Sanskrit from 1816 and that of his Latin translation of the episode of Nal and Damayanti from the *Mahabharata* of 1819; he alludes in an ironic aside to the mythological origin of the caste system in India. One feels that with all the ironic color, however, a soft strain of longing pervades the whole passage, even in the wry and exaggerated self-identification of the poet with his "Indic" forebears: the entire passage wears an aura of parody. The Indic allusions are sophisticated and knowledgeable, but are haunted by the mythical image.

In *Die romantische Schule* (1833) Heine finds the poetry of the Orient to be a Romantic poetry: "Bei den Völkern, wo die Poesie ebenfalls das Unendliche darstellen wollte, and ungeheure Ausgeburten der Phantasie zum Vorschein kamen, z.B. bei den Skandinaviern und Indiern, finden wir Gedichte, die wir ebenfalls für romantische halten und auch romantisch zu nennen pflegen" (VII, 15). Heine emphasizes the feeling of kinship the Romanticists felt with India through the mythical image. One remembers Friedrich Schlegel's exhortation to seek the highest expression of the Romantic in the Orient. Heine compliments Friedrich on the accomplishment of bringing Sanskrit poetry in its original meters to the attention of German readers: "Durch sein tiefes Anschauungsvermögen erkannte er ganz die Bedeutung der epischen Versart der Indier, der Sloka, die so breit dahinflutet wie der Ganges, der heilige klare Fluss" (VII, 67). He compares the poets of Romanticism with the mystics of India:

Die einen Dichter versenkten sich mit allen ihren menschlichen Gefühlen in die Natur hinein.... Sie waren die eigentlichen Mystiker und glichen in vieler Hinsicht den indischen Religiosen, die in der Natur aufgehen, und endlich mit der Natur in Gemeinschaft zu fühlen beginnen.... Zu ihnen gehörte zunächst Novalis.... Novalis sah überall nur Wunder und liebliche Wunder; er belauschte das Gespräch der Pflanzen, er wusste das Geheimnis jeder jungen Rose, er identifizierte sich endlich mit der ganzen Natur. (VII, 105)

It is interesting, and significant, that Heine associates the Romantic appreciation and awareness of nature, and its receptivity to the idea of *Wunder*, with India.

Heine seems, despite the frequent ironical touches, to be earnest in his yearning for the India perceived in the mythical image. This belief is borne out by the aphorisms contained in "Gedanken und Einfälle," published after his death. He acknowledges the quest of India among the intellectuals of his day and is aware of the incompleteness of the image of India: "Wir haben das körperliche Indien gesucht, und haben Amerika gefunden; wir suchen jetzt das geistige Indien—was werden wir finden?" (X, 253). He is cognizant of the historical value of Hindu epics with their symbolic representation of the infinite:

Die epischen Gedichte der Indier sind ihre Geschichte; doch können *wir* sie erst dann zur Geschichte benutzen, wenn wir die Gesetze entdeckt haben, nach welchen die Indier das Geschehene ins phantastisch Poetische umwandelten. Dies ist uns noch nicht bei der Mythologie der Griechen gelungen, doch mag es bei diesen schwerer sein, weil diese das Geschehene beständig zur Fabel ausbildeten in immer bestimmterer Plastik. Bei den Indiern hingegen bleibt die phantastische Umbildung immer noch Symbol, das das Unendliche bedeutet, und nicht nach Dichterlaune in bestimmteren Formen ausgemeiselt wird. (X, 253-254)

He acknowledges the antiquity of the Hindu epic fragments by comparing them with mammoth fossils: "Die Mahabaratas, Ramayanas und ähnliche Riesenfragmente sind geistige Mammutsknochen, die auf dem Himalaya zurückgeblieben" (X, 254). That the Hindu permeated the whole world with poetry was testimony to

his character as a contemplative being and evidence of the immanent nature of his God: "Der Indier konnte nur ungeheuer grosse
Gedichte liefern, weil er nichts aus dem Weltzusammenhang
schneiden konnte, wie überhaupt der Anschauungsmensch. Die
ganze Welt ist ihm ein Gedicht, wovon der Mahabarata nur ein
Kapitel" (X, 254).

The mythical image of India as reflected in Heine has acquired
a new lyricism as well as a shade of irony. The lyricism makes the
image more sublime and the irony illuminates the image with a
brighter discernment. Both are manifestations of Heine's sincere
longing for the magic world of the image, filled with strains of love
and cultural splendors.

*3. Da fiel mir ein ... ich wollte nach dem Himalaia gehen. Ich
wollte die riesenhaften und unschuldigen Pflanzen Gottes
sehen.* —STIFTER

The first recognition of the Orient by Adalbert Stifter (1806-1868),
perhaps under the influence of Herder, is found in *Haidedorf* (1840),
where exotic lands appear for the first time in his writings.[1] In *Feld-
blumen* (1840) is his earliest expression of longing for distant lands,
among them India: "Italien fiel mir ein und Indien und Griechen-
land und Amerika und die ganze schöne Kugel und die Meere
darauf und die Palmenwälder—und dass ich all Das nie in meinem
Leben werde sehen können" (I, 141). There is no question here of
attainment; the longing is acknowledged to be beyond the possibility
of realization. In the same work, in the episode entitled "Baldrian,"
Stifter lets a character, Emil, describe East India, where he had
been born but which he had not seen since his childhood:

Dann sagte er ihr von fernen Ländern, in denen er geboren worden, und
von den schönen Menschen, die dort wohnen. Auf einmal verlangte er
selber nach Ostindien. Alle Werke über dieses Land, die er habhaft
werden konnte, las er durch und entzündete sich immer mehr und mehr,

---

1. Adalbert Stifter, *Sämmtliche Werke*, ed. August Sauer *et al.* (25 vols.; to 1960;
Prag, 1904-), I, xxxix-xl. Further references are given parenthetically by volume and
page of this edition.

ja, als er im nächsten Jahre von Paris kam, redete er zum Erstaunen des Oheims ziemlich gut die Sprache der Bramanen. (I, 158)

When Emil returns to Europe after several years in India, he speaks of "indische Märchen . . . voll fremden Dufts und fremder Farben" (I, 159). These references to India, however, are only preliminary to the forlorn longing one finds in the story of the unfortunate pariah maiden, Chelion.

It is in this tale in *Die Narrenburg* (1843) that Stifter's yearning for India is defined. Aspects of the mythical image appear, but tinged with an attitude of hopeless nostalgia. The time when the fulfilment of the longing might have been realized is past. The delicate mythical image, transplanted to the West, perishes from home-sickness and the rigors of the northern climate. The synthesis of the Orient and the West results in a lovely but half-wild, home-less, and forlorn creature.

The story of Chelion, found in the frame of *Die Narrenburg,* seems to have been based on the actual experience of an Abyssinian girl, Machbubah, who was bought at Gondar by Hermann von Pück-ler-Muskau in 1836. Chelion is brought from India by Jodok, an ancestor of the actual hero of the story, Heinrich, who has come to inspect the family castle, called the "Narrenburg" by local residents, which has been without inhabitants for many years. From the old caretaker, Ruprecht, and from an autobiographical sketch written by Jodok, Heinrich is able to reconstruct the story of Chelion.

She was the daughter of a pariah, the lowest social class of the Hindus, but Stifter has given her the qualities usually ascribed in the mythical image to the high-born caste of the Brahman. She is gentle, devoted, and childishly naïve. Heinrich is shown a portrait of her:

Eine kleine weibliche Figur war auf dem Bilde gemalt, wie ein Kind in sanfter Trauer, und doch wie ein vermähltes glühendes Weib. Ueber dem schwarzen Seidenkleide hielt sie ein lichtes Antlitz, so seltsam und schön, wie eine Blume über dunklen Blättern. Die kleine, weisse Hand lag auf Marmor und spiegelte sich drinnen. Die Augen sahen fremd und erschreckt. Zu ihren Füssen, als friere er, schmiegte sich ein Goldfasen.
(II, 74)

The comparison of her features with a flower, evoking the lotus, marks the portrait unmistakably as a reflection of the mythical image. The quiet grief of the girl and the apparently freezing pheasant symbolize the nostalgia for India and the baleful influence of an enervating climate on a fragile foreign organism. Ruprecht compares the fairness of Chelion to a white lily contrasting with the dark waters of a swamp (II, 74-75). Jodok, in his notebook, can find no words to describe the beauty of Chelion:

Das Land Indien war es, wo mir der Engel meiner schwersten That erschien;—unter dunklem Schatten fremder Bäume war es, an einem Fluss, der so klar floss, als walle nur dichtere Luft längs der glänzenden Kiesel—das Schlechteste und Verachtet'ste, was die Menschheit hat, war dieser Engel, die Tochter eines Paria; aber schön war sie, schön über jeden Ausdruck, den eine Sprache ersinnen mag, und über jedes Bild, das in Jahrtausenden einmal in eine wallende Phantasie kommt.
(II, 100)

In the narrative Jodok tells how he went to India and met the lovely pariah maiden Chelion. The mythical image of India shimmers throughout the account:

Da fiel mir ein . . . ich wollte nach dem Himalaia gehen. Ich wollte die riesenhaften und unschuldigen Pflanzen Gottes sehen . . .
Ich kam nach dem Himalaia. Dort lernte ich die Hindusprache, dort sah ich das Bramanenleben . . . und dort ging auch die Paria zwischen Riesenpalmen nach dem Flusse, um Wasser für den Vater zu schöpfen. Sie hat, seit sie lebte, sonst nichts getan, als dass sie durch die Palmen ging, um Wasser zu holen und für den Vater Datteln zu lesen und Kräuter zu pflücken.
"Rühre mich nicht an und rede nicht mit mir," hatte sie zu dem fremden Manne gesagt, "dass Du nicht unrein werdest,"—und dann stellte sie den Wasserkrug auf ihre Schulter neben den glänzenden, unsäglich reinen Nacken und ging zwischen den schlanken Stämmen davon.
. . . Als er [der Vater] eines Tages todt war, und sie nicht zu dem Fluss kam, so ging ich zu ihr und berührte sie doch; denn ich nahm ihre Hand, um sie zu trösten—ich redete mit ihr, dass sie erschrak und zitterte und mich ansah, wie ein Reh. (II, 101)

The disarming naïveté of the Hindu is illustrated in the conversation he has with Chelion. Jodok, wanting to take her to Europe with him, speaks to her about the Christian God, Who does not desire the death of the wife when a husband dies. Chelion's reply is childlike: " 'Wenn sie aber freiwillig geht, so nimmt er sie doch mit Wohlgefallen auf?' fragte sie und heftete die Augen der Gazelle auf mich" (II, 102). The guileless and persistent tenacity with which Chelion clings to her beliefs, her inability to accept intellectual persuasion betokens her physical inability to adapt to the harsh northern climate.

Jodok relates how he spirited Chelion from the idyllic life in India and how she, with her sense of cleanliness and purity, was shocked at having to bathe in and drink the dirty water aboard ship on the voyage to Europe: "Sie kannte kein anderes Glück, als im Walde zu leben, Früchte zu geniessen, Blumen zu pflücken and die Pflanzenspeisen zu bereiten, die ihr sanfter, reinlicher Glaube vorschrieb. . . . Das weiche Blumenblatt nahm ich mit mir fort, unter einen fremden Himmel, unter eine fremde Sonne" (II, 102-103). When Jodok has his Indic flower safely in Europe, he builds for her a strange, temple-like structure and surrounds it with a marvelous garden planted with the flowers and shrubs of her homeland. The innkeeper first describes the temple, now fallen to ruin, as it had been:

Da hat er innerhalb der Schlossfriedigung abseits den andern Gebäuden einen seltsamen Tempel aufgeführt, mit vielen Säulen, wie man sie oft als Lusthaus in hochherrschaftlichen Gärten sieht, und in diesem Tempel hat er gewohnt, wie man sagt, in ungewöhnlicher Pracht und Ueppigkeit, mit seiner Frau, einer wunderschönen Zigeunerin, die er einmal brachte —und dieses Bauwerk hat er dann angezündet. (II, 17)

Ruprecht leads Heinrich to what remains of the exotic garden: " 'Hier ist das Thor; Ihr könnt ja gleich in den indischen Garten des bösen Jodok kommen. Seht, der Garten ist so schön.' . . . Es war ein reicher Garten . . . voll der sanftesten Sträuche und Bäume nebst Resten verkommener, ausländischer Gewächse. Mitten in dem Garten stand ein grosser, weisser Würfel aus dem feinsten Marmor gehauen, mit der Inschrift: 'Jodok und Chelion' " (II, 83).

In Jodok's journal is a description of the garden and an account of the pains taken to make of it an artificial Eden to protect his transplanted blossom:

Auch einen Garten legte ich rund herum an. . . . Ich zog schwarze Mauern und Terrassen, um die Sonnenhitze zu sammeln; ich warf Wälle auf, um den Winden zu wehren; ich baute ganze Gassen von gläsernen Häusern, um darin Pflanzen zu hegen, dann liess ich kommen, was ihr theuer und vertraut war: die schönsten Blumen ihres Vaterlandes, die weichsten Gesträuche, die lieblichsten Vögel und Thiere—aber ach, den dunkelblauen Himmel und die weissen Häupter des Himalaia konnte ich nicht kommen lassen, und der Glanz meiner Wohnung war nicht der Glanz ihrer indischen Sonne. (II, 103)

Chelion lived for a time in the man-made Paradise, but she faded with longing for India: "So lebte sie nun fort. Sie ass kein Fleisch. . . . höher hätte sie mich gewiss geachtet, wenn ich es ebenfalls vermocht hatte, nur ihre Pflanzengerichte, ihre Früchte und ihr Obst zu geniessen. . . . Oft sagte mir eine Stimme ganz deutlich in das Ohr: 'Gehe wieder mit ihr nach Indien, sie stirbt vor Heimweh' " (II, 104). The Romantic mythical image was essentially subjective; the Romantic poet ignored the unpleasant aspects of the image, aware of them but choosing to overlook them. If he mentions the pariah, it is with sorrow and pity. But he would not have confused the pariah with the Brahman, as Stifter does in his portrayal of Chelion. An outstanding difference between the castes, emphasized by travelers and Herder himself, was that the Brahman ate no meat; the lowly pariah not only ate of meat but even slaughtered animals.

When he realizes that Chelion has been seduced by his brother, Jodok enters her chamber with a poison, intending to kill her; but her gentle beauty and her simple, essentially innocent heart disarm him: "Ihre Hand, wie ein Blatt der Lotosblume, lag auf der reinen Decke ihres Lages. . . . sie regte sich, öffnete die Augenlider und sah mich mit den schönen, heimathlosen Augen an" (II, 108-109). He departs to dispose of the poison, and his wrath abates, but the Indic plants in the garden regard him reproachfully (II, 109). When Jodok returns to her room he finds Chelion crouching on the floor, holding a dove to her breast. He vows to make her unsmirched heart forget the horrors of the night, with the realization that simple, artless, and pure things are most easily and most irrevocably destroyed (II, 113). Despite the protective care she finds lavished upon her, Chelion meets the same fate which befell the old hermit's wife in *Heinrich von Ofterdingen*. Like the transplanted fragile tropical plant, she perishes under the rigors of an inhospitable climate.

The granddaughter of Jodok and Chelion, Pia, lives with Ruprecht, the caretaker. She is about ten years old, a wild and untamed child whose best friend is a dog. When she is first glimpsed by Heinrich, on his visit to the castle, she is described as follows: "Sie blieb stehen, als bemerke sie die Fremden erst jetzt, zögerte, sah sie eine Zeit lang mit wilden, schwarzen Augen an, dann aber ging sie zuerst langsam um die Mauerecke, scheu und wild, wie eine junge, schlanke Pantherkatze, dann fing sie an, den jenseitigen Rasenhang hinabzulaufen—der Hund hinter ihr" (II, 113).

Pia, the shy and animal-like child, the ruined garden, and the fallen, burned temple, the graves, the legend, and the portrait are all that remain of Chelion. When Ruprecht and Heinrich have gazed upon Chelion's portrait, the caretaker says, as they are about to depart: "Wartet nur, ich will zuerst den blauen Vorhang herablassen, weil er nicht offen stehen bleiben darf . . ." And then he says: "Hüll' Dich ein . . . Du schöne Sünde, hüll' Dich ein, Du Apfel des Paradieses" (II, 77-78).

This seems to be Stifter's regretful farewell to the Romantic mythical image itself; the story of Chelion is filled with a mood of helpless mournfulness mixed with a gently grievous longing. The mythical image remains, but only as a tantalizing portrait in the poet's mind, mantled with the blue drapery of poesy.

Postscript

From the time of unrecorded prehistorical cultural currents, through the magnificence of Greek conquest, through the restless and relentless loquaciousness of traveling missionaries, merchants, and mercenaries to the period of perspicacious, scholarly preoccupation with its language and culture, India exerted a gentle and persistent pressure on the consciousness and intellect of the West. At the ripe and appropriate moment the diverse and ubiquitous flow crystallized in the catalytic hands of Herder in the form of a lodestone which irresistibly claimed the minds and hearts of many German Romanticists.

The magnetic image, ideal and appealingly mythical, attracted the fancifulness and inventiveness of Romantic authors. It was mirrored, refracted, transmitted, metamorphosed, and synthesized in the eye of each. Glimpsed as an inherent attribute of Romanticism by literary theorists, the mythical image received the accolade of their pronouncements of its innate Romantic properties. It was absorbed into the style and metaphor of Romantic poetry and prose. It animated nature, suffused characters with the blush of sophisticated naïveté, furnished a deep root for the genesis of religion, and released a steady flow from bottomless wells of mythology. The magical mixture of the marvelous and the mundane produced by Romanticists conjuring under the sign of the mythical image dazzled the eyes of a generation of readers. Its own persuasive metaphysics gave direction and contour to Romantic philosophy.

In the foreword to the second edition of Forster's *Sakontala* in 1803, Herder unwittingly defined the phenomenon of the mythical image:

Nah und fern wirken Geister auf Geister; die sie umgebenden, darstellenden Hüllen und Formen sind—*Maja*, eine liebliche Täuschung. In dieser Vorstellungsart, in der Alles sich so leise und zart berühret, kann mit Beibehaltung ewiger Urformen Alles aus Allem werden. Ein Wechseln des Spiels für die Sinne wird das grosse Drama der Welt; der innere Sinn, der es am tiefsten, innigsten geniesst, ist *Ruhe der Seele, Götterfriede.* (XXIV, 578-579)

The mythical image of India might be called, then, "a sweet illusion," an illusory world in which everything touched gently and tenderly, a contact of spirits which brought infinities and eternities out of temporal and spatial prototypes. On the world stage the grand striding of history entertained the senses with artful and variable play. The essential and inescapable dissolution of the mythical image was manifest in the unattainable pleasure of the inner sense: the quietude of soul, the peace of the gods. The illusion was sweet, and it endured for a time, leaving an indelible imprint on Romantic thought and endeavor, transforming its own illusory essence into an adamantine poetic brilliance.

The dissolution of the mythical image did not mean the end of India's influence—the years when the image flourished were the first stage. After the disappearance of the image, serious and earnest scholars such as August Wilhelm Schlegel, Franz Bopp, and Friedrich Max Müller labored fruitfully with Sanskrit, to be followed by generations of linguists. The enchantment of Indic mythology and the beauties of Sanskrit poetic literature were echoed in the works of minor poets such as Otto Heinrich Graf von Loeben and Joseph von Hammer-Purgstall. They found new voice in the poetry and prose of Friedrich Rückert, who published the *Gita-Govinda* (a translation) in 1837, *Die Weisheit des Bramanen* (an original collection of aphorisms, parables, and tales in the Indic tradition) between 1836 and 1839, and who became professor of Oriental philology at the University of Erlangen. In 1845-1856 appeared Adolf Holtzmann's *Indische Sagen*, which became an enduring source book. Some authors counterfeited Indic backgrounds, as did Karl Gutzkow in his novel *Mahagura* (1832), J. V. Widmann in the epic poem *Buddha* (1869), and Karl Bleibtreu in the dramas *Karma* (1901) and *Heilskönig* (1903), none of which contain a valid portrait of Indic culture. However, most authors who concerned themselves with Indic subjects sincerely tried to fathom Indic thought or sought to fit Hindu ethics into analogous Western terms, as did Friedrich Hebbel in the year of his death (1863) with the poem "Der Brahmine," which celebrates the equality of man and beast in creation.

The mythical image of India embraced only Hindu and Brahmanical branches of Indic religion. New information about India filtered through the German Pietist missionaries in the nineteenth century. Around 1850 the revelation of Buddhist philosophy through Eugène Burnouf's *Introduction à l'histoire du Bouddhisme* (1844) and Carl Friedrich Köppen's *Die Religion des Buddha und ihre Entstehung* (1857), as well as through Schopenhauer's philosophy, opened a fresh source of legendary and historic Indic substance. Richard Wagner, in the dramatic sketch *Die Sieger*, took an Indic tale as his model. The characters of the sketch appear transformed in *Parsifal*, which glimmers with images from Buddhist lore. In the opera *Götterdämmerung*, too, an Indic patina of thought is discernible. Further treatment of the theme of Buddha is found in three plays by Karl Gjellerup, *Pilger Kamanita* (1903), *Das Weib des Vollendeten* (1906), and *Die Weltwanderer* (1922). Other authors illuminate with various skill and success various elements in the thought and life of Buddha: Fritz Mauthner in *Der letzte Tod des Gautama Buddha* (1912) and Max Albert Schreiber in his novel *Kunala* (1910).

The works of authors of international repute are witnesses to

India's inexhaustible fund of literary and mythological charms: Max Dauthendey in the twelve stories collected in *Lingam* (1909), Waldemar Bonsels in *Die Biene Maja* (1912) and the travel narrative *Indienfahrt* (1916), Hugo von Hofmannsthal in the fantasy *Die Frau ohne Schatten* (1919), Franz Werfel in the drama *Der Spiegelmensch* (1920), Stefan Zweig in the legend *Die Augen des ewigen Bruders* (1921), and Alfred Döblin in the epic *Manas* (1927). The tantalizing enigma of India exerted its lure on Hermann Hesse (*Siddhartha* [1922] and other works) and Thomas Mann (*Die vertauschten Köpfe*, 1940) and will doubtless involve future poets who sense the pulse that throbs still in India, who will seek to measure that ancient rhythm whose essence ever remains a sweet illusion.

Bibliography

[*1. General*]

Burnet, John. *Early Greek Philosophy*. New York, 1957.

Frenzel, Elisabeth. *Stoffe der Weltliteratur*. Stuttgart, 1962.

Graves, Robert. *The Greek Myths*. 2 vols. New York, 1959.

Harrison, Jane. *Prolegomena to the Study of Greek Religion*. New York, 1955.

Tindall, William York. *The Literary Symbol*. New York, 1955.

Ueberweg, Friedrich. *Grundriss der Geschichte der Philosophie*. 12th ed., rev. T. K. Oesterreich. Berlin, 1923. IV. Das neunzehnte Jahrhundert und die Gegenwart.

Voltaire, François. *Oeuvres complètes*, ed. Louis Moland. 52 vols. Paris, 1877-1885.

Voragine, Jacobus de. *The Golden Legend*, trans. Granger Ryan and Helmut Ripperger. 2 vols. London, 1941.

[2. *Travel Literature and Works on India*]

Adelung, Friedrich von. *An Historical Sketch of Sanscrit Literature.* Oxford, 1832.

Allgemeine Historie der Reisen zu Wasser und zu Lande. See J. J. Schwabe.

Auswahl der besten ausländischen geographischen und statistischen Nachrichten zur Aufklärung der Völker- und Länderkunde. See M. C. Sprengel.

Avalon, Arthur [John George Woodroffe]. *The Serpent Power.* London, 1924.

Bailly, Jean Sylvain. *Lettres sur l'origine des sciences et sur celle des peuples de l'Asie, adressées à M. Voltaire.* Paris, 1777.

Baldeus, Philipp. *Beschreibung der ostindischen Kusten* [sic] *Malabar und Coromandel* ... Aus dem Niederländischen. Amsterdam, 1672.

Barnett, L. D. *The Heart of India.* London, 1908.

Behr, Johann von der. *Diarium einer neuenjährigen Ostindianischen Reise von 1641 bis 1650.* Jena, 1668.

——. *Johannis von der Behr Neun-jährige ostindianische Reise.* Frankfurt, 1689.

Beiträge zur Völker- und Länderkunde. See Reinhold Forster.

Bernier, François. *Voyages de François Bernier.* 2 vols. Amsterdam, 1699.

Bernoulli, Jean. *Description historique et géographique de l'Inde.* 3 vols. Berlin, 1786-1789.

Bohlen, Peter von, ed. *Bhartriharis Sententiae.* Berlin, 1833.

——, trans. *Die Sprüche des Bhartrihari.* Hamburg, 1835.

Boyd, Hugh. *Hugh Boyd's Gesandtschaftsreise nach Ceylon.* Hamburg, 1801.

——. *Miscellaneous Works.* With an account of his life and writings by Lawrence Dundas Campbell. 2 vols. London, 1800.

Bruyn, Cornelius de. *Reizen over Moscovie door Persie en Indie.* Amsterdam, 1711.

——. *Travels into Muscovy, Persia, and divers parts of the East Indies.* London, 1759.

——. *Voyages par la Moscovie, en Perse et aux Indes-orientales.* Amsterdam, 1718.

Das Buch der Weisheit, ed. Rudolf Payer von Thurn [originally published in 1483]. Vienna, 1925.

Dapper, Olfert [Oliver.] *Asia, oder ausführliche Beschreibung des Reichs des grossen Mogols, und eines grossen Theils von Indien,* trans. [from the Dutch] Johann Christoff Beern. Nürnberg, 1681.

Dauer, Dorothea W. "Buddhistic Influence on German Literature and Thought to the End of the Nineteenth Century." Unpublished

Ph.D. dissertation, University of Texas, 1953.

Degrandpré, B. [*sic*, L.] *Reise nach Indien und Arabien in den Jahren 1789 und 1790.* Berlin, 1803.

Dellon, V. *Nouvelle relation d'un voyage fait aux Indies orientales* [Amsterdam, 1699], in *Allgemeine Historie der Reisen*, ed. J. J. Schwabe.

Description historique et géographique de l'Inde. See Jean Bernoulli.

Doberentz, O. "Die erd- und völkerkunde in der weltchronik des Rudolf von Ems," *Zeitschrift für deutsche Philologie*, XIII (1882), 29-57, 165-223.

Dow, Alexander. *Dissertation sur les mœurs, les usages, le langage, la religion et la philosophie des Hindous*, trans. M. B. . . . Paris, 1769.

——. *The History of Hindostan*, translated from the Persian [of Firishtah, Muhammad Kāsim ibn Hindū Shāh]. 3rd ed. 3 vols. Dublin, 1792.

Downing, Clement. *History of the Indian Wars, with an Account of Angria the Pyrate.* London, 1737.

——. *Die neuesten Unruhen auf der Ost-Indischen Küste oder Geschichte vom . . . See-Räuber Torrengei Angria* [from the Dutch]. Nürnberg, 1738.

Duperron, Anquetil. *Oupnek'hat* (*id est, Secretum tegendum*). Strassburg, 1801.

L'Ezour Vedam ou Ancient Commentaire du Vedam, contenant l'exposition des opinions religieuses et philosophiques des Indiens, Traduit de Samscretan par un *Brame.* Yverdon, 1778.

Ezour-Vedam, oder die Geschichte, Religion und Philosophie der Indier, trans. J. Ith. Leipzig, [1779].

Forster, Georg and M. C. Sprengel, eds. *Neue Beyträge zur Länder- und Völkerkunde.* 8 vols. Leipzig, 1790-1793.

——. *Sketches of the Mythology and Customs of the Hindoos.* London, 1785.

Forster, Reinhold, and M. C. Sprengel, eds. *Beiträge zur Völker- und Länderkunde.* 14 vols. Leipzig, 1781-1784, 1786-1790.

——, trans. and ed. *Magazin von merkwürdigen neuen Reisebeschreibungen.* 16 vols. Berlin, 1790-1798.

Fricken, Christoph. *Ostindische Reisen und Kriegsdienste von 1680-1685.* Ulm, 1692.

Gatterer, Johann Christoph. *Allgemeine historische Bibliothek.* 16 vols. Halle, 1767-1771.

Gentil [de la Galaisière], Guillaume [Joseph] le. *Reisen in den indischen Meeren 1761-69*, in Vols. II and IV of *Neue Sammlung von Reisebeschreibungen.* Hamburg, 1781.

——. *Voyage dans les mers de l'Inde.* 2 vols. Paris, 1779-1781.

Gerbett, G. F. *Ostindische Naturgeschichte, Sitten und Alterthümer.* Halle, 1752.

Gowen, Herbert H. *A History of Indian Literature.* New York, 1931.

Halhed, Nathaniel Brassey, trans. *A Code of Gentoo Laws, or, Ordinations of the Pundits.* London, 1776.

——. *Gesetzbuch der Gentoos,* trans. Rudolf Erich Raspe. Hamburg, 1778.

Hamilton, Alexander. *A New Account of the East Indies, from 1688 to 1723* [Edinburgh, 1727], in *Voyages and Travels,* ed. John Pinkerton, VIII.

Hertel, Johannes. *Das Pañcatantra, seine Geschichte und seine Verbreitung.* Leipzig, 1914.

Hofmann, J. C. *Ostindianische Voyage.* Cassel, 1680.

Holwell, J. Z. *Merkwürdige historische Nachrichten von Hindostan und Bengalen,* trans. J. F. Kleucker. Leipzig, 1778.

Houtmann, C. *Erste Reise nach Ostindien* [*De erste Schep Vaert . . .* Amsterdam, 1595], in *Allgemeine Historie der Reisen,* ed. J. J. Schwabe, III.

Hüttner, Johann Christian, trans. *Hindus-Gesetzbuch* [from the English trans. by Sir William Jones]. Weimar, 1797.

Ives, Edward. *Reisen nach Indien und Persien,* trans. Christian Willhelm Dohm. 2 vols. Leipzig, 1774.

Jones, Sir William. *Institutes of Hindoo Law, or the Ordinances of Menu.* Calcutta, 1794.

——. *Poeseos asiaticae commentariorum libri sex.* Leipzig, 1777.

——. *Poems consisting chiefly of Translations from the Asiatick Languages.* Oxford, 1772.

——. *Ueber die Musik der Indier,* trans. F. H. von Dalberg. Erfurt, 1802.

——. *Works.* 6 vols. London, 1799.

Kleucker, J. F., trans., with Johannes Fick. *Abhandlungen über die Geschichte und Alterthümer der Künste, Wissenschaften . . . Asiens.* Riga, 1795.

[Macintosh, William.] *Travels in Europe, Asia and Africa.* 2 vols. London, 1782.

——. *Reisen durch Europa, Asia und Africa.* 2 vols. Leipzig, 1785.

Magazin von merkwürdigen neuen Reisebeschreibungen. See Reinhold Forster.

Mandelslo, Johann Albrecht. *Mandelslos Schreiben von seiner ostindischen Reise an Ad. Olearius,* ed. Adam Olearius. [Schleswig], 1645.

——. *Oft begehrte Beschreibung der newen* [*sic*] *orientalischen Reise,* ed. Adam Olearius. Schleswig, 1647.

——. *Des . . . Johann Albrecht von Mandelslo morgenländische Reisebeschreibung,* ed. Adam Olearius. Schleswig, 1658.

——. *Travels.* See Olearius, *The Voyages and Travels of the Ambassadors.*

McCrindle, J. W., trans. and ed. *Ancient India as Described by Megasthenês and Arrian.* London, 1877.
Neue Beyträge zur Länder- und Völkerkunde. See Georg Forster.
Neue Sammlung von Reisebeschreibungen. Hamburg, 1781.
Niebuhr, Carsten. *Reise nach Arabien.* 3 vols. Copenhagen, 1774-1778.
Olearius, Adam. *Viel vermehrte Moscowitische und Persianische Reisebeschreibung.* Hamburg, 1696.
——. *The Voyages and Travels of the Ambassadors,* trans. John Davies. London, 1662.
Pagés, Pierre-Marie-François. *Voyages autour du monde 1767-1776.* Paris, 1782.
Paulinus a Sancto Bartholomaeo. *Viaggio alle Indie orientali.* Rome, 1796.
——. *Reise nach Ostindien,* trans. Reinhold Forster, in *Magazin von merkwürdigen neuen Reisebeschreibungen,* XV. Berlin, 1798.
——. *A Voyage to the East Indies,* trans. [from the German] William Johnston. London, 1800.
——. *Darstellung der Brahmanisch-Indischen Götterlehre.* Gotha, 1797.
Pinkerton, John, ed. *Voyages and Travels.* 17 vols. London, 1808-1814.
Polo, Marco. *The Book of Ser Marco Polo,* trans. and ed. Col. Sir Henry Yule, 3rd ed. rev. Henri Cordier. 2 vols. London, 1926.
Poullé, Méridas [Mariyadāsa Piḷḷai], trans. *Bagavadam ou Doctrine Divine.* Paris, 1788.
——. *Le Bhâgavata,* ed. Père H. Hosten. Société de l'Histoire de l'Inde Française, IV, 1. Pondichéry, 1921.
Robertson, William. *An Historical Disquisition concerning the Knowledge which the Ancients had of India.* London, 1791.
——. *W. Robertson's historische Untersuchung über die Kenntnisse der Alten von Indien,* [trans. D. M. Liebeskind]. Berlin, 1792.
Rochon, Abbé [Alexis-Marie]. *Des Abbé Rochon Reise nach Madagaskar und Ostindien* [original French edition, 1791], in *Magazin von merkwürdigen neuen Reisebeschreibungen,* XIV. Berlin, 1792.
Rogerius, Abraham. *De Open-Deure tot het Verborgen Heydendom* [originally published 1651], ed. W. Caland. Linschoten-Vereeniging, X. 'S-Gravenhage, 1915.
——. *Offne Thür zu dem verborgenen Heydenthum,* trans. Christoph Arnold. Nürnberg, 1663.
——. *Le Theatre de l'Idolatrie, ou la Porte Ouverte,* trans. Thomas la Grue. Amsterdam, 1670.
Saar, J. J. *Ost-Indianische fünfzehenjährige Kriegs-Dienste.* Nürnberg, 1672.
Schouten, Gautier. *Voyage de Gautier Schouten aux Indes Orientales* (1658-1665) [Rouen, 1725], in *Allgemeine Historie der Reisen,* ed. J. J. Schwabe, XII.

Schroeder, Leopold von. *Indiens Literatur und Kultur.* Leipzig, 1887.

Schulz, Arthur. "Schiller and the Literature of Travel." Unpublished Ph.D. Dissertation, University of Wisconsin, 1940.

Schwabe, J. J., ed. *Allgemeine Historie der Reisen zu Wasser und zu Lande oder Sammlung aller Reisebeschreibungen.* 21 vols. Amsterdam, 1747-1777.

Schweitzer, Christophorus. *Journal und Tagebuch seiner sechsjährigen Ostindianischen Reise.* Tübingen, 1688.

Sonnerat, M. [Pierre de]. *Voyage aux Indes Orientales.* 2 vols. Paris, 1782.

——. *Reise nach Ostindien und China.* 2 vols. Zürich, 1783.

Sprengel, M. C. *Allgemeines historisches Taschenbuch.* Berlin, 1786.

——. *Auswahl der besten ausländischen geographischen und statistischen Nachrichten zur Aufklärung der Völker- und Länderkunde.* 14 parts in 7 vols. Halle, 1794-1800.

——. *Beiträge zur Völker- und Länderkunde,* ed. with Reinhold Forster. 14 vols. Leipzig, 1781-1784, 1786-1790.

——. *Neue Beyträge zur Länder- und Völkerkunde,* ed. with Georg Forster. 8 vols. Leipzig, 1790-1793.

Stavorinus, Johan Splinter. *Voyages to the East Indies,* trans. Samuel Hull Wilcocke. 3 vols. London, 1798.

Valentin, François. *Beschryving van't Nederlandsch Comptoir op te Kust van Malabar.* Amsterdam, 1726.

Valle, Pietro della. *Travels,* trans. George Havers. London, 1665. This work is the third part of the author's *Viaggi cioè la Turchia, la Persia, e l'Inde.* Rome, 1650.

Voyages and Travels. See Pinkerton.

Wilkins, Charles, trans. *The Bhagvat-Geeta, or Dialogues of Kreeshna and Arjoon.* London, 1785.

——. *The Heetopades of Veeshnoo-Sarma.* Bath, 1787.

——. *The Story of Dooshwanta and Sakoontala.* London, 1795.

Windisch, Ernst. *Geschichte der Sanskrit-Philologie.* Strassburg, 1917.

Zimmer, Heinrich. *Philosophies of India.* New York, 1956.

[3. *Periodicals*]

Asiatisches Magazin, ed. Julius Klaproch [Louis de L'Or, Wilhelm Lauterbach]. 2 vols. Weimar, 1802.

Athenäum, eine Zeitschrift, ed. A. W. Schlegel and Friedrich Schlegel. 3 vols. Berlin, 1798-1800.

Europa, ed. Friedrich Schlegel. 2 vols. Frankfurt a.M., 1803-1805.

Oster Taschenbuch von Weimar, ed. Leopold von Seckendorff-Aberdar. Weimar, 1801.

Poetisches Journal, ed. Ludwig Tieck. Jena, 1800.
Thalia, ed. Friedrich Schiller. 3 vols. Leipzig, 1787-1791, Heft X.

[*4. Poets, Mythologists, and Philosophers*]

Arnim, Achim von. *Achim von Arnim und die ihm nahe standen*, ed. Reinhold Steig. 3 vols. Stuttgart, 1894-1904.
Creuzer, Friedrich. *Deutsche Schriften*, 3rd ed. 4 vols. Leipzig, 1836-1843.
Creuzer, Friedrich, and Karoline von Günderode. *Briefe und Dichtungen*. ed. Erwin Rohde. Heidelberg, 1896.
Dalberg, Friedrich von, trans. *Gita-Govinda* [from the English of Sir William Jones]. Erfurt, 1802.
——, trans. and ed. *Über die Musik der Indier. Eine Abhandlung des Sir William Jones.* Erfurt, 1802.
Fichte, Johann Gottlieb. *Sämmtliche Werke*, ed. J. H. Fichte. 11 vols. Berlin, 1845-1846.
Forster, Georg. *Sämmtliche Schriften.* 9 vols. Leipzig, 1843.
Goethe, Johann Wolfgang von. *Werke.* 141 vols. Weimar, 1887-1912.
——. *Goethes Gespräche, Gesamtausgabe*, ed. Flodoard Freiherr von Biedermann. 4 vols. Leipzig, 1910.
Görres, Johann Joseph von. *Mythengeschichte der asiatischen Welt.* 2 vols. Heidelberg, 1810.
Günderode, Karoline von. *Gesammelte Dichtungen*, ed. Dr. Elisabeth Salomon. München, 1923.
Happel, Everhard Guerner. *Der asiatische Onogambo.* Hamburg, 1673.
Hartlieb, Johannes. *Alexander*, in *Deutsche Literatur*, Reihe Volks- und Schwankbücher, Vol. II: *Volksbücher von Weltweite und Abenteuerlust*, ed. Franz Podleiszek. Leipzig, 1936.
Hegel, Georg Wilhelm Friedrich. *Sämtliche Werke*, ed. Hermann Glockner. 20 vols., plus 2 supplementary vols. and one register vol. Stuttgart, 1927-1929.
Heine, Heinrich. *Sämtliche Werke*, ed. Oskar Walzel. 10 vols. Leipzig, 1911-1915.
Herder, Johann Gottfried. *Sämtliche Werke*, ed. Bernhard Suphan. 33 vols. Leipzig, 1877-1913.
——. *Von und an Herder. Ungedruckte Briefe aus Herders Nachlass*, ed. Heinrich Düntzer and F. G. von Herder. 3 vols. Leipzig, 1861.
Hoffmann, E. T. A. *Dichtungen und Schriften*, ed. Walther Harich. 15 vols. Weimar, 1924.
——. *Werke*, ed. Dr. Viktor Schweizer. 3 vols. Leipzig, [1896].
Hölderlin, Friedrich. *Sämtliche Werke*, ed. Friedrich Beissner. 6 vols. Stuttgart, 1943-1961.

Jean Paul [Friedrich Richter]. *Sämtliche Werke,* ed. Eduard Berend. 32 vols. Weimar, 1927-1960.

Kanne, Johann Arnold. *Erste Urkunden der Geschichte oder allgemeine Mythologie.* 2 vols. Baireuth [*sic*], 1808.

———. *System der indischen Mythe, oder Chronus und die Geschichte des Gottmenschen in der Periode des Vorrückens der Nachtgleichen.* Leipzig, 1813.

Majer, Friedrich. *Allgemeines mythologisches Lexicon.* 2 vols. Weimar, 1803-1804.

———. "Der Bhaguat-Geeta," in Vols. I and II of *Asiatisches Magazin,* ed. Julius Klaproth. 2 vols. Weimar, 1802.

———. *Brahma, oder die Religion der Indier als Brahmaismus.* Leipzig, 1818.

Meyern, Wilhelm Friedrich von. *Dya-Na-Sore oder die Wanderer, eine Geschichte aus dem Sam-skritt übersetzt.* 3 vols. Leipzig, 1787-1791.

Novalis [Friedrich Leopold Freiherr von Hardenberg]. *Schriften,* ed. Jakob Minor. 4 vols. Jena, 1923.

———. *Schriften,* ed. Paul Kluckhohn. 4 vols. Leipzig, [1929].

———. *Schriften. Die Werke Friedrich von Hardenbergs,* ed. Paul Kluckhohn (†) and Richard Samuel, with Heinz Ritter and Gerhard Schulz. Stuttgart, 1960. Edition in progress.

Schelling, Friedrich. *Sämmtliche Werke,* ed. K. F. A. Schelling. 14 vols. Stuttgart, 1856-1861.

Schlegel, August Wilhelm. *Sämmtliche Werke,* ed. Eduard Böcking. 12 vols. Leipzig, 1846-1847.

———. *Vorlesungen über schöne Litteratur und Kunst,* ed. Jakob Minor. 3 vols. Heilbronn, 1884.

———. *Briefe von und an August Wilhelm Schlegel,* ed. Josef Körner. 2 vols. Zürich, 1930.

Schlegel, Friedrich. *Kritische Friedrich-Schlegel-Ausgabe,* ed. Ernst Behler, with Jean-Jacques Anstett and Hans Eichner. Paderborn, 1958-1963. Edition in progress.

———. *Sämmtliche Werke.* 2nd ed. 15 vols. Wien, 1846.

———. *Literary Notebooks 1797-1801,* ed. Hans Eichner. London, 1957.

———. *Seine prosaischen Jugendschriften* (1794-1802), ed. Jakob Minor. 2nd ed. 2 vols. Wien, 1906.

———. *Die Brüder Schlegel: Briefe von und an Friedrich und Dorothea Schlegel,* ed. Josef Körner. Berlin, 1926.

———. *Friedrich Schlegels Briefe an seinen Bruder August Wilhelm,* ed. Oskar Walzel. Berlin, 1890.

Schleiermacher, Friedrich. *Werke, Auswahl in vier Bänden,* ed. Dr. Otto Braun and Prof. Dr. Joh. Bauer. 4 vols. Leipzig, 1911.

Schopenhauer, Arthur. *Sämtliche Werke,* ed. Eduard Grisebach. 3rd ed. 6 vols. Leipzig [1921-1924].

——. *Handschriftlicher Nachlass*, ed. Eduard Grisebach. 4 vols. Leipzig, [1926-1931].

——. *Schopenhauer-Briefe. Sammlung meist ungedruckter oder schwer zugänglicher Briefe von, an und über Schopenhauer*, ed. Ludwig Schermann. Leipzig, 1893.

Schubert, Gotthilf Heinrich. *Ansichten von der Nachtseite der Naturwissenschaft*. Dresden, 1808.

Stifter, Adalbert. *Sämmtliche Werke*, ed. August Sauer and others. 25 vols. Prag, 1904-1960. Edition in progress.

Tieck, Ludwig. *Ausgewählte Werke*, ed. Georg Witkowski. 4 vols. Leipzig, [1903].

——. *Schriften*. 20 vols. Berlin, 1828-1846.

——. *Werke*, ed. Eduard Berend. 6 vols. Leipzig, [1908].

——. *Ludwig Tieck und die Brüder Schlegel* [letters], ed. H. von Lüdeke. Frankfurt a.M., 1930.

Wackenroder, Wilhelm Heinrich. *Werke und Briefe*, ed. Friedrich von der Leyen. 2 vols. Jena, 1910.

Ziegler und Kliphausen, Heinrich Anslem von. *Asiatische Banise, oder blutiges doch muthiges Pegu*. Leipzig, 1707, in *Deutsche National-Litteratur*, ed. Joseph Kürschner. Berlin, n.d. Vol. XXXVII.

[5. *Secondary Sources*]

Böhm, Wilhelm. *Hölderlin*. 2 vols. Halle/Saale,, 1928-1930.

Brandes, George. *Main Currents in Nineteenth Century Literature*, trans. Diana White and Mary Morison. 6 vols. London, 1901-1905. Vol. II: The Romantic School.

Ederheimer, Edgar. *Jakob Boehme und die Romantiker*. 2 vols. Heidelberg, 1904.

Enders, Carl. *Friedrich Schlegel, die Quellen seines Wesens und Werdens*. Leipzig, 1913.

Fiesel, Eva. *Die Sprachphilosophie der deutschen Romantik*. Tübingen, 1927.

Grundmann, Johannes. "Die geographischen und völkerkundlichen Quellen und Anschauungen in Herders 'Ideen zur Geschichte der Menschheit.'" Dissertation, Leipzig, 1900.

Haering, Theodor. *Novalis als Philosoph*. Stuttgart, 1954.

Haym, Rudolf. *Die romantische Schule*, 3rd ed. Berlin, 1914.

Haywood, Bruce. *Novalis: The Veil of Imagery*. Cambridge, Mass., 1959.

Hecker, Jutta. *Das Symbol der Blauen Blume im Zusammenhang mit der Blumensymbolik der Romantik*. Jena, 1931.

Hiebel, Friedrich. *Novalis, der Dichter der blauen Blume*. Bern, 1951.

——. "Zur Interpretation der 'Blauen Blume' des Novalis," *Monatshefte*, XLIII (1951), 327-334.

Hoffmann, Paul T. "Der indische und der deutsche Geist von Herder bis zur Romantik." Dissertation, Tübingen, 1915.

Huch, Ricarda. *Die Romantik*. 2 vols. Leipzig, 1924.

Imle, F. *Friedrich von Schlegels Entwicklung von Kant zum Katholizismus*. Paderborn, 1927.

Jaeger, Hans Peter. *Hölderlin-Novalis, Grenzen der Sprache*. Zürich, 1949.

Kranz, Walther. *Empedokles, antike Gestalt und romantische Neuschöpfung*. Zürich, 1949.

Lehmann, Emil. *Hölderlins Lyrik*. Stuttgart, 1922.

Lerch, Paul. "Friedrich Schlegels philosophische Anschauungen in ihrer Entwicklung und systematischen Ausgestaltung." Dissertation, Friedrich-Alexanders-Universität, Erlangen, 1905.

Petersen, Julius. *Die Wesensbestimmung der deutschen Romantik*. Leipzig, 1926.

Regen, Erich. *Die Dramen Karolinens von Günderode*. Berlin, 1910.

Remy, Arthur F. J. "The Influence of India and Persia on the Poetry of Germany." Dissertation, Columbia University, 1901.

Ritter, Heinz. *Novalis' Hymnen an die Nacht*. Heidelberg, 1930.

Rouge, I. *Erläuterungen zu Friedrich Schlegels Lucinde*. Halle, 1905.

Salzberger, L. S. *Hölderlin*. New Haven, 1952.

Sommerfeld, Susanne. "Indienschau und Indiendeutung romantischer Philosophen." Dissertation, Zürich, 1943.

Spenlé E. *Novalis*. Paris, 1904.

Strich, Fritz. *Deutsche Klassik und Romantik*. München, 1928.

——. *Die Mythologie in der deutschen Literatur von Klopstock bis Wagner*. 2 vols. Halle a.S., 1910.

Walzel, Oskar. *German Romanticism*. New York, 1932.

Zeydel, Edwin H. *Ludwig Tieck, The German Romanticist*. Princeton, 1935.

Index